Aaron Copland and the American Legacy of Gustav Mahler

Aaron Copland and the American Legacy of Gustav Mahler

Matthew Mugmon

University of Rochester Press

The University of Rochester Press gratefully acknowledges generous support from the American Musicological Society.

First published 2019

University of Rochester Press
668 Mt. Hope Avenue, Rochester, NY 14620, USA
www.urpress.com
and Boydell & Brewer Limited
PO Box 9, Woodbridge, Suffolk IP12 3DF, UK
www.boydellandbrewer.com

ISBN-13: 978-1-58046-964-7
ISSN: 1071-9989

Library of Congress Cataloging-in-Publication Data

Names: Mugmon, Matthew, author.
Title: Aaron Copland and the American legacy of Gustav Mahler / Matthew Mugmon.
Other titles: Eastman studies in music ; v. 160.
Description: Rochester : University of Rochester Press, 2019. | Series: Eastman studies in music, 1071-9989 ; volume 160 | Includes bibliographical references and index. | Summary: "Although Aaron Copland (1900–1990) is often credited with creating an unmistakably American musical style, he was strongly attracted to the music of Gustav Mahler. Drawing extensively on archival and musical materials, this is the first detailed exploration of Copland's multifaceted relationship with Mahler's music and its lasting consequences for music in America. Matthew Mugmon demonstrates that Copland, inspired by Mahler's example, blended modernism and romanticism in shaping a vision for American music in the twentieth century, and that he did so through his multiple roles as composer, teacher, critic, and orchestral tastemaker. Copland's career-long engagement with Mahler's music intersected with Copland's own Jewish identity and with his links to such towering figures in American music as Nadia Boulanger, Serge Koussevitzky, and Leonard Bernstein"—Provided by publisher.
Identifiers: LCCN 2019023205 | ISBN 9781580469647 (hardcover)
Subjects: LCSH: Copland, Aaron, 1900–1990—Criticism and interpretation. | Mahler, Gustav, 1860–1911—Influence. | Music—United States—20th century—History and criticism.
Classification: LCC ML410.C756 M84 2019 | DDC 780.92—dc23
LC record available at https://lccn.loc.gov/2019023205
This publication is printed on acid-free paper.
Printed in the United States of America.

To Madeleine, Owen, and Emmett

CONTENTS

ACKNOWLEDGMENTS

This book's journey began almost twenty years ago, when I first encountered—and fell in love with—music history and the music of Gustav Mahler. This introduction came courtesy of two inspirational and generous educators at the University of Pennsylvania, Larry Bernstein and the late Norman Smith. As a graduate student at Harvard University, in a seminar on American music historiography led by Carol Oja, I explored Aaron Copland's role in Serge Koussevitzky's American premiere of Mahler's Ninth Symphony, which took place in Boston in 1931. Under Carol's sage guidance, I developed this local history project into a larger one of transatlantic resonance that also involved figures like Leonard Bernstein and Nadia Boulanger. I treasured the opportunity to consult frequently with the late Gil Kaplan, and I relied on many members of Harvard's wonderful faculty, especially Tom Kelly and Alex Rehding, who have always made themselves available to me. I feel privileged that to this day I can count on Carol, Tom, and Alex as mentors and friends.

Fruitful discussions with and support from many individuals have shaped this book in both overall thrust and specific details. As this project developed, I depended heavily on ideas and feedback from my Harvard colleagues, including Emily Abrams Ansari, Ryan Bañagale, Andrea Bohlman, Davide Ceriani, Will Cheng, Chris Chowrimootoo, Glenda Goodman, Jack Hamilton, Sheryl Kaskowitz, Tom Lin, Drew Massey, Luci Mok, and Meredith Schweig. I owe a special debt of gratitude to Elizabeth Craft, Louis Epstein, Frank Lehman, and Hannah Lewis for their advice and comradeship throughout many stages of this project, and to my academic role models Ben Gross, and Freeden Oeur, and Sarah Suhadolnik. Also, I recall fondly my conversations with scholars such as Jeanice Brooks, Richard Crawford, Dorothy Lamb Crawford, Kimberly Francis, Karen Painter, Dave Paul, Thomas Peattie, Howard Pollack, and Judith Tick. Many individuals, including Bridget Carr and Barbara Perkel (Boston Symphony Orchestra Archives), Barbara Haws and Gabe Smith (New York Philharmonic Archives), Charlotte Kolczynski (Boston Public Library), Anne Rhodes (Oral History of American Music), Nathalie Castinel, Christiane Kriloff, and Laurence

Languin (Médiathèque Nadia Boulanger), Eileen Ganter (Interlochen Center for the Arts), Mark Horowitz (Library of Congress), and Alexandra Laederich (Centre international Nadia et Lili Boulanger), went out of their way to provide me with guidance, perspective, resources, and materials.

I have been lucky to call the University of Arizona my home for the last several years, and I thank my wonderful and wise colleagues for creating such a warm and intellectually invigorating environment—and for their interest in, and advice concerning, both my overall progress and the specific details of my research. I have also learned much about Mahler, Copland, Bernstein, and American music from the many exceptional students I have had the privilege of teaching. Ed Reid, director of the Fred Fox School of Music, arranged for crucial financial assistance for this book's publication through a subvention from the Alan C. and Daveen Fox Endowment. I am also grateful for a grant from the University of Arizona Provost Author's Support Fund, made possible by Andrea Romero, vice provost for faculty affairs. In the earlier stages of this project, I was fortunate to receive an award from the American Musicological Society's Jan LaRue Travel Fund to conduct research in Europe.

Some material in this book was presented at conferences and in other venues; other material was published previously and is reprinted here with the permission of the publishers. A version of chapter 2 appeared as "An Imperfect Mahlerite: Nadia Boulanger and the Reception of Gustav Mahler," *Journal of Musicology* 35, no. 1 (2018), published by the University of California Press. A version of chapter 7 appeared as "Beyond the Composer-Conductor Dichotomy: Bernstein's Copland-Inspired Mahler Advocacy," *Music & Letters* 94, no. 4 (2013), published by Oxford University Press. And a portion of chapter 6 appeared in "Abridging Mahler's Symphonies: A Historical Perspective," in the collected volume *Rethinking Mahler*, edited by Jeremy Barham and published by Oxford University Press. I am thankful to the many scholars and editors who, both formally and informally and at various stages, have engaged with and helped me improve this book's content.

For making this book possible, I wish to thank Ralph Locke, senior editor of the Eastman Studies in Music series, both for his support for this project and for his indispensable guidance concerning details large and small, as well as Sonia Kane, editorial director of the University of Rochester Press, for steering this project through the publication process from the time of our earliest conversations at musicology conferences. I am also grateful to Julia Cook, Tracey Engel, and Jacqueline Heinzelmann for their expert behind-the-scenes work in matters relating to this book's production. I appreciate Chris Kayler for his patient and thorough work in generating the musical examples, Carrie Crompton for her careful and sensitive copyediting, and Marilyn Bliss for the superb index she created.

My grandfather Louis Jacobs would have been first in line for a copy of this book. He was a pianist and music aficionado who, for as long as I can remember, shared his musical gift with everyone around him, and he was my leading correspondent about musicological matters. My grandfather Leo Mugmon served his community for decades as a beloved physician, and from him I gained an appreciation for short-order cooking and time in the swimming pool. They are no longer with us, but their memory lives on in these pages; like both of my grandfathers, Aaron Copland and Leonard Bernstein were the children of Jewish immigrants from Eastern Europe. I know that Grandpa and Poppy would get nachas from reading this book.

Turning to the brains of the operation, I have relied on my wife, Madeleine deBlois, for her love, her enthusiasm for my endeavors, her analytical brilliance, and her incisive ability to clarify my own thoughts and words. With affection, humility, and incalculable gratitude, I dedicate this book, first and foremost, to her. Madeleine is the amazing mother of our kind and charming children Owen and Emmett, whose voracious appetite for books inspired me to finish writing this one; I also dedicate this book to them. My parents, Ellen and Marc Mugmon, have made everything possible through their unconditional love, support, and generosity (and proofreading). My brother Michael has been my lifelong source for advice, perspective, and inspiration; I hope this book has a chance of finding a spot on one of my hero's bookshelves.

Thanks, finally, to the Washington Capitals, who were kind enough to help me celebrate the completion of this manuscript by winning the Stanley Cup.

NOTE ON MUSICAL EXAMPLES

For ease of reference within the musical examples from Mahler's compositions, measure numbers drawn from the critical editions published by the International Gustav Mahler Society are included in the examples. Rehearsal figures (boxed and in bold), and distances from them, are also included in those captions to assist readers who have access to the many editions that contain such figures. (For instance, **4**-2 indicates two measures before **4** appears, while **4**+1 denotes either the measure containing the figure or the first measure after it.) For musical examples by composers other than Mahler, where source scores include rehearsal figures but measure numbers are unavailable, captions include only rehearsal figures; in these cases, the rehearsal figures are reproduced in the examples if they also appear in those passages in the source scores themselves. In one unusual case, example 5.9, I have treated the measure numbers provided in the score of Copland's *Clarinet Concerto* as rehearsal figures because these measure numbers pause for the cadenza, a portion of which is included in the example. In example 5.10, from Copland's *Piano Fantasy*, the source score does not contain measure numbers or rehearsal numbers, so the measure numbers provided reflect my own count.

To save space, individual editions of musical scores have not been cited in notes or the bibliography, but dependable and widely available editions have been consulted for this book. For the sake of accuracy and consistency, minor details in musical examples have at times been altered silently from how they appear in scores.

INTRODUCTION

In 1925, the composer Aaron Copland (1900–1990), then twenty-four years old, wrote a letter to the *New York Times* vehemently defending the music of Gustav Mahler (1860–1911) against what Copland viewed as critics' unmerited attacks on the late-romantic Austrian composer's music. Copland conceded that Mahler's works were sometimes "bombastic," "long-winded," "banal," and beset with "old-fashioned romantico-philosophical conceptions." These common views of Mahler's music as overwrought and outmoded, he wrote, were "quite justified." But Copland then made a striking pivot, arguing that it was what the critics "leave unsaid that seems to me unfair." He was referring to the technical details of Mahler's music, which, according to Copland, placed Mahler squarely in the world of modern composition—and therefore gave his music value. "If one looks at the music qua music," Copland wrote, "then it is undeniable that Mahler is a composer of today." Copland's evidence for Mahler's contemporary resonance included his economical orchestration and his polished use of counterpoint, both of which countered Mahler's reputation as an archaic romanticist. Copland cited "so recent a score as [Arthur] Honegger's 'Pacific 231,'" at the time a sensation in the United States, as "proof of Mahler's living influence." He singled out movements of Mahler's Fourth, Seventh, and Ninth Symphonies, as well as all of the symphonic song cycle *Das Lied von der Erde,* as containing "the stuff of living music"—a powerful assertion of Mahler's contemporary relevance.[1]

Despite his endorsement of Mahler, Aaron Copland's name remains synonymous, for many, with a strain of American music composition clearly distinct from Mahler's Austro-German idiom. His studies with Nadia Boulanger in France in the early 1920s primed him to return to the United States and develop a musical language seen as characteristically American, first through the incorporation of jazz and, in the later 1920s, through his use of dissonance and linear writing, with the music of Igor Stravinsky as a clear precedent.[2] In the 1930s, Copland adopted a more accessible style associated with Americana, most notably in the ballets *Billy the Kid, Rodeo,* and *Appalachian Spring.* And after World War II, Copland turned, as did many of his colleagues, to twelve-tone composition. Although he composed little in the 1970s and 1980s, he remained a significant figure in American composition into his later years, having been commissioned to write a significant work—although it never came into being—for the United States Bicentennial in 1976.[3]

This account of Copland's stature would seem to leave little room for the Austro-German romantic tradition, especially for a composer like Mahler, in the story of twentieth-century American music. At first glance, Mahler and Copland make an incongruous pair. A musical icon of late romanticism and the turbulent *fin de siècle* in Austria, Mahler was the fiery conductor whose personal tribulations and ruminations on life and death seem to pervade his vast symphonies and impassioned songs. Copland, by contrast, has come to represent an unfussy, straightforward, and modern American musical disposition. Born almost forty years after Mahler, and aged ten when Mahler died, Copland is typically seen to embody a streamlined aesthetic, one more readily connected to the modernism and neoclassicism of the early twentieth century than the romanticism of the late nineteenth. In 1953, the composer Arthur Berger, one of the first figures to explore Copland's music in detail, extolled "his economy of means, the transparency of his textures, the preciseness of his tonal vocabulary." Painting Copland as a serious modernist, Berger referred to "the disciplined mentality of a sober artisan."[4] More recently, the outspoken and widely performed American composer John Adams wrote of Copland's "personal style" as an orchestrator, calling it "characteristically simple and free of the excess . . . of much European fin-de-siècle symphonic practice." Setting Copland apart from his European ancestors as both an American icon and an anti-romantic, Adams continued by defining Copland in terms of a specific kind of dispassionate "American" spirit. "In comparison to a Strauss tone poem, with its swirling currents of inner voices, mercurial shifts of mood, and constant upending of harmonic stasis, Copland's orchestral works are like pieces of Shaker furniture, simple to the point of being humble, but sturdy and effective and free of excess emotional baggage. They are typical of the American grain, not unlike the prose of Ernest Hemingway or the poetry of Robert Frost."[5]

Popular conceptions of Copland's work reinforce a sense of distance between his distinctively sober American music and the effusively romantic musical imagination of composers like Mahler. In the 2009 PBS documentary *Keeping Score: Aaron Copland and the American Sound*, the conductor Michael Tilson Thomas called Copland's short, iconic orchestral work *Fanfare for the Common Man* "unmistakably American." Tilson Thomas portrayed this "sound" as the conscious creation of Copland himself; free from assumptions of eminent European visitors like Antonín Dvořák and Gustav Mahler about how American music *should* sound, Tilson Thomas suggested, Copland developed the powerful and recognizable sonic world found in *Appalachian Spring, Billy the Kid,* and the Third Symphony.[6]

It is tempting to think of Copland, with his signature sound, as the chief representative of a new American musical idiom unhindered by the country's Austro-German cultural past. In the Young People's Concert "What Is American Music?" broadcast in 1958, Leonard Bernstein provided an inviting narrative of the history of American composition since the late nineteenth century, describing American composers such as George Whitefield Chadwick (1854–1931) as writing "straight European stuff." The discovery of jazz, Bernstein continued, unlocked "an American folk music that belonged to all Americans" and that became a natural part of composers' vision. Bernstein later introduced Copland, referring to him as the "dean of all American music," and invited him to conduct an excerpt from his Third Symphony. In his introduction, Bernstein noted the work's "American qualities" such as "jazz rhythms, and wide open optimism, and wide open spaces, and the simplicity, and the sentimentality," as well as a distinctly American compound of internationally derived vernacular traditions ("a mixture of things from all over the world—a noble fanfare, a hymn—everything").[7]

The straightforward story of American composers like Copland forging their own path in opposition to the grand European tradition—and drawing on uniquely American materials and sensibilities to do so—has already received much-needed nuance. Specifically, commentators have complicated the sense of distance between Copland's so-called American musical idiom and the realm of European art music by drawing on evidence of his strong connections with French music and aesthetics and, more broadly, contemporary European music. To name a few, Annegret Fauser has shown the specific ways in which the formative years Copland spent in Europe—especially as a student of the noted musician Nadia Boulanger in Paris—shaped his American identity.[8] Carol J. Oja demonstrated that Copland was part of a network of modernists who viewed the creation of new American music as a transnational enterprise that drew clout from linkages with Europe.[9] A recent study by Gayle Murchison outlines Copland's direct musical debts to Igor Stravinsky.[10] In their book on musical nationalism, Matthew Riley and Anthony D. Smith view Copland's "influential American national style" as a result of pan-Americanism, vernacular styles, and Copland's interest in modernists like Stravinsky and Anton Webern.[11] And Nadine Hubbs has placed Copland in a network of gay composers who shared a sense of French musical heredity.[12]

The narrative of twentieth-century American music has also seen important revisions that invite us to find in it a sense of heritage in a Europe-informed American musical past, rather than a clean break from an ancestry that was supposedly dominated by a European sensibility. Despite the fact that Leonard Bernstein announced Chadwick, one of the composers of the late-nineteenth century's so-called Second New England School, as having written "straight European stuff," composers of that period were in fact seeking to develop a distinctive American music. In a frequently quoted passage, Edward MacDowell (1860–1908), another figure associated with the Second New England School, spoke of the need for "absolute freedom from the restraint that an almost unlimited deference to European thought and prejudice has imposed upon us."[13] Furthermore, lineages can be readily drawn from the composers of the Second New England School to twentieth-century American composers, as in the case of Charles Ives, whose teacher was Horatio Parker.[14] Looking even further back, Douglas W. Shadle recently explored a body of music created by American composers of the nineteenth century, confronting a widespread dismissal of pre–twentieth-century American music—a dismissal that, as Shadle showed, Copland himself perpetuated in upholding a narrative of American music coming into its own in the twentieth century.[15] And Beth Levy has challenged, through the idea of the frontier, the narrative of a monolithic American art music.[16]

As the French sources of Copland's American idiom have come to light, the relationship of that idiom with Austro-German music—especially of the romantic era—has remained obscured. Consistent with a tendency to paint much twentieth-century music as an about-face from the fiery extravagance, ardent emotion, and longing nostalgia of the nineteenth century, Copland and his colleagues are typically viewed as opponents of romanticism, even if their admiration for certain nineteenth-century music is sometimes acknowledged (and even if Bernstein, in his Young People's Concert, did mention Copland's "sentimentality").[17] This is a narrative to which Copland himself contributed; in 1954, he said that Mozart, Haydn, and Beethoven "were followed in turn by the fervent romantics of the Nineteenth Century, and the past fifty years have brought an anti-romantic reaction and a major broadening of all phases of music's technical resources."[18] An expanded version of this argument appeared in 1941 in Copland's book *Our New Music,* whose thesis *New York Times* critic Olin Downes then summed up as the claim that romanticism, alive and well in the nineteenth century, was "as dead as a doornail" in the twentieth.[19]

France's reputation as Germany's aesthetic polar opposite helps explain Copland's claim, as an American composer, that romanticism had reached its endpoint. Along with the growing cultural relationship between France and the United States after World War I came the prominence of neoclassicism—a term that developed in France in the late 1910s to encapsulate and validate musical characteristics associated with France, such as clarity, economy, and objectivity, against those of Austro-German romanticism, which was seen as stuffy, longwinded, and subjective.[20] In such an environment, little room remained for an unqualified acceptance of recent Austro-German music. Combined with both strong anti-German sentiment after World War I and a longstanding anxiety about American musical culture as simply having descended from German culture, the conditions would seem to have been in place in the 1920s and beyond for American figures to express a strong sense of distance from romanticism.

But as scholars have shown, the real extent to which World War I shattered the deep-seated prestige of Austro-German culture in the United States is questionable. The European origins of American orchestras, which were founded by and initially consisted of German-speaking musicians, are well documented.[21] And the music of esteemed Austro-German composers such as Ludwig van Beethoven, Richard Wagner, and Johannes Brahms has long commanded the repertoires of these institutions. Looking beyond the concert hall, much of the music of Hollywood has strong Austro-German roots.[22] And as Jessica Gienow-Hecht has discussed, World War I did temporarily exert a negative effect on concert programming of music by Austrian and German composers. And it did sour the attitudes of a number of Americans toward German musicians—with Karl Muck, the German conductor of the Boston Symphony Orchestra, emerging as one of the most prominent victims of an anti-German climate with his imprisonment and deportation. But very shortly after the war ended, German music returned to its privileged place in orchestral repertoires.[23]

Shifting narratives of the development of American music, along with the cultural presence of European and specifically Austro-German music in the United States, invite a new look at how that presence persisted beyond the world of concert programming and into the sound worlds of American composers like Copland. This book is the first to center on how twentieth-century American composers such as Copland drew on, rather than rejected, Austro-German musical romanticism. I examine Copland's relationship with the music of Mahler as a lens through which to observe the role—until now, a largely hidden one—of Austro-German music in the development of American music in the twentieth century.

This is not to say that Copland's debts to Mahler or to the nineteenth century have been ignored entirely; on the contrary, such debts have been documented, albeit sporadically. Such scattered acknowledgments of Copland's romantic heritage usually serve as exceptions in larger narratives that foreground his distinctively anti-romantic attitude, while I see them here as invitations to probe more deeply into Copland's identity as both a modernist and a romanticist. Indeed, his lifelong encounter with Mahler puts pressure on the binaries that have long governed music historiography—particularly those of American/European, French/Austro-German, and modernism/romanticism. Neither Mahler nor Copland, for instance, fits securely in the ever-fluctuating categories of romanticism and modernism—terms that I treat fluidly, as mixtures of stylistic attributes and attitudes toward music that the discussions below suggest were in force during Copland's time, and that sometimes overlap. For the purposes of this study, romanticism points to lush orchestration, sweeping melodic lines, expressiveness, nature, and nostalgia—fixtures of the nineteenth-century orchestral canon; Copland himself identified "lushness of texture," "tonal painting," "the enactment of elemental emotions," and "overpowering climaxes of sound" as "Romantic traits" in Stravinsky's *Rite of Spring*, of all pieces.[24] Broadly speaking, and following what Copland saw as Stravinsky's anti-romantic idiom, musical modernism here connects to spare orchestration, angular melodic writing, and a sense of objectivity. Copland noted Stravinsky's "sharply defined colors" as an orchestrator, as well as "something brutally unsentimental that separated his music from music of the Romantic era" and "an objective quality in the composer's attitude that separates it completely from the 19th-century Romantic attitude.[25] But more broadly, modernism also, as Carol J. Oja has described it, represents "iconoclastic, irreverent innovation, sometimes irreconcilable with the historic traditions that preceded it."[26] Also helpful is Daniel Albright's definition of modernism as "the testing of the limits of aesthetic construction," in terms of both rejecting and exaggerating traits that are often linked to romanticism—making room in modernism, for instance, for both expressionism and objectivity.[27]

For their part, both Mahler and Copland are difficult to pin down in terms of romanticism and modernism. Signature elements of Mahler's music, such as its expressiveness and irony, have been fruitfully understood as both extensions of and departures from romanticism.[28] And Arthur Berger wrote cautiously that Copland's "economy is determined as much by an almost Romantic concern with expression as by the disciplined mentality of a sober artisan." Linking Copland's "Romantic element" to Mahler's example (as opposed to Wagner's), Berger even traced "the combination of leanness and a certain grandiosity" in Copland's Third Symphony to his admiration for Mahler.[29]

What remains remarkable is that although Copland attempted to isolate and then promote those aspects of Mahler's music that he believed pointed to the twentieth century—characteristics such as economical orchestration—his own music, along with his comments on Mahler, tells a more complex story that belies his deep investment in romanticism and the debt he and other American figures owed to it.

My discussion of Copland's relationship with Mahler, and of larger questions that concern American musical life, takes place in several overarching contexts—contexts that embrace Copland's wide range of activities as an American musical figure. Indeed, I view American music in this study not as a fixed aesthetic or set of compositional practices, but rather as an intersection among ideas and activities that includes transatlantic musical encounters, concert programming conventions, and the reception of European music in America. I therefore contend with Copland in many roles, not simply or even primarily as a composer. I consider Copland as a student; archival evidence reveals that he first encountered Mahler's music, oddly enough, in Paris—the hub of French musical restraint—as a young musician in the 1920s. I address Copland as an advocate; correspondence shows Copland to have worked behind the scenes to make Mahler's music more widely known in America as a writer, as a lecturer at the New School for Social Research in New York, and as a tastemaker in the orchestral world—and that these activities were part of a larger project to develop a secure future for the performance of American music. I examine Copland as a composer; musical evidence shows that Copland drew directly on compositional tools he learned from his study of Mahler's music in creating the sound world often identified as distinctly Copland and unmistakably American. I contemplate Copland in terms of Jewishness; Copland drew on his admiration for Mahler, in the context of their shared Jewish identity, to shape his own musical persona. I discuss Copland as a mentor; he played a crucial but under-recognized role in shaping his protégé Leonard Bernstein's approach to Mahler. And I briefly consider Copland as a performer; a little-known but striking detail is that between the 1950s and 1970s, when Leonard Bernstein made his own name as a Mahler conductor, Copland also led performances of Mahler's works. Of course, he did not do so to the same extent as his younger colleague, or with anything approaching the same visibility. But Copland's programming of Mahler does shed light on his own musical priorities.

Copland is the protagonist of the story that unfolds here. Chapter 1 focuses on his early experiences as a musician and as a student of Nadia Boulanger (1887–1979), the French composer, organist, and teacher who taught so many American students in her time that

Virgil Thomson called her "a one-woman graduate school so powerful and so permeating that legend credits every U.S. town with two things—a five-and-dime and a Boulanger pupil."[30] It was in her studio that Copland's first documented encounter with Mahler's music took place. Chapter 2 centers on Boulanger's experience with Mahler in the context of post–World War I internationalism, and on how that experience filtered into her teaching of Copland. Chapter 3 turns to the nuts and bolts of Copland's advocacy of Mahler, particularly as a teacher, and his gradual shift in the 1930s toward a more open embrace of Mahler's romanticism. Chapter 4 considers Copland's Jewishness and its relationship with his vision of Mahler's romanticism in the 1920s, and chapter 5 explores how that romanticism turned up in Copland's own music.

The final two chapters of this book return to Copland's relationships with other significant figures. Chapter 6 concentrates on the Russian conductor Serge Koussevitzky (1874– 1951), a European celebrity who ran a major contemporary music concert series in Paris before he crossed the ocean in 1924 to take over as conductor of the eminent Boston Symphony Orchestra. In that role, he forged a link between romanticism and modernism in the concert hall, promoting Mahler as an exponent of both. Copland likely convinced Koussevitzky to perform Mahler in the first place, and supported his perspective. Chapter 7 considers Copland's and Bernstein's shared vision of Mahler as simultaneously modern and romantic. When it comes to American figures, it is Bernstein, not Copland, who tends to receive most of the recognition for advocacy of Mahler's music. In addition to conducting his works, in 1960 he presented the national CBS broadcast of the Young People's Concert "Who Is Gustav Mahler?" In the following years, he presented numerous audio and video recordings, including a powerful testimonial on Mahler's importance as part of the Norton Lectures at Harvard University in 1973. Indeed, Mahler and Bernstein have been inextricably linked in the annals of twentieth-century music.[31] This book explores a missing link between them: Aaron Copland.

Because Copland's relationship with Mahler's music is the main subject of this book, Bernstein, Koussevitzky, and other figures are considered here primarily for the ways in which their musical activities intersected with Copland's. Much room remains, of course, for research into their own connections with Mahler's music. Far from being an exhaustive investigation into Mahler's American legacy—a study in which these personalities would certainly play significant roles, along with Otto Klemperer in the conducting realm, George Rochberg in concert music, Erich Wolfgang Korngold in film music, and many others—this book maintains a focus on Copland and Mahler as a case study into broader issues that concern American music scholarship. Taken together, the fascinating network of musical figures I consider in this book shapes our understanding not only of Copland's interaction with Mahler, but of its larger implications for American music and its strong—but easily missed—Austro-German romantic roots.

Chapter One

MAHLER AND COPLAND IN NEW YORK

Aaron Copland was only seven years old when Gustav Mahler crossed the Atlantic Ocean and arrived in New York to begin what would turn out to be the final phase of his conducting career. With Mahler's death in 1911, the overlap between the two composers' lives, even if they shared the same city during part of that time, turned out to be quite brief. Although Copland and Mahler likely never came into contact with each other personally, Copland's early years, including Mahler's time in America, were a time of significant developments in ideas about both American musical identity and Mahler's musical value. Mahler's works—despite his central role in New York's musical life—occupied a space on the periphery of the symphonic world as the product of a composer whose long, rarely heard compositions stood at some distance from the established Austro-German tradition. Whether Copland first encountered Mahler's music in New York or when he traveled to Europe in 1921, the fact that Mahler's work was at this time on the outskirts of the orchestral mainstream allowed him to respond to it with fresh ears, and without undue influence from critics or Copland's teacher, Rubin Goldmark.

In Copland's childhood years, Mahler's legacy in the United States was beginning to form, with mixed commentary on the artistic value of his music. In his time with the New York Philharmonic, Mahler introduced his own first two symphonies to the United States in 1908 and 1909. (The first Mahler work to be heard in the United States was his Fourth Symphony, in 1904, with Walter Damrosch conducting the New York Symphony Society and soprano Etta de Montjau singing the fourth movement; in 1906, Wilhelm Gericke led the Boston Symphony Orchestra in Mahler's Fifth Symphony.) Mahler's refusal to sanction program notes irritated the critic Henry Krehbiel, who considered his First Symphony impenetrable without the help of explanatory details.[1] Krehbiel did have positive things to say about Mahler; he noted an "exquisitely lovely and profoundly moving" melody in the First

Symphony's finale, but he also called Mahler "a naïve though unoriginal melodist, who, had he not been drawn into the latter-day swirl by a desire to exploit new colors, new harmonies and new notions about form, would have become a true symphonist."[2] A few years earlier, an unsigned review in the *New York Tribune*, perhaps also by Krehbiel, pointed to another sticking point in discussing Mahler's symphonies—their sheer length. On November 7, 1904, the writer called the Fourth Symphony "brilliantly ingenious in spots, but its habit of drooling along after a rational and longed-for resting place has repeatedly been reached brings weariness before the end of nearly every movement."[3]

Mahler also came under fire as a conductor by some critics for altering the scores of classic symphonists like Ludwig van Beethoven and Franz Schubert. Here again, Krehbiel was a significant voice; he famously wrote of Beethoven's Fifth Symphony that Mahler "phlebotomized" the brief oboe cadenza in the first movement's recapitulation "by giving it to two oboes and beating time for each note—not in the expressive adagio called for by Beethoven, but in a rigid andante."[4] A defender of Beethoven as an inviolable paradigm of high art, as Joseph Horowitz has discussed in detail, Krehbiel is readily pictured as Mahler's unqualified enemy.[5] In his infamously insensitive obituary for Mahler, Krehbiel wrote (referring to the Metropolitan Opera and the New York Philharmonic) that "the investment was a poor one for the opera company that brought him to America and the concert organization which kept him here."[6] But Krehbiel's opinion of Mahler as a conductor was not universally negative. Returning to the Fifth Symphony, Krehbiel actually praised Mahler's doubling of the bassoons with cellos and his transposition of the piccolo an octave higher in the symphony's final movement, writing that through these changes Mahler "secured sonority, which aided him in building up a thrilling climax, but did not materially disturb Beethoven's color scheme. The question of the artistic righteousness of his act may be left to the decision of musicians. Yesterday's audience accepted the result with gladness."[7]

Although controversial, the liberties Mahler took with the scoring of symphonic classics point to a significant aspect of early American discussions of Mahler as a composer: his inventiveness as an orchestrator. A preview of Mahler's Fourth Symphony in 1904 by Richard Aldrich of the *New York Times* highlighted several aspects of Mahler's music that Copland would later discuss in his own writings on Mahler: orchestration, simplicity, counterpoint, and apparent borrowings from the style—and sometimes the actual music—of earlier Austro-German composers. Aldrich called Mahler "intimately familiar with all the modern resources of musical expression, with the refinements of orchestral technique as well as with the most daring of modern harmonic combinations and the manipulation of thematic material. With this goes an unmistakable predilection for the naïve, the folk-tune, the simplicity and sometimes the bareness of the archaic." Turning specifically to the Fourth Symphony, Aldrich praised it, writing that "the scoring is extremely ingenious and goes into numberless subtleties of orchestral technique and unusual instrumental effects." Detecting similarities that the symphony's first two themes bear to the music of Beethoven and Mozart, Aldrich gushed that Mahler's "development of these themes, to which he has joined further brief bits of similar naïve melody, is extremely ingenious, and is full of contrapuntal devices, employing the themes in fragments in which the different voices of the orchestra are treated with utmost independence." Later in the preview, he praised the "learned and adroit contrapuntal devices" in the third movement. And he concluded with a strong endorsement that foreshadows Copland's own commentary: referring to Mahler as a "strangely attractive personality," he added, "His achievements in composition are such that it is time his music was introduced to the attention of American music lovers."[8]

Conductors including Gericke, Josef Stransky (Mahler's successor at the New York Philharmonic), Karl Muck, and Ernst Kunwald brought Mahler's symphonies to American audiences in the years leading up to and during World War I. But the signature event in Mahler's early American reception was the American premiere of Mahler's monumental Eighth Symphony, performed by the Philadelphia Orchestra with Leopold Stokowski conducting on March 2, 1916—five years after Mahler's death and almost sixteen years into Copland's life. Stokowski even took his show on the road to New York on April 9, thanks to the patronage of Mrs. J. F. D. Lanier, leader of the Society of Friends of Music. In her history of the Philadelphia Orchestra, Frances Anne Wister recounted of the orchestra's trip to New York that "such a journey was never before undertaken in musical circles here and abroad. Twelve hundred people left Philadelphia by private trains, totalling seventeen cars . . . and at 8.15 appeared before a packed audience which included all the musicians then in America."[9]

There is no evidence that Copland attended this event, and any suggestion that he may have done so is pure speculation. But it is enticing to consider the possibility that the then-fifteen-year-old musician seized the opportunity, or that at least he became exposed to aspects of Mahler's music at a time of such excitement about Mahler in New York. As Howard Pollack has noted, Copland rarely visited Manhattan from Brooklyn for concerts until 1917, when he began composition lessons with Goldmark. But as an active young composer and pianist who gained experience with classical and romantic repertoire through his studies with Leopold Wolfsohn, Copland did take the opportunity to hear Ignacy Paderewski perform in 1915.[10] It seems likely that a high-profile event like the New York premiere of Mahler's Eighth Symphony with the Philadelphia Orchestra in 1916 would have been on a musically hungry Copland's radar. And he was certainly aware of the event later in his career; his handwritten notes for a lecture on Mahler's Eighth Symphony, which he delivered in 1929 at the New School for Social Research, mention Stokowski's American premiere of the work.[11]

The American composer Rubin Goldmark—soon to be Copland's teacher—was reported to have attended the premiere of Mahler's Eighth Symphony in 1916.[12] His published comments on Mahler illustrate his admiration for Mahler's multifaceted work as a musician, and Goldmark even endorsed Mahler as a composer, if reservedly. In a pamphlet published by the Society of Friends of Music to coincide with the performance, a short commentary by Goldmark included the remark that the "production of his Eighth Symphony is sure to arouse the interest of every serious lover of music." Goldmark spoke effusively about Mahler's conducting, demonstrating that Mahler's reputation for taking liberties with standard scores did not scar his long-term reputation as a performer or a composer. As Goldmark commented,

> Gustav Mahler's unique personality dominated every musical work of art with which he came in contact. Among the greatest of my musical experiences I shall ever consider a performance of "Tristan und Isolde" under his direction at the Court Opera in Vienna some fifteen years ago. It is a striking tribute to his genius as a conductor that another work, heard about the same time—one which stands emotionally at the opposite extreme of operatic literature—Nicolai's "Merry Wives of Windsor," should likewise have produced a remarkable impression. The contrast between the impassioned sweep in the reproduction of the one work, with the exquisite charm and refinement of the other, afforded a strong insight into the versatility of his musicianship.

Connecting these contrasts in Mahler's conducting work to his compositions, Goldmark continued, "His own style of composition seems to abound in similar contrasts (my knowledge of his orchestral works is limited to the First and Fourth Symphonies). Simplicity and faithfulness of theme, combined with an ultra-modern harmonic sense and a truly marvelous orchestral palette."[13] Goldmark's reflections on Mahler's "simplicity" and mastery of the orchestra hark back to Aldrich's preview from more than ten years before. Goldmark's comment that Mahler's Eighth Symphony should "arouse the interest of every serious lover of music" echoes Aldrich's preview of the Fourth Symphony in 1904 that "it is time his music was introduced to the attention of American music lovers." Thus for Goldmark, room existed for Americans to become more familiar with Mahler's works. And Goldmark was not alone among pamphlet contributors in highlighting Mahler's treatment of the orchestra. George Whitefield Chadwick, whose *Melpomene* Mahler conducted with the New York Philharmonic in 1911, referred to Mahler's "enormous orchestral technique, in which he was surpassed by no one." Howard Brockway, another composer, wrote that Mahler "scored with the sure touch of a great master of modern orchestral resources." Ernst Kunwald mentioned Mahler's "wonderfully brilliant and effective orchestration." The pianist Ossip Gabrilowitsch wrote that Mahler's "style of orchestration is unlike any other, and so is his polyphonic treatment of ideas."[14]

In light of this praise, and of his experience hearing Mahler conduct in Vienna, Goldmark's central position in a network of figures that embraced Mahler—as one indirect link between Mahler and Copland—is worth noting. Goldmark was one of the founders of the Bohemians, an organization of musicians in New York; on January 23, 1909, while Goldmark was president of the group, the Bohemians held a gathering in honor of Mahler at the Astor Hotel in New York.[15] Goldmark might have heard the First and Fourth symphonies, to which he referred in the Society of Friends of Music pamphlet, when Mahler himself conducted those works in New York around the time of the gathering—the First Symphony in December of 1909, and the Fourth Symphony in January of 1911, both with the New York Philharmonic. Having been a resident of New York, he may also have attended the American premiere of Mahler's Fourth Symphony in 1904. (Goldmark's claim of familiarity with only the First and Fourth symphonies suggests that he did not hear Mahler conduct the Second Symphony with the New York Symphony Society in December of 1908, the month before the Bohemians event.) What is more, Goldmark's family had ties to Mahler in Europe. His uncle, the Hungarian composer Karl Goldmark (1830–1915), was a prominent figure in Vienna whose operas Mahler championed as a conductor.

By categorizing Mahler's harmonic language as "ultra-modern," Rubin Goldmark—if indeed he discussed Mahler's music at all with Copland—may well have made Mahler more attractive to Copland in the long run. Copland later recalled that his teacher shied away from compositions that seemed to be on the cutting edge. Of studying with Goldmark, Copland wrote, "The one drawback—a serious one from my standpoint—was that [Goldmark] had little if any sympathy for the advanced musical idioms of the day, and frankly admitted the fact."[16]

Copland called his teacher "a rather conventionally minded composer and musician. . . . He was a good teacher but I, of course, was interested in the newest music, as all good students should be."[17] Goldmark apparently discouraged Copland from exploring Charles Ives's *Concord Sonata*; Copland wrote that Goldmark feared that, as a young composer, Copland might "be contaminated by stuff like that."[18]

Picturing his own teacher—one who was deeply invested in German romanticism—as helplessly conservative served a narrative in which Copland would later emerge as a distinctly twentieth-century American who escaped the shadow of the Austro-German canon. This is despite the fact that Copland's knowledge of counterpoint—central both to neoclassicism and to his defense of Mahler, as will be seen in chapter 3—owed much to his studies with Goldmark.[19] While Copland may well have sold short his mentor's quite robust interest in composers of the early twentieth century, it is also possible that Goldmark never made that interest known to him. After Goldmark's death in 1936, another of his students, the composer Frederick Jacobi, painted him as more open-minded than closed off to modernism: "Contrary to a fairly general impression, he was not intolerant of the more advanced music of his contemporaries. . . . In his youth he had been a champion of [Richard] Strauss and Debussy and he knew the works of these masters thoroughly. . . . He was conscious of his reputation of belonging to the 'right wing' and this troubled him . . . unnecessarily, we believe."[20] That Jacobi would recall Goldmark as tolerant of and even receptive to newer music is not surprising. It reflects Jacobi's own stance as a composer who embraced new music but was—as he acknowledged in the first sentence of his article "In Defense of Modernism"—"at heart a conservative."[21]

Mahler may even have been one of the composers Copland, looking back in 1939 on his studies with Goldmark, saw as temptingly off limits, and thus enough to "whet any young man's appetite"—especially any young man who, like Copland, had "something of the reputation of a musical rebel, in Goldmark's eyes at any rate."[22] If Copland did glean from any conversations with Goldmark that his teacher perceived Mahler's work as harmonically "ultra-modern," then Mahler's stock was sure to rise for him. And it seems likely, though it is again a matter of speculation, that in four years of lessons, Mahler and even the experience of the American premiere of the Eighth Symphony turned up at some point in their discussions. Copland specifically recalled that Goldmark's "inexhaustible fund of stories and anecdotes made him a favorite toastmaster at musical gatherings."[23] Indeed, as Krehbiel wrote in his history of the Bohemians, Goldmark was known as "the Club's oracle, the laudator of its guest, the spokesman of its president" after he turned over the office to Franz Kneisel in 1910.[24] Although that role postdates the Club's 1909 event in honor of Mahler, Krehbiel's statement suggests that Goldmark had his personal testimony on a large number of significant musicians—including Mahler—at the ready.

But as a figure whom Goldmark linked with the term "ultra-modern," Mahler probably would have rested comfortably outside the perimeter of composers Goldmark considered worthy of emulation by his students. Thus for Copland in his late teens, Mahler was on the musical frontier, waiting to be fully discovered. The performance of Mahler's Eighth Symphony was one of the few opportunities Copland would have had to hear Mahler in New York during his teenage years—a circumstance that perhaps added to Mahler's mystique as a little-known composer. Indeed, between the latter part of 1917 and the spring of 1921, the period during which Copland studied with Goldmark, the only Mahler symphony programmed by the New York Philharmonic was the First Symphony, in December of 1920 and January of 1921, conducted by Josef Stransky. The New York Philharmonic was in fact slated to perform Mahler's Third Symphony in the 1917–18 season, but the performance did not materialize.[25]

To be sure, other groups did take on Mahler's music while Copland was a teenager. Before his time with Goldmark, in February of 1916, Marcia van Dresser sang Mahler's *Lieder eines fahrenden Gesellen*, with Walter Damrosch conducting the New York Symphony. And in January of 1917, Artur Bodanzky led members of the Metropolitan Opera orchestra in a performance of the same cycle (sung by Johannes Sembach), as well as *Kindertotenlieder* (with Tilly Koenen), at the Ritz Carlton Hotel, in a concert sponsored by the Society of Friends of Music—the same group that had made possible the Philadelphia Orchestra performance of Mahler's Eighth Symphony the previous year. But in general, Mahler was not often performed in New York during Copland's Goldmark years.[26]

Geopolitics may have played a temporary role in reducing the amount of Mahler Copland would have had the opportunity to experience while he studied with Goldmark. W. J. Henderson, a Mahler skeptic, wrote in the *New York Herald* in 1922 that "New York underwent a heavy bombardment of Mahler in the season of 1916–17. During the participation of the United States in the world war the Austrians and friends of Austrian music in this city enjoyed a period of enforced rest."[27] The "enforced rest" for Mahler's music happened to begin at the same time as Copland's studies with Goldmark. Zooming out from Mahler, Copland connected the idea of music "forbidden" by Goldmark to the broader point that World War I made recent music from Europe—specifically, by Debussy, Ravel, and Scriabin—prohibitively expensive to obtain. As Copland wrote, "The fact that the music was in some sense forbidden only increased its attractiveness. Moreover, it was difficult to get. The war had made the importation of new music a luxury; Scriabin and Debussy and Ravel were bringing in high prices."[28] Thus, it was not only Goldmark's tentativeness about certain music that made composers like Mahler potentially attractive for Copland at the time; it was the mere fact that, as with Mahler's symphonies, such music was challenging to access.

A significant shift in Mahler's American reception took place in the early 1920s. The turning point was the arrival in the United States of the Dutch conductor Willem Mengelberg, one of the most ardent supporters of Mahler's music and one of his closest colleagues. From 1921 to 1930 in New York, Mengelberg conducted several of Mahler's compositions, first as conductor of New York's National Symphony Orchestra and then with the New York Philharmonic.[29] In his first month leading the NSO, in January of 1921, Mengelberg led Mahler's First Symphony. Later that year, the New York Philharmonic merged with the NSO, and Mengelberg conducted Mahler with the group nearly every year until 1930 (1924 and 1928 were exceptions). Meanwhile, Bruno Walter, who had assisted Mahler at the Vienna Court Opera, led the New York Philharmonic in Mahler's First Symphony in 1924.

But Copland did not witness the beginnings of this shift firsthand. Mengelberg's arrival in New York coincided with Copland's departure for Paris, where he would study with Nadia Boulanger from 1921 to 1924. As he did not leave for Europe until June of 1921, he would have been present in New York for both major orchestras' performances of Mahler's First Symphony earlier that year—although no evidence exists to suggests he attended any Mahler performances before his departure. But by the time he returned to the United States in June of 1924, he had missed the New York premieres of both Mahler's Third Symphony (February 1922) and Seventh Symphony (March 1923). The Seventh Symphony was a recent newcomer to the United States; it had its American premiere in 1921, with Frederick Stock conducting the Chicago Symphony Orchestra. (This was a delayed American premiere; Mahler himself intended to perform the Seventh in New York but discarded that plan because of concerns that audiences were not ready for the work.)[30] Perhaps the most significant missed opportunity for Copland was a collection of performances of *Das Lied von der Erde*—which would become his favorite Mahler work—in concerts sponsored again by the Society of Friends of Music. The performances were conducted by Artur Bodanzky and all featured contralto Sara

Cahier, who also performed at the work's premiere on November 20, 1911, in Munich, alongside tenor William Miller, with Bruno Walter conducting. The New York performances took place in February 1922 (the New York premiere, with tenor Orville Harrold), February 1923 (with Jacques Urlus), and January 1924 (with Curt Taucher).

Despite the uptick in Mahler performances in the early 1920s, negative attitudes toward Mahler in the United States—although not new to this period—thrived, setting the stage for Copland's public embrace of his music. Critic Lawrence Gilman summed up the situation in July of 1921 in terms of a transatlantic divide, with Europeans embracing Mahler but Americans rejecting him. Gilman wrote that "the 'Mahler Question' is no nearer settlement than it ever was. Discussion concerning his qualities as a musician persists with unabated fury, dividing those who (like Mr. Mengelberg, Mr. Stokowski, and innumerable European musicians of eminence and experience) regard him as one of the great men of music, from those who (like most of our American critics) regard him as the abomination of desolation."[31] In a biting review of Mengelberg's performance of Mahler's Seventh Symphony in 1923, Richard Aldrich of the *New York Times* wrote colorfully (and surprisingly, given his enthusiasm for Mahler in 1904) that the composition, full of "the laborious manipulation of trivial ideas that have no issue in musical beauty or musical significance or expression," ought to "lead to the hope that the times and labor and funds of the Philharmonic shall not further be expended upon this sort of music, Dead Sea fruit that turns to ashes in the hands of him who would grasp it."[32] And while, as Edward R. Reilly has noted, Mahler's songs tended to receive better press than the numbered symphonies, Aldrich questioned even the merits of *Das Lied*, writing that it "disclosed again a certain few passages of striking though not very original beauty, and many more passages of dull and tiresome music-making, pure manufacture."[33] Commercial considerations also presented a problem for Mahler's supporters; the New York Philharmonic's executive board refused Mengelberg permission to program Mahler in the 1923–24 season because of concerns about Mahler's lack of appeal—which the orchestra's manager, Arthur Judson, relayed directly to Mengelberg."[34]

Of course, not all assessments of Mahler's music were negative. In his 1921 article, Gilman wrote glowingly of Mahler's Second Symphony and a recent performance by Stokowski and the Philadelphia Orchestra. But the music certainly faced an overwhelmingly antipathetic critical landscape when Copland returned in June of 1924 from his studies with Nadia Boulanger. And it was a landscape Copland was eager to enter; less than a year after his return to New York, in the spring of 1925, he heard Mengelberg conduct the New York Philharmonic in

Mahler's Second Symphony and wrote his letter to the *New York Times* defending Mahler from his harsh critics.

Copland's burgeoning appreciation for Mahler, which led to the *Times* letter, is the subject of the next chapter. But as we have seen, a number of factors came together to pave the way for Copland to respond positively to the music by the mid-1920s. Since Copland held a strong interest in music outside the mainstream, Mahler's lack of a reliable place in the American orchestral canon likely gave the music an additional allure. Mahler's outsider status in the symphonic canon, both as a composer and as a controversial conductor, perhaps insulated his legacy from any concern that he fit securely in the Austro-German tradition that had long dominated American orchestras' repertories. And despite some prominent successes for Mahler's music, such as Stokowski's performances of the Eighth Symphony, concerts of Mahler's music were unusual in the United States in the late 1910s, partly owing to anti-German sentiment after World War I. Much of Mahler's music—including the Sixth, Seventh, and Ninth symphonies, had yet to be heard in America by the time the war ended in 1918. And the increase in Mahler's musical visibility in the New York happened to coincide with Copland's absence; he simply did not participate in the surge of interest in Mahler in his home country in the early 1920s. By the time Copland left for Paris, Mahler was new and marginal enough in the United States to resonate with Copland and to avoid a stigma of Austro-German dominance.

Chapter Two

MAHLER IN NADIA BOULANGER'S STUDIO AND BEYOND

If Copland's deep relationship with Mahler's music had its roots in New York in the 1910s, it blossomed quickly and powerfully in the context of his European training, and in a setting that seems unlikely at first: the studio of Nadia Boulanger in Paris. When Copland arrived in Paris in June of 1921, Mahler's music—and indeed that of other Austro-German composers closely linked to the late nineteenth century—was likely far from his mind. Setting off for Paris was in part an assertion of his own status as a young American composer who consciously avoided Austro-German precedents. In this passage from a 1976 interview, Copland recalled his decision: "All the new music seemed to be coming from Paris in those days . . . so I decided to go to Paris to study. The older generation had all gone to Germany to study—in Leipzig, Munich, or Berlin where Strauss was. That was where they headed for. But my own generation began to see pieces by Debussy and Ravel and I guess some Roussel at that time, and so we wanted to go to Paris."[1] Little more than a week after reaching Paris, he began his study at the Conservatoire américain at Fontainebleau for the summer of 1921, which led him to the most important figure in his development as a composer: the noted organist and teacher Nadia Boulanger, who was on the faculty there. As he wrote to his parents, that introduction made clear that "she understands the kind of modern music I like to write," making her "the teacher I was looking for."[2]

As it happened, Mahler's music was fresh in Boulanger's mind in 1921—a circumstance that, as we will see, translated directly into Copland's own relationship with Mahler. In May of 1920, just the year before Copland arrived in her studio, Boulanger's first documented introduction to Mahler's music took place at a pivotal moment in Mahler's musical afterlife. Over the course of two weeks, Willem Mengelberg, as leader of the Royal Concertgebouw Orchestra in

Amsterdam, conducted the nine completed symphonies, *Das Lied von der Erde, Kindertotenlieder,* and *Lieder eines fahrenden Gesellen.* The occasion was Mengelberg's twenty-fifth anniversary as the orchestra's conductor, and he chose to mark it by honoring Mahler. His choice was fitting because the orchestra was as deeply connected with Mahler and his music as any in the world—including the Vienna Philharmonic and the New York Philharmonic, two groups for which Mahler had served as music director. The festival also included speeches on his significance by notable figures who were closely linked to Mahler and his works, including Guido Adler, Richard Specht, and Alfredo Casella.[3]

It was not the first opportunity Boulanger would have had to experience Mahler's music; Mahler himself conducted his music in Paris when Boulanger was twenty-two years old. In a striking example of international collaboration that foreshadowed the Amsterdam festival, Elisabeth Comtesse Greffulhe and the Italian musician Alfredo Casella brought Mahler to Paris to lead his monumental Second Symphony for orchestra, soloists, and chorus on April 17, 1910.[4] The concert was, for the most part, a critical success.[5] But while Mahler was conducting, several eminent French figures, including Gabriel Pierné, Paul Dukas, and Claude Debussy, reportedly left in disgust.[6] This story may be apocryphal; as Henry-Louis de La Grange suggested, it is doubtful that Pierné, who conducted part of the concert himself, would have made such an insolent show of disdain—or that Dukas, who had praised Mahler's music the year before, would have done the same. Still, La Grange's research into the incident turned up a witness who corroborated the story that Debussy indeed excused himself mid-concert.[7] Whatever the case, this anecdote about French musicians giving Mahler the cold shoulder is emblematic of a larger friction between French and Austro-German musical traditions that can be traced back to at least the 1870s, and that makes Paris an unusual source of Copland's interest in Mahler. This longstanding friction was marked by both the Franco-Prussian War of 1870–71 and intense debates in France about the merits of Richard Wagner's music.[8]

Notwithstanding her status as one of the twentieth century's most influential French musicians, Nadia Boulanger has been almost completely omitted from discussions of Mahler's reception, and indeed of most late-nineteenth-century Austro-German music. Jeanice Brooks has demonstrated that Boulanger admired Brahms's music—but with a keen awareness of her own aesthetic distance from it.[9] Boulanger's only extended commentary on Mahler's music is apparently critical in tone. In a frequently cited passage from her 1920 review of the Royal Concertgebouw Orchestra's Mahler festival, she asserted Mahler's incompatibility with French preferences: "The architecture, the aesthetics of Mahler, by its dimension, its size, go against the French mind, made of moderation, of harmony."[10]

This passage reveals a disconnect between Mahler's Austro-German expansiveness and a French inclination toward restraint, making it all the more surprising that Copland would have been in a position to encounter that music in Boulanger's studio. But the full review and its context in Boulanger's teaching suggest a more complex story. Her apparent rejection of Mahler contradicts a tantalizing detail: at least three of Boulanger's students came into contact with Mahler's scores under her direction. The first two were Copland and Virgil Thomson, who, in traveling to France rather than Germany for a musical education in the early 1920s, took part in a shift of American musical allegiance away from Germany after World War I.[11] In doing so they helped confirm Boulanger's primary position in international musical communities "at the forefront of a burgeoning conduit of Franco-American cultural exchange," as Kimberly Francis put it.[12] The third was Elliott Carter, Boulanger's student from 1932 to 1935, who reported that she noted the "care with which Mahler indicated everything in his orchestral scores."[13]

Despite the doubts about Mahler's music that Boulanger expressed along national lines, documentary evidence regveals that a post–World War I attitude of internationalism pervaded her engagement with Mahler, with far-reaching consequences for his twentieth-century reception. Through archival material at the Fonds Boulanger of the Bibliothèque nationale de France and at the Amsterdam City Archives, this chapter explores the Mahler festival held in Amsterdam in 1920 and led by Dutch conductor Willem Mengelberg—Boulanger's earliest known encounter with Mahler's music, and the event that prompted her review. Correspondence between Boulanger and Mengelberg reveals that she attended the festival as a journalist and Mengelberg's French colleague. A reexamination of Boulanger's review of the festival demonstrates that, far from indicating distaste for Mahler, she encouraged her readers to explore his music precisely because of the discrepancy between Mahler's aesthetic world and French expectations.

Boulanger's library tells an important part of the story. Housed at the Conservatoire national supérieur musique et danse (CNSMD) in Lyon, the library includes several Mahler scores that she brought from Amsterdam to Paris, including a copy of the Fourth Symphony in which Boulanger assigned numerical labels to motives—an analytical approach that, in Mahler's case, highlights the music's polyphonic fabric. Correspondence preserved in the Copland Collection at the Library of Congress and in the Bibliothèque nationale then shows that Boulanger served as a sounding board for Copland's exploration of Mahler's works, encouraging his agenda of promoting Mahler publicly.

In addition to illustrating the roots of Copland's fascination with Mahler, Boulanger's engagement with that music serves as a case study in broadening research on musical reception beyond the nexus of public performances and journalistic accounts to include evidence from more private realms. Reception in general—and Mahler's in particular—is usually assessed in terms of concerts and published reactions to public events.[14] For instance, evaluating Mahler's reception in France, La Grange considered the composer's music to have been virtually "dormant" there until the 1960s, measured strictly by the scarcity of public performances.[15] As Mark Everist has pointed out, "For much of the last half of the twentieth century, 'reception' was almost synonymous with the study of the press."[16] In this chapter, the account of Boulanger's encounter with Mahler blends discussions of public and private realms to help collapse what Jeanice Brooks has identified as a "public/private dichotomy" in music history.[17]

Boulanger's first known experience with Mahler, at the Mahler festival in Amsterdam in 1920, took place in the context of a new international solidarity following World War I. The festival's official message was that Mahler's music could bring together citizens of all nations.[18] The Treaty of Versailles had been signed less than a year earlier, on June 28, 1919; the festival served as a cultural parallel to this moment of political reconciliation.[19] Casella's recollection of delivering remarks alongside Guido Adler and Paul Stefan elucidates this feeling of camaraderie. Referring to himself initially in the third person, Casella wrote, "The Italian spoke in French and the two Viennese in German. A tight spiritual solidarity reunited these enemies of the day before. And at the end of this event one could see the Frenchman Florent Schmitt walking arm-in-arm with the Austrian Arnold Schoenberg."[20]

This sense of international rapprochement through music was ubiquitous at the Mahler festival. Casella (representing Italy), Schoenberg (Austria), and Schmitt (France) all signed the Manifesto of the foreign guests at the Mahler Festival, a document whose ideals have been connected to those surrounding the League of Nations, established in Paris the year before.[21] Although Boulanger was not selected as the manifesto's French signatory (each nation had just one representative), its themes were central to the event and would certainly have shaped her experience. David C. Paul has characterized the manifesto as an "official testimony to the internationalist aspirations of the occasion."[22] Its text mentions the "common worship of a single genius" and credits the festival with helping to "rebuild the broken spiritual bridges between the peoples." Moreover, it extols "the opportunity afforded to all of us—for the first time since the long years of war and isolation—to shake the hands of our brethren in art, irrespective of nationality and race."[23] The document's signatories represented several nations and musical vocations; they included the English critic Samuel Langford and the American pianist Olga Samaroff Stokowski. And the Russian violinist Alexander Schmuller coordinated a set of five chamber music concerts that featured works by living composers from several nations.[24] Boulanger surely attended concerts in that series; her copy of the separate program for the chamber-music events survives at the CNSMD.[25]

Boulanger had a personal stake in the festival's success. Correspondence suggests that at Mengelberg's request, she facilitated French attendance at the festival. On January 6, 1920, Mengelberg asked her to identify twenty-five to thirty important French composers and critics.[26] In his letter, emblazoned with a Mahler-festival insignia, he cautioned her that invitations would be limited. Boulanger's response has not been found, but her name is the first in a two-page, non-alphabetized, handwritten list of invitees residing in France, found among planning documents in the Amsterdam City Archives—further suggesting that she helped shepherd French attendance.[27] In assisting Mengelberg she was supporting the work of a member of her own musical network. Boulanger had been a close associate of the pianist Raoul Pugno, who died in 1914.[28] Mengelberg was one of many prominent musicians in the orbit of Pugno's family.[29] Whether or not Mahler turned up in discussions between Boulanger and Mengelberg, the two probably interacted at La Maison Blanche, Pugno's summer home in Gargenville. Indeed in Léonie Rosenstiel's biography of Boulanger, Mengelberg is pictured at La Maison Blanche with Pugno and Boulanger's mother, Raissa.[30]

Boulanger's regard for Mengelberg emerges clearly in her review of the festival in *Le monde musical*. She begins by noting that Mengelberg's popularity and technical ability had been evident throughout his tenure at the Concertgebouw, which started in 1895, and she praises Mengelberg as a "tireless worker" (travailleur infatigable) and "bright mind" (esprit lumineux). Boulanger dwells on the quality of the performances in the works she heard (as she explains, she arrived in Amsterdam in time to hear only some of the offerings, including the Sixth through Ninth Symphonies, *Das Lied von der Erde*, and the *Kindertotenlieder*). Of the performance of *Das Lied*, sung by Sara Cahier and Jacques Urlus, she writes that it was "impossible to imagine a more moving interpretation."[31]

Other personal relationships may also have prepared Boulanger to paint Mahler's music in a positive light. Boulanger had been friends with Casella since their time as students at the Paris Conservatoire.[32] She clearly valued his musical insights; she would later praise Casella's "admirable" 1924 book, titled *The Evolution of Music throughout the History of the Perfect Cadence.*[33] Casella's study reflects the same international sensibility of the 1920 festival: he presents the full text in English, French, and Italian. He praises Mahler, considering a passage from the second movement of the Eighth Symphony to have been "delicious in its grace and harmonic freshness."[34] It is possible—although no documentation has yet emerged to demonstrate this—that Boulanger and Casella conferred about Mahler's music and even that she was present at the notable 1910 performance of Mahler's Second Symphony in Paris.

Indeed, Boulanger was a member of a larger network of French musicians who showed interest in music originating from across the Rhine. Maurice Ravel and Arthur Honegger were invested in Mahler's music, difficult though it was for them to access it in the 1910s and 1920s. Honegger sought a copy of Mahler's Second Symphony while in Paris in 1917.[35] In an interview in the *Neue Freie Presse* on October 29, 1920, Ravel expressed hope that Mahler's music would cross national borders: "Unfortunately, the symphonies and lieder of Gustav Mahler have not penetrated our important musical centers."[36] Schmitt, as noted above, served as France's official representative at the festival. And in 1922, a favorable overview of Mahler's symphonies by the composer Édouard Combe appeared in *La revue musicale.*[37] French interest in non-French music also extended well beyond Mahler; as Barbara Kelly has discussed in the context of Darius Milhaud's advocacy of Arnold Schoenberg's *Pierrot lunaire*, the members of *Les Six* "craved to hear and keep abreast of contemporary European music after the restrictions of war."[38]

In her review, Boulanger grappled with Mahler in the context of a larger discussion of musical nationality and universality; she considered Mahler a genius but questioned whether his genius was "universal."[39] Leaning toward the negative, she declared, "It is certain that as concerns Mahler and French artists, there is one part lack of knowledge and one part incompatibility."[40] The divergence she observed between Mahler and French aesthetics stemmed from the subjectivity she detected in Mahler; she drew on the festival as a vehicle for delineating a regional musical identity based on a "Latin" tradition that omitted Mahler:[41] "The architecture, the aesthetics of Mahler's music, by its size, its expansion, go against the French mind, made of moderation, of harmony. In other words, here [in France], style must dominate feeling, whereas there [in Germany], everything must give way to feeling: hence a mode of neo-romanticism that the Latin races seem to flee, just as they try to renounce the predominance of the 'self.'"[42] Here Boulanger positioned Mahler as Teutonic rather than Latin, implicitly excluding him, through her use of the term "neo-romanticism," from neoclassicism, her preferred aesthetic universe.[43] And still other evidence reveals Boulanger's concerns about—or at least her keen awareness of—the immense scale of Mahler's music. She reported, with an exclamation point, that the performances involved 156 instrumentalists and 717 choral singers.[44] These figures were not advertised at the festival; Boulanger apparently arrived at them herself, as if to prove, wryly, her point about scale. In her program book (fig. 2.1), she manually tallied the number of singers.[45]

Boulanger placed the inexperience of the French with Mahler into a broader internationalist context, what she called "the intellectual rapprochement that is necessary not to equalize the races, but to allow them to determine the reasons for their different characters."[46] In referring to the junction of nationalist and internationalist outlooks, she evinced an attitude similar to one later expressed by Ralph Vaughan Williams, who wrote in 1942, "I believe that all that is of value in our spiritual and cultural life springs from our own soil; but this life cannot develop and fructify except in an atmosphere of friendship and sympathy with other nations."[47]

For her part, Boulanger identified two typical reactions to Mahler, presumably on the part of the French: simply condemning his music without getting to know it, and struggling earnestly but in vain to come to terms with it.[48] Rejecting these approaches, she insisted that Mahler deserved a fair hearing: "Our independence is one of our sources of pride—it allows us to forget our grievances and sympathies alike in the sincere desire to understand well."[49] This did not mean Mahler was compatible with French tastes, but rather that the French, despite their aesthetic distance from Mahler, could comprehend and even appreciate his music.[50] For Boulanger, the festival took place at a time when "the conditions of existence demand that each people endeavors to understand the mentality of other peoples."[51]

Boulanger ultimately came to terms with Mahler's music not through musical style but through an emotional potency that bridged national divides. The passage in which she attempted to find value in Mahler merits quoting in full:

> His music demands respect, for it expresses itself deeply, with an undeniable sincerity, and it appeals to hearts, for it has concentrated in itself the greatest human feelings. Our anxiety in the face of our misery, in the face of the unknown that we sense from all sides, our pain in the face of death, and our love for the child are the first

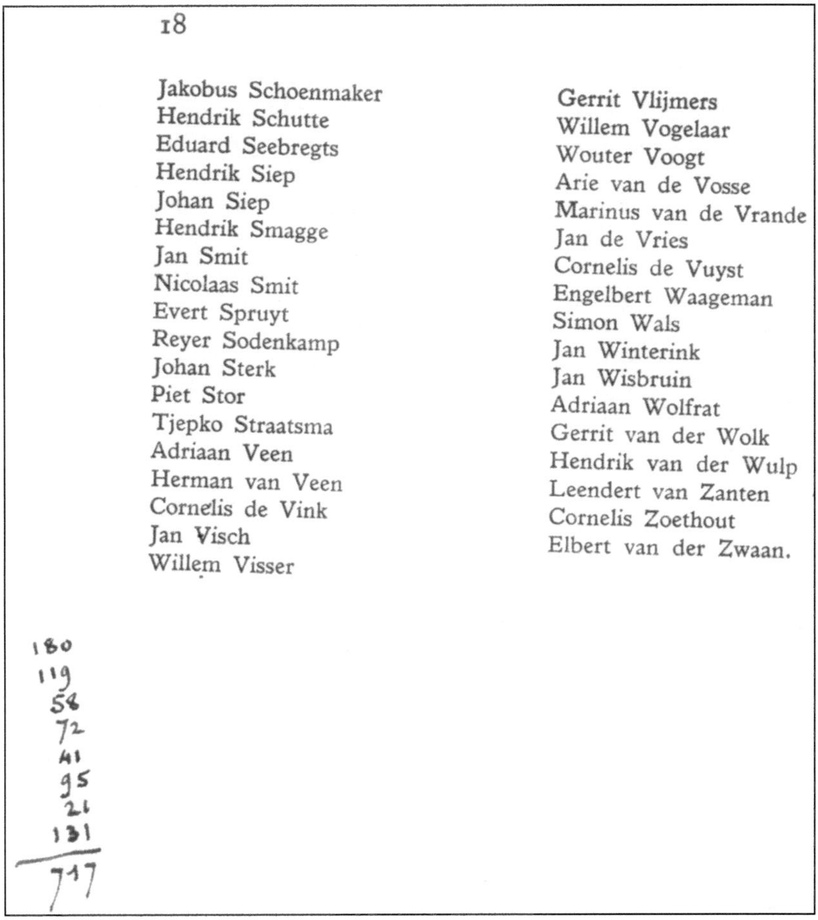
18

Jakobus Schoenmaker
Hendrik Schutte
Eduard Seebregts
Hendrik Siep
Johan Siep
Hendrik Smagge
Jan Smit
Nicolaas Smit
Evert Spruyt
Reyer Sodenkamp
Johan Sterk
Piet Stor
Tjepko Straatsma
Adriaan Veen
Herman van Veen
Cornelis de Vink
Jan Visch
Willem Visser
Gerrit Vlijmers
Willem Vogelaar
Wouter Voogt
Arie van de Vosse
Marinus van de Vrande
Jan de Vries
Cornelis de Vuyst
Engelbert Waageman
Simon Wals
Jan Winterink
Jan Wisbruin
Adriaan Wolfrat
Gerrit van der Wolk
Hendrik van der Wulp
Leendert van Zanten
Cornelis Zoethout
Elbert van der Zwaan.

180
119
58
72
41
95
21
131
717

Figure 2.1. Boulanger's count of singing forces in the Mahler festival program book, 1920. Photo courtesy of Médiathèque Nadia Boulanger, CNSMD de Lyon, UFNB L MAH 3 M.

things we notice. Next appear our serene and religious resignation, our haughty and lonely strength, which go through wild bursts of outrage, of passion, and finally, our faith, this faith giving peace to all instances of mourning, radiance to all joys. That all this is not sometimes tarnished by a questionable melodic turn, by longueurs and heavy passages, is impossible to argue, but must we persist in criticizing when we can love? . . . There are, then, a thousand reasons to love Mahler who, in any case, is one of the great modern composers—let us strive to feel the profound emotion of his work.[52]

Despite the "longueurs and heavy passages" (markers of Mahler as Teutonic), Boulanger identified a multidimensional expressive palette. (Combe's published discussion of Mahler in 1922 echoed Boulanger's detection of an "undeniable sincerity"; Combe found in his music "a profound and persuasive sincerity" [une sincérité profonde et persuasive].)[53] In the context of Copland's lessons with Boulanger, Annegret Fauser has pointed to the "fine line" Boulanger navigated "between universalism and national specificity."[54] In Boulanger's case, the lack of universalism she found in Mahler's expansive musical fabric was compensated for by an emotional appeal that carried with it a universal resonance.

Boulanger's defense of Mahler persisted and indeed strengthened well into the 1920s. Beginning in January 1925, she toured the United States as an organist and lecturer. Her trip included three talks on modern music at Rice University, versions of which were published in English. (As Kimberly Francis has noted, these differed considerably from the spoken texts; the discussion here considers the published texts).[55] In the first published lecture, Boulanger likened the prejudicial attitude of the "Anglo-Saxon or German" toward Gabriel Fauré's music to the "impatience and irritation which the music of Brahms or Malher [*sic*] tends to provoke in a Frenchman." She continued with a plea for open-mindedness, as in her Mahler review, only here she admitted Mahler into the "universal" category: "But in all such cases of national differences, longer acquaintance is an easy and a certain remedy, and in the end one finds oneself loving the very qualities which at first seemed so repellent. Also we must remember that, as [André] Gide has said, 'it is in being the most individual that one is the most universal.'"[56] Further, Boulanger expressed "regret" for omitting non-French composers from her discussion: "France has always been quick to recognize beauty and merit wherever they happened to be found and I feel almost as though I were being unfaithful to the traditions of my country in not speaking of such men as de Falla, Malipiero, Szymanowski, Bartok, Schoenberg, etc."[57] This passage in the Rice lectures reflects Boulanger's belief in "eclecticism as a powerful French character trait," as Fauser has described it in this context.[58] Her willingness to come to terms with Mahler fits squarely within that context.

Boulanger's personal library at the CNSMD in Lyon contains a nearly complete set of scores of Mahler's compositions, and her annotations can serve as a private supplement to her public commentary on Mahler. The collection includes full scores of the First through the Ninth Symphonies and *Das Lied von der Erde*, as well as piano-vocal scores of *Das Lied* (in French, as *Le chant de la terre*), *Des Knaben Wunderhorn, Lieder eines fahrenden Gesellen*, and *Kindertotenlieder* (two copies, including one in French as *Aux enfants morts*). Boulanger's markings suggest that she acquired most of these scores at the festival: on the inside title page of her copy of Mahler's First Symphony, she wrote her initials, the year 1920, and the word Amsterdam (fig. 2.2). The full scores of all the other numbered symphonies, as well as *Aux enfants morts*, also have her initials and "1920" on either the inside title page or the first page of music, suggesting that she obtained these, too, at the time of the festival. (She probably added "Amsterdam" to the score of the First Symphony because she viewed it as the beginning of a set.) Moreover, the prices of the scores on the front covers of the Ninth Symphony and the piano-vocal score *Aux enfants morts* are indicated by Dutch stamps. Some of the scores that Boulanger marked with her initials but did not date "1920" were also likely acquired at the time of the festival. Her full score of *Das Lied von der Erde* is one such case. Copland later recalled that Boulanger had in her possession a score of *Das Lied* as early as 1922; he wrote that he and Boulanger carefully reviewed its orchestration, a task for which the full score was needed.[59]

The makings of an analysis, probably dating from the early 1920s, appear on a portion of the Fourth Symphony's first movement. As Francis has suggested in her discussion of Boulanger's analytical work on Igor Stravinsky's *Symphony of Psalms*, Boulanger generated a number of strategies for analyzing music from thematic, harmonic, and rhythmic standpoints.[60] In the Mahler annotations she operated on a motivic level, assigning numbers to individual melodic fragments and marking them each time they appeared by writing the corresponding number and, typically, by circling the number. (In this discussion I indicate the location of markings in terms of their distance in measures from rehearsal numbers, which are boxed and in bold.) Boulanger made annotations from the beginning of the composition to measure 175, in the development section, after which her markings abruptly cease for unknown reasons. In addition to twenty-three numbered motives, she identifies two introductory motives (I1 and I2) and another that she calls i″ or i^{bis}. She also labeled the movement's primary theme complex, beginning in the first violins, with the letter A. Figure 2.3 shows Boulanger's identification of motives on the score's first page, which includes I1 and I2 in the flutes; A, 1, and 2 in the first violins; and i″ or i^{bis} in the second violins.

Boulanger's identification of motives establishes the movement's texture as a polyphonic latticework of melodic fragments; relationships surface between melodic fragments that sound in succession or simultaneously. This is especially evident on the sixth page of her score (fig. 2.4). Beginning at measure 28, the first violins play motive 6 and then 3. When they repeat motive 6, the other strings take up motive 3.

Figure 2.2. Boulanger's label on the inside title page of Mahler's First Symphony (Universal Edition, no. 946). Photo courtesy of Médiathèque Nadia Boulanger, CNSMD de Lyon, ME MAH 400 UFNB.

Figure 2.3. Annotations in Mahler, Fourth Symphony, mvt. 1, mm. 1–4 (Universal Edition, no. 952). Photo courtesy of Médiathèque Nadia Boulanger, CNSMD de Lyon, ME MAH 400 UFNB.

Figure 2.4. Annotations in Mahler, Fourth Symphony, mvt. 1, mm. 27–31 (2-5 to 2-1), strings (Universal Edition, no. 952). Photo courtesy of Médiathèque Nadia Boulanger, CNSMD de Lyon, ME MAH 400 UFNB.

Figure 2.5. Annotations in Mahler, Fourth Symphony, mvt. 1, mm. 67–71 (5+1 to 5+5) (Universal Edition, no. 952). Photo courtesy of Médiathèque Nadia Boulanger, CNSMD de Lyon, ME MAH 400 UFNB.

At measure 67, Boulanger indicated the interlacing of several pairs of melodies—motives 19 and 20, then 19 and 17, and finally 21 and 16 (fig. 2.5).

In illustrating the simultaneous appearance of different motives, her analysis calls attention to the music's contrapuntal quality—a quality enhanced by Mahler's characteristic orchestration, in which the sounds of a small number of instruments or orchestral sections are juxtaposed in an otherwise sparse, lucid texture. In the passage shown in

Figure 2.5, motive 16 is heard in the clarinets; three measures later it is heard in the cellos, under motive 21 in the first bassoon; it then sounds alone in the double basses in the following measure. Meanwhile motive 19 is heard in the clarinets over motive 20 in the bass clarinet before migrating to the English horn over motive 17 in the harp.

By labeling and tracing individual motives in different voices, Boulanger demonstrated that Mahler's music shares characteristics with that of the composers she admired most, including Stravinsky and Johann Sebastian Bach. Indeed, she began the task of evaluating the Fourth Symphony graphically using the same criteria with which she discussed Stravinsky's Octet in 1923. In the Octet Boulanger found "precise, simple, and classic lines" and "sonorities opposed and blended"; she proposed for this work an impressive lineage going back to "the old masters of the Renaissance and Johann Sebastian Bach."[61] When speaking of modern French music, particularly that of Albert Roussel, Boulanger fixed on linear rather than harmonic aspects; she wrote in the published version of her Rice University lectures that to understand Roussel's music "one must hear it 'horizontally,' must follow lines rather than chords."[62] Such a horizontal approach is one way of understanding her motivic labels in Mahler, in that she traced melodic fragments over time, witnessing their successive and simultaneous appearances in forming a polyphonic web.

What I am describing as Boulanger's horizontal approach to Mahler's Fourth Symphony coincided with an aspect of her method for understanding Bach, whose music was of deep-seated significance in France—an intriguing layer in the complex network of French attitudes toward German music. Indeed, Brooks has pointed out that in France Bach had long "served as a reference for absolute musical values," and that he was "the poster boy for anti-Romantic aesthetics"—suggesting a sense of distance from what were perceived as Teutonic musical sensibilities.[63] Katharine Ellis has explored a surge in French admiration for Bach's music at the end of the nineteenth century that coincided with Boulanger's formative years.[64] The link between Boulanger's approaches to Bach and Mahler emerges clearly in her annotations to the first movement of Bach's cantata *Wie schön leuchtet der Morgenstern*, BWV 1, also housed at the CNSMD in Lyon. In her analysis, dated 1930–31, Boulanger labeled and traced individual motives, just as she had in Mahler's Fourth Symphony. Using letters rather than numbers, she identified ten motives (A–J) in the cantata, as opposed to more than twenty in just a portion of the first movement of the Mahler symphony. Figure 2.6, which shows the first page of her cantata score, includes motives A–F. (Boulanger also used numbers in the Bach score, here to identify the individual phrases of the chorale.)

Figure 2.6. Annotations in Bach, *Wie schön leuchtet der Morgenstern*, BWV 1, mm. 1–3 (*Kirchencantaten, Erster Band* [Leipzig: Breitkopf & Härtel, 1851]). Photo courtesy of Médiathèque Nadia Boulanger, CNSMD de Lyon, UFNB U MON BACH 01.

In analyzing Mahler's Fourth Symphony, she occasionally identified a motive as having been derived from another: "de 5" in the bass clarinet signals a fragment related to motive 5 (fig. 2.7). We find the same practice in the cantata, where Boulanger labeled material related to the chorale's third phrase ("3") as "de 3" (fig. 2.8).

If Boulanger was at all hesitant to engage Mahler's often overpowering aesthetic, highlighting the development of and interaction among brief melodic fragments perhaps suggested a fruitful avenue into his

Figure 2.7. Annotations in Mahler, Fourth Symphony, mvt. 1, mm. 125–31 (10+1 to 10+7) (Universal Edition, no. 952). Photo courtesy of Médiathèque Nadia Boulanger, CNSMD de Lyon, ME MAH 400 UFNB.

Figure 2.8. Annotations in Bach, *Wie schön leuchtet der Morgenstern*, BWV 1, mm. 34–36 (*Kirchencantaten, Erster Band* [Leipzig: Breitkopf & Härtel, 1851]). Photo courtesy of Médiathèque Nadia Boulanger, CNSMD de Lyon, UFNB U MON BACH 01.

works. What is more, despite her comment that Mahler's music challenged French preferences with its "neo-romanticism that the Latin races seem to flee," she evidently followed her own advice to readers—that they dismiss prejudices and grapple directly with his music.

As with her experience of Mahler at the Amsterdam festival and private exploration of the Fourth Symphony, Boulanger's encouragement of Copland occurred in the context of post-World War I internationalism, when figures such as Copland were developing identities as members of cosmopolitan musical communities.[65] Perhaps it is not surprising, then, that Mahler's music surfaced in Boulanger's teaching shortly after her firsthand experience at the Amsterdam festival. Some of her earliest American pupils recalled that Mahler figured in the lessons in her home on 36 rue Ballu in Paris. As Virgil Thomson,

Boulanger's student from 1921 to 1922, later wrote: "And there, of a Wednesday afternoon, took place weekly gatherings of pupils (strictly by invitation) at which the most modern scores of the time (by Stravinsky and Schoenberg, and Mahler) were analyzed and played on the pianoforte, and the rarest madrigals of the Renaissance (by Monteverdi, Luca Marenzio and Gesualdo di Venosa) were sung in class."[66] Copland remembered reading "torturously through Mahler orchestra scores at the piano with Mademoiselle insisting I go on to the end without stopping, no matter how slowly."[67] Copland gave one hint about the specific content of these Mahler sessions: that in 1922 he and his teacher "pored over" *Das Lied von der Erde*—"especially the orchestration."[68]

Boulanger had cultivated in Copland a flexible outlook that left significant room for him to evaluate Mahler and other German-speaking composers, some of them quite recent. In 1930 Copland wrote of Boulanger's teaching that she "seeks . . . the profound personality that can create great music and considers such a personality as beyond a question of territorial boundaries."[69] Boulanger's success as what Fauser has called a "teacher and cultural mediator" is clear in a letter from September 1922, when Copland wrote her from Berlin after hearing Bruno Walter conduct *Das Lied von der Erde.*[70] Copland told her he was "quite carried away by it, particularly the first few movements."[71] He informed her of his efforts to obtain copies she had asked for of Franz Liszt's *Faust Symphony* and symphonic poems, and of Schoenberg's *Harmonielehre*; and he discussed hearing "interesting performances" of operas by Franz Schreker (*Der Schatzgräber*) and Carl Maria von Weber (*Der Freischütz*), and looking forward to Schoenberg's *Pierrot lunaire.* He said he would bring back works by Egon Wellesz and Béla Bartók that she had not specifically requested.[72]

In 1925, the year after Copland's return to the United States, he notified an approving Boulanger of his advocacy efforts for Mahler. After hearing Mengelberg and the New York Philharmonic Orchestra play Mahler's Second Symphony at Carnegie Hall, Copland published the letter in the *New York Times* on April 5, discussed above, to complain about Mahler's treatment in the press.[73] Copland had written Boulanger two days earlier to credit her for his intervention: "How very modern the orchestration is! Thirty years ahead of its time. How I wish I could hear all the others, especially the 'Seventh' The music critics treat Mahler badly in New York. I shall write an article 'In Defense of Mahler.' Once more I have you to thank for discovering Mahler for me!"[74] In his *New York Times* letter, Copland highlighted the first movement of the Seventh Symphony. He also praised the Fourth Symphony's finale and the Rondo-Burleske movement of the Ninth, as well as the counterpoint in the first movement of the Eighth.[75] In a response to Copland, Boulanger wrote, "Bravo for Mahler—it's a much-needed perspective" (Bravo pour Mahler—c'est une attitude bien nécessaire).[76] Her brief acknowledgment of Copland's efforts aligns with her published Rice University lectures from the same year.

The substance of Copland's defense of Mahler may also have emerged from his experiences with Boulanger. His remarks, which are discussed in more depth in chapter 3, focused on compositional techniques that are discernible from her annotations to the Fourth Symphony: textural clarity and interactions between individual instruments. Specifically, he wrote that in the Second Symphony Mahler "orchestrates on big, simple lines, in which each note is of importance," and—drawing on terminology associated with neoclassicism—that he "manages his enormous number of instruments with extraordinary economy, there are no useless doublings, instrument is pitted against instrument, group against group."

In the years following Boulanger's lectures at Rice and Copland's letter to the *New York Times*, Copland continued to treat Boulanger as a sounding board for his enthusiastic musings about Mahler. On January 5, 1927, he wrote to her, "Just now I am completely overcome by the marvels—technical and orchestral—of Mahler's 8th Symphony," and that he "would go a long ways to hear it played."[77] In a letter to Boulanger sent from Germany on August 22 of the same year, Copland drew a sharp contrast between Mahler and Richard Strauss: "There is an article to be written on the difference between the naive, sympathetic banality of Mahler compared with the cold, heartless banality in Strauss."[78]

Mahler's role in Boulanger's teaching filtered into the public activities of other students and colleagues. One of Virgil Thomson's assessments of Mahler's music suggests the extent to which Boulanger shaped transatlantic ideas about Mahler's significance. In a vivid passage from a 1941 review, Thomson called Mahler's Ninth Symphony

> utterly German and Viennese and strangely not so at the same time. In reviewing *Das Lied von der Erde* some time back, I opined that there were some French influences in the particular contrapuntal approach Mahler employed. Naturally, I pulled down on my head a flood of abusive correspondence from the Mahlerites, who will have no analyzing of their idol and certainly no aspersions cast upon his hundred-per-cent Germanism. I suppose they don't count his Israelite birth or his professional travels (he conducted here at the Metropolitan Opera house and at the Philharmonic for something like three years) as factual evidence of a certain internationalism in his culture. Nevertheless, as I listened to the Ninth Symphony last night,

> I was still aware of French influences. Certain of these are technical, like the no-doubling orchestration. Others are aesthetic. I know the protest mail I shall get for saying this, but I must say it. Mahler has a great deal in common with the French impressionists. As an Italian musician to whom I mentioned the matter put it, "He comes as near being an impressionist as a German could."[79]

This passage presents an international Mahler much like the one Thomson's teacher encountered at the Amsterdam Mahler festival; in mentioning counterpoint and spare orchestration, Thomson hints, like Copland, at the vocabulary of neoclassicism. But Thomson goes further than Boulanger, directly highlighting both Mahler's Jewishness ("his Israelite birth") and his musical Frenchness. In 1941, mentioning Mahler's Jewish background was simultaneously a positive gesture, given the menace of Nazi Germany, and a dismissive one, considering the shades of anti-Semitism that have been detected in Thomson's discussions of Copland's music.[80] (Copland, himself Jewish, did not center his discussion of Mahler on Jewish identity, but the issue did surface, and is the subject of chapter 4 of this book.) And in vaguely connecting Mahler to the "French impressionists," Thomson implicitly links Mahler to Debussy—an unusual but compelling observation. Thomson did not elaborate, but more recently, Donald Mitchell made a similar comment. Referring to Mahler's song "Ich atmet' einen Linden Duft," Mitchell wrote that the "degree of delicate instrumental shading, in which colour is handled with the finest touch, almost drives one to drag in impressionism as a label. . . . The low dynamics, the delicacy and subtlety of the sound—the very preoccupation with timbre—these are qualities and characteristics that mark much of what one recognizes as impressionist features in other composers' music."[81] To be sure, the exquisite final passages of both the Ninth Symphony and *Das Lied von der Erde* (which are considered further in chapter 5) could serve as apt examples of this almost Debussyan subtlety. Speaking specifically of harmony, Debussy's "Pagodes" from the collection of piano pieces *Estampes* (1903), which like *Das Lied* points to the Far East in its subject matter, ends in a major chord with an added second and sixth (outlining the pentatonic scale), which the conclusion of *Das Lied* echoes.[82] Overall, Thomson's interest in Mahler seems not to have been indebted solely to Boulanger; indeed, he did not take to Boulanger's teaching of Mahler, recalling that "her attentive efforts to lead me in the directions of Fauré and Mahler were not successful."[83] Yet it is likely that Boulanger prepared Thomson to challenge the "Mahlerites" for what he saw as their belief in Mahler's "hundred-percent Germanism."

Whereas Boulanger had motivated Copland and others of his generation to explore Mahler, she does not seem to have encouraged Leonard Bernstein—or others who were in her orbit after Elliott Carter's time as her student in the early 1930s—to do the same. Indeed, the contrast between what would become Bernstein's passion for Mahler, especially beginning in the 1960s, and Boulanger's apparently growing apathy toward Mahler, is a striking one. Bernstein and Boulanger apparently did not meet until 1946.[84] Jay Gottlieb, who studied with Boulanger intermittently from 1967 to 1976, recalled a dynamic that accords with what is already known about Bernstein's strong sense of self-identification with Mahler: "She did not speak much about Mahler in the last decade (when I worked with her) of her life. . . . The subject came up when her dear 'Lenny B' was around, and I more than gathered that this was not really to her taste. . . . I can tell you what those conversations sounded like: [Boulanger] telling [Bernstein] that he should calm down and stop claiming to be the reincarnation of Mahler!"[85]

Further evidence that Boulanger's enthusiasm waned over time emerges from comments by La Grange, who authored a vast, multi-volume biography of Mahler; *New York Times* critic Harold Schonberg compared his Mahler advocacy to Bernstein's.[86] La Grange studied with Boulanger in the late 1940s and early 1950s and recalled that she "didn't like [Mahler's] music in the least."[87] He later clarified his perception of her attitude: "I of course told her once that I was writing a biography of Mahler, but she seemed to disapprove (silently) so much that I never mentioned Mahler's name again in her presence. Neither did she ever mention it in any of her letters to me."[88]

Boulanger's declining interest in Mahler's music may be traced back as far as the 1930s. In notes for a music history course from 1935, the American composer Louise Talma captured Boulanger's ambivalence toward Mahler, which tended toward rejection; according to Talma's notes, Boulanger said this of Mahler: "One cannot not admire + not hate . . . When bad so awful."[89] Just when and why Boulanger's attitude shifted from appreciation to disapproval remains a matter of speculation. It is possible that her affinity for Mahler's music—music she had linked to a Teutonic spirit—declined with the growth of fascism in Germany, the approach of World War II, and, eventually, the German occupation of France in 1940.[90] And perhaps her steadfast support for Stravinsky, in the face of skepticism on the part of music critics in the 1930s toward both his music and French neoclassicism, hardened her aversion to Mahler's overtly late-romantic aesthetic.[91] Of course, Boulanger's tastes did not gravitate toward late-romantic Austro-German music in the first place.[92] Once the novelty of Mahler's music had worn off, perhaps so, too, did Boulanger's interest.

Nonetheless, Boulanger's score collection suggests that her relationship with Mahler's music remained complex during the 1940s and beyond, for she continued to add copies of his works to her library. One of these was an orchestral score of *Kindertotenlieder* in English translation; an annotation in her hand, on the inside title page, indicates that she obtained it in Los Angeles in 1944. Her score of the *Lieder eines fahrenden Gesellen*, in English translation and published by Josef Weinberger Ltd., bears a copyright date of 1959. Thus, Boulanger acquired the *Gesellen* score in her later years—perhaps in the United States or England, countries she visited frequently.[93] Although there is no evidence to suggest that Boulanger encouraged her students to pursue Mahler's music from the 1940s to the 1970s, these scores leave the question somewhat open.

Even if Boulanger's interest in Mahler had faded entirely by the period of her association with Bernstein and La Grange, her activities earlier in the century demonstrate how considering the intersection between private and public realms can help us draw a more complete picture of a composer's reception. Through the lens of her interaction with Mahler's music and her relationship with Copland, Boulanger's Mahler story points the way toward a promising avenue of research: exploring how private conversations about music—and its value—could have public implications. However intangible and elusive as compared to concert programs and attendance records, Boulanger's studio turns out to have been a realm in which she and her students shaped and refined discourses about music, with wide-ranging implications.

Chapter Three

COPLAND IN DEFENSE OF MAHLER

It was on March 28, 1925, within a year of his return to the United States in June of 1924, that Aaron Copland attended the performance of Mahler's Second Symphony that prompted his letter to the *New York Times.* Copland used critics' distaste for Mahler's music as a launching pad for a detailed defense of it: "The music critics of New York City are agreed upon at least one point—Gustav Mahler, as a composer, is hopeless. Year in and year out, the performance of one of Mahler's works is invariably accompanied by the same disparaging reviews."[1]

Such "disparaging reviews" came courtesy of prominent critics such as Lawrence Gilman in the *New York Herald Tribune,* Richard Aldrich in the *New York Times,* and Deems Taylor in the *New York World.*[2] Gilman wrote that Mahler's "tragedy" was that despite his "tremendous reveries," "mystical and passionate aspirations," and "apocalyptic concepts," he could not create "living and eloquent music."[3] Copland's letter to the *Times* was published a few days later, on April 5; but his was not the only voice in sympathy with Mahler. In the *New York Telegram-Mail,* the day after Copland's letter appeared, Pitts Sanborn wrote of the Second Symphony that "taken by and large, the work in question is impressive and engrossing. . . . We are now richer in our artistic knowledge and experience because of this occasion."[4] And the next year, a more elaborate endorsement of Mahler, by Allen Lincoln Langley, appeared in *Musical Quarterly.* There, Langley called Sanborn's positive review "the first temperate criticism of Mahler it has been my pleasure to see in a New York newspaper during the last five years."[5]

Taking note of the generally hostile critical environment toward Mahler, Copland embarked, in the remainder of his letter, on a career-long advocacy of Mahler in which he navigated the challenges of pitching Mahler simultaneously as a progenitor of musical modernism and a paragon of romanticism. The *Times* letter offers a compelling starting point for examining this complicated mission. It featured a cluster of ideas meant to convince others that Mahler's music was worthwhile; these were an appeal to internationalism, an emphasis on Mahler's forward-looking orchestration, and a claim for Mahler's originality. As we shall see, these arguments would shift—often dramatically—as Copland's own musical identity developed over the following decades.

Copland began his defense of Mahler in the *Times* with a hint of the same post–World War I sense of international reconciliation that mattered so much to his mentor, Nadia Boulanger. Suggesting that the New York critics' dismissal of Mahler reflected an insular attitude toward music, he wrote that "no critic has been able to explain just what it is that Mengelberg—and for that matter, all of Germany, Austria, and Holland[6]—finds so admirable in Mahler's music." By remarking on Europe's approval of Mahler, Copland pointed to Americans' need to take stock of their place in a transatlantic musical world. And by invoking the nations where Mahler's music had already found a fertile home, and seeming to value the opinions of members of those communities, Copland proposed a transnationally inclusive, rather than narrowly national, take on musical value. He seemed to witness an appreciation gap: if sophisticated German, Austrian, and Dutch listeners could accept Mahler, Americans ought to be enlightened enough to do so as well.

Such an interpretation suggests that Copland used Mahler in 1925 in part to emphasize the significance of Europe, and particularly his training with Boulanger, in constructions of musical worth in a transatlantic world. As Carol J. Oja has shown, Copland himself positioned musical value in mid-1920s America in terms of a venerable European tradition. She notes that his article "What Europe Means to the Aspiring Composer" appeared the same year as the Mahler letter, and in it Copland "listed the virtues of European training and described in detail the inadequacies that most Americans faced when encountering a European teacher."[7] By referring to the Mahler appreciation gap between Europe and America, Copland was perhaps implying that for Europeans to accept Mahler but Americans to reject him offhand was evidence of a narrow view on the American side of the Atlantic. And by specifically naming Mengelberg, Copland was drawing on the reputation of an eminent musician with a transatlantic reputation, one whose musical tastes he thought critics and readers should have to contend with rather than dismiss. Not only was Mahler advocacy a central part of Mengelberg's persona as a conductor in America, but as seen in chapter 2, Copland was first introduced to Mahler's music in part as a consequence of Boulanger's attendance at Mengelberg's 1920 Mahler festival in Amsterdam. Thus, encouraging observers to take stock of European tastes—particularly those in Holland, Germany, and Austria—was a position with close ties to Copland's own outlook.

To depart from Copland's letter for a moment, the following year, Oscar Sonneck, founder and editor of *Musical Quarterly*, offered one answer to the question of the apparent imbalance in estimations of Mahler's importance on either side of the Atlantic: he suggested that Mahler's brand of romanticism was alien to the United States. Sonneck, in an analysis Langley printed in his detailed apologia, pointed to Mahler's romantic roots as the source of both Europe's sympathy for Mahler's music and America's apparent resistance to it. He called Austro-German romanticism an "unknown sphere" in America, adding that "if an auditor has no knowledge or spiritual connection with that romanticism he will never be able really to appreciate Mahler entirely."[8] As if in direct response to Copland's query from the year before, Sonneck called this distance from Austro-German romanticism "the principal reason why in Central Europe and Holland Mahler's music sounds at home and strikes such a sympathetic note in the listeners. Inversely, it is why it is so difficult to transplant and export Mahler to any other country." Sonneck added that Mahler "did not shrink from a refined sort of banality when his ideas demanded it" and that listeners must keep "the German folk-song in mind which he so loved and tried to reflect faithfully."[9]

While Sonneck appealed to romanticism and a relationship with folk music to explain why American audiences apparently had difficulty with Mahler, Copland did the opposite in his *Times* letter, at least on the surface: he attempted to create a divide between romanticism and modernism, placing Mahler firmly on the modernist side of that divide. Copland agreed with the critics that Mahler "has at times written music which is bombastic, longwinded, banal." By using these adjectives, Copland met Mahler's critics halfway, acknowledging Mahler's connections to what some may have viewed as an outmoded romantic aesthetic that favored expansiveness over concision. But he only did so to then downplay those connections: "If one discounts for the moment the banal themes, the old-fashioned romantico-philosophical considerations so dear to Mahler—if one looks at the music qua music—then it is undeniable that Mahler is a composer of today." Certain of Mahler's works, moreover, "have in them the stuff of living music"—a comment some may have read as a direct response to Lawrence Gilman's claim, quoted above, that Mahler could not write "living and eloquent music."

When Copland wrote of "the music qua music" and referred to Mahler as a "composer of today," he was shaping an argument that linked Mahler to a burgeoning vision of new music that centered on modernism—what David C. Paul, in examining the same letter, has aptly called "a patently modernist approach to musical value" in its shunning the matter of musical meaning.[10] Specifically, Copland was linking Mahler to neoclassicism as a strain of modernism, using a network of terms and ideas that, as Oja has suggested, became an avenue for Copland to position himself within an international musical community.[11]

To be sure, the pairing of Mahler and neoclassicism was a counterintuitive one, given both the immensity of Mahler's typical symphonic forces and his strong ties to Austro-German romanticism. But delving into musical specifics, Copland established a powerful link between Mahler and neoclassicism. He claimed that Mahler based his method of orchestration on "big, simple lines, in which each note is of importance." He wrote that Mahler "manages his enormous number of instruments with extraordinary economy." And although Copland did not specifically use the term neoclassicism in the *Times* letter, he did add, in a flourish that might be reserved for commentary on Palestrina or J. S. Bach rather than Mahler, that the "present-day renewed interest in polyphonic writing cannot fail to reflect glory on Mahler's consummate mastery of that delicate art." Indeed, as Oja has discussed, many American musicians in the 1920s partook of the ideology of neoclassicism without using the term itself.[12]

In linking Mahler's orchestration to neoclassicism, Copland transformed an existing discourse in the United States about Mahler's orchestration and counterpoint. American critics had long praised these aspects of Mahler's writing, and some of their comments even prefigure Copland's argument. In 1906, Richard Aldrich wrote after hearing the Fifth Symphony that Mahler "writes freely in that modern style of counterpoint that gets its themes and subjects and countersubjects together anyhow, whether euphoniously or not."[13] As seen in chapter 1, Copland's teacher, Rubin Goldmark, even referred to Mahler's "truly marvelous orchestral palette" in 1916. Later, Aldrich criticized Mahler's handling of the orchestra using terms that Copland, given his attraction to neoclassicism, might well have viewed as positive attributes. Reviewing Mahler's Seventh Symphony in 1923, Aldrich complained, "Unskillfulness in orchestration results in sound that is by turns hollow, thin, airy, overladen, raucous, noisy, fragmentary, noisy, and strident."[14] Although Aldrich's statement attacks inconsistencies in Mahler's textures, his use of the adjectives "hollow," "thin," and "airy," although likely meant disparagingly, became something positive for Copland, who in 1930 would write that Mahler's "was the first orchestra to play *without pedal*" and that "his instrumentation possesses that sharply-etched and clarified sonority that may be heard again and again in the music of later composers."[15]

In the *Times* letter, Copland appealed to transatlantic sensibilities as well as neoclassicism by naming the Swiss composer Arthur Honegger, one of *Les Six*, as an important musical descendant of Mahler. "So recent a score as Honegger's 'Pacific 231' is proof of Mahler's living influence," Copland wrote. His strategic reference to this tone poem—the only specific work by a composer other than Mahler that Copland mentioned in the letter—implied a strong connection between Mahler and a European composer who was highly regarded at the time, and whose music resonated with Americans at that moment; Honegger's *Pacific 231* was viewed as a groundbreaking work and even a point of reference for American musical achievement. Less than a year before Copland's letter, on May 8, 1924, Serge Koussevitzky had led the world premiere of *Pacific 231* in Paris, a performance Copland attended.[16] Then, in his much-anticipated debut as the Boston Symphony Orchestra's conductor on October 10, 1924, Koussevitzky conducted it again, and others in the United States did so shortly afterward.[17] Underscoring the work's American credibility, Olin Downes wrote in the *New York Times* that Honegger's composition achieved for American music what American composers had not yet accomplished for themselves. He wrote, "In America there has been raised the hue and cry of a national music which should be racy, authentic, contemporaneous in its accents. And lo and behold, it is a Frenchman who gives us, in tones, a quality of our civilization."[18]

What is more, by associating Mahler with a member of *Les Six*, Copland was granting a certain cultural currency to Mahler, who, despite Mengelberg's advocacy, remained on the periphery of the established orchestral canon. *Les Six* had gained popularity in the United States in the early 1920s as a group that reflected "the latest artistic trends in Paris" and "articulated a disdain for the hallowed traditions of high art that probably appealed to a populist streak in Americans," as Oja put it.[19] By summoning Honegger, Copland was by no means attempting to disconnect Mahler from America's high art traditions. On the contrary, he implicitly tethered Mahler to a web of new music, imported from France, that he viewed as contemporarily relevant and that he noticed had the potential to seep into America's venerable art music institutions.

By invoking Honegger's name in the *New York Times* letter to bolster his case for Mahler, Copland was drawing on his own experience in Paris. In Boulanger's studio, he had had opportunities to explore scores by figures like Stravinsky, Honegger, Milhaud, and Roussel (in addition to Mahler) and to interact with the composers themselves. "One had the feeling in her Paris studio, being her student, that you were sitting in the center of the musical life of Paris in 1921," he later recalled. "You weren't just studying a thing that had happened in the past. It was happening around you."[20] For Boulanger, Honegger was especially significant; in the published version of her Rice University lectures, she considered him to be "unquestionably" the "most important figure" in *Les Six* for his absorption of a range of composers' music into his own style ("Bach, Handel, Wagner, Debussy, Schoenberg, and Strawinsky have all contributed to the formation of his language"); his "power of construction, richness of polyphony, athletic rhythms and contrapuntal dissonance"; and "the very catholicity of the composer's culture" that has aided him in continuing to develop "a perfected and more highly personal idiom."[21] For his part, Copland even pointed to Honegger as a precedent for his own compositional decisions; in a letter to Boulanger in 1924, he updated her on his *Symphony for Organ and Orchestra,* whose premiere Boulanger would later perform, telling her that the three-movement structure was related to that of Honegger's First Violin Sonata.[22] This structure, as Howard Pollack has pointed out in discussing this work and Honegger's possible influence on Copland, became "one of [Copland's] most characteristic gestures."[23]

A central aspect of Copland's defense of Mahler as an ancestor of modernism, then, meant invoking a composer, Honegger, whose formal structures Copland imitated in his own music—paradoxically so, as Copland placed a high value on originality. (Oja has noted a similar pattern in her discussion of the critic Paul Rosenfeld, whom Copland admired: "At the same time as Rosenfeld criticized some contemporary American composers for being too derivative of European modernists, he was unable to break free of constant comparisons with Europeans.")[24] In the *Times* letter, Copland pointed forcefully to Mahler's originality as a composer, countering claims that Mahler's music was derivative: "As for the banality of Mahler's thematic material, I have found that generally no matter how ordinary the melody may be, there is always somewhere, either in the beginning or end, one note, one harmony, one slight change which gives the Mahler touch," he wrote, adding parenthetically, "Every page he wrote has that individual quality that we demand from every great composer—he was never more Mahler than when he was copying Mozart." Later, Copland would observe about his time witnessing Koussevitzky's concerts in Paris, where he first encountered *Pacific 231,* that the "watchword in those days was 'originality.' The laws of rhythm, or harmony, of construction had all been torn down. Every composer in the vanguard set out to remake these laws according to his own conceptions. And I suppose that I was no exception despite my youth—or possibly because of it."[25]

Copland's argumentative thread seems complex and contradictory, in part because of the difficult balance between picturing a composer simultaneously as a pioneering genius and an artist grounded in the past. This is not to dismiss his argument but rather to highlight the blurred boundary, and even the symbiotic relationship, between originality and emulation. Copland pictured Honegger, apparently a twentieth-century original, as a musical descendant of Mahler, the latter also an original despite "copying Mozart." At the same time, Copland attempted to explain away the criticism that Mahler's music was suspiciously reminiscent of that of earlier European composers by referring to the so-called "Mahler touch." That criticism had been articulated in 1923 in an autobiography by Walter Damrosch, the first conductor to have performed Mahler's music in the United States. Damrosch wrote that Mahler perhaps "occupied himself so intensely and constantly in analyzing and interpreting the works of the great master that he lost the power to develop himself as composer on original lines." He added that Mahler "could write cleverly in the style of Haydn or Berlioz or Wagner, and without forgetting Beethoven, but was never able to write in the style of Mahler."[26] Copland, by writing that Mahler was "never more Mahler than when he was copying Mozart," invoked originality to respond directly to claims like those of Damrosch—a specific take on the notion, long and frequently attributed to Voltaire, that "originality is nothing but judicious imitation."

Honegger's ties to romanticism may have been strong enough to make the Mahler comparison seem more reasonable to Copland's knowledgeable readers. Honegger's *Les Six* colleague Darius Milhaud singled him out as the champion of "German romanticism," placing himself, by contrast, in the vein of "Mediterranean lyricism," rehearsing the cliché of the artistic rift between so-called Teutonic and Latin strains in European music.[27] (Milhaud, like Copland, found aspects of Mahler's music to appreciate in terms of neoclassicism; in a 1952 interview, he praised "the beauty, the richness, the clarity of his orchestration" and located instances of "extraordinary economy" in that area.)[28] Honegger, evidently aware of the stigma of the nineteenth century, still accepted his own role as the "romantic" member of *Les Six*; of the second movement of his First Symphony, he wrote, "Here I abandoned myself to what people smilingly refer to as 'my *romanticism*'; it's a crime I don't repent at all. The song takes wing, the tunes embrace, then separate, the song comes to earth again, and it's all over."[29]

The programmatic nature of *Pacific 231* makes Copland's link between Mahler and Honegger especially plausible. As Howard Pollack has pointed out, Copland viewed *Pacific 231* as "a quintessential example of twentieth-century program music."[30] In that sense, it is a composition that points in conception toward Mahler's Austro-German romantic tradition. To be sure, the work's driving rhythms and ostinati recall Igor Stravinsky's *Le sacre du printemps*. Its French ancestry in pictorial works like Debussy's three-movement *La mer* (1905) is also evident. And its obvious dialogue with machine sounds ties *Pacific 231* to a contemporary American fascination with the "mechanical picturesque," which hardly intersects with Mahler's idiom.[31] But *Pacific 231* is an orchestral tone poem, a genre with firm roots in the romantic period; the modern (for the time) subject matter of train travel belies the work's relationship with its nineteenth-century predecessors. As a symphonic poem, it finds its conceptual heritage partly in the Austro-German romantic tradition, dating back to works such as Franz Liszt's *Les préludes* (completed in 1854). Despite Mahler's own ambivalence toward program music, his *Totenfeier* (1888), which became the first movement of his Second Symphony, is also an example of the genre.

What is more, the brevity of *Pacific 231,* which takes under ten minutes to perform, furnished Copland with a means of divorcing the usually "longwinded" Mahler from "old-fashioned romantico-philosophical conceptions." Although Copland did not spell out what he meant by such "conceptions," the sense of Mahler contending with profound questions of existence, pain, death, and resurrection in hour-long symphonies certainly contrasts with a mostly lighthearted orchestral vignette about a mode of transportation. In this sense, Copland's approach here departed from that of Boulanger, who extolled Mahler's explorations of deeper issues. Perhaps further supporting the Mahler–Honegger connection for Copland's readership was the fact that a number of individual movements in Mahler's symphonies are about as brief as *Pacific 231.* In the *Times* letter, as we have seen, Copland referred to two of these movements—the final movement of the Fourth Symphony and the Rondo-Burleske from Mahler's Ninth Symphony.

A comparison of Honegger's orchestration in *Pacific 231* to one of those movements, the finale of Mahler's Fourth Symphony, reveals that Copland's comparison of Honegger to Mahler was not just conceptually reasonable, but musically convincing, too. Although Copland did not identify specific passages from either work, Mahler's practice as an orchestrator in the finale aligns with portions of Honegger's *Pacific 231.* Throughout Mahler's movement, usually only one or two instruments at a time dominate the texture along with the vocal line, and Mahler quickly divides his melodies among the instruments—perhaps a reflection of what Copland, in the *Times* letter, called Mahler's practice of having instruments and groups "pitted" against each other. Varying the presentation of melodic fragments by alternating the instruments that present them is also a hallmark of Mahler's style of orchestration.[32] Toward the movement's conclusion, as shown in example 3.1a, the main countermelody to the vocal line moves from violin to flute to English horn to clarinet to viola to cello, settling on a

Example 3.1a. Mahler, Fourth Symphony, mvt. 4, mm. 169–77 (15+5 to 15+13).

call and response between cello and bass clarinet that begins at measure 174. Meanwhile, an arpeggiated motif begins with pizzicato in the cellos and migrates to the harp in measure 171.

A similar foregrounding of individual instruments or combinations as audibly identifiable but quickly switching entities occurs throughout Honegger's *Pacific 231*. At measure 97, one of the movement's main melodies—a series of repeated notes followed by a pair of ascending leaps (originally stated earlier by the bassoons)—is heard successively in a stretto-like manner in several instruments (ex. 3.1b, which only shows selected woodwind and brass instruments). And although Copland did not refer specifically to melodic similarities between *Pacific 231* and Mahler's works, striking commonalities shed some light on how Copland may have come to associate these composers in the first place—or, at least, hoped to convince others that linking the two was sensible. At measure 119 in *Pacific 231*, repeated descending seconds and scalar lines dominate the melodic landscape (see ex. 3.2a, which shows selected woodwinds only). This gesture closely mirrors the winding melodic character of one of the main themes of the Mahler finale, where descending seconds come in the form of grace notes at measure 48 (see ex. 3.2b, which shows only the woodwinds and first horn).

For Copland, Mahler's orchestration stood in sharp contrast to that of Richard Strauss. Copland chose Mahler over Strauss because—he claimed—Mahler was the romantic-era composer whose orchestration transcended that very era and offered much to the twentieth century. He called Mahler "head and shoulders above Strauss, whose orchestral methods have already dated so perceptibly." Specifically, by referring to the avoidance of "useless doublings" in Mahler's music, Copland implied that Strauss overused doubling to create dense textures that lacked Mahler's "extraordinary economy." Sixteen years later, Copland wrote of Strauss's "overrich" orchestra that his "scores are uneconomical, weighted down with notes, super-Wagnerian in effect" with "little relationship to the more sober and precise orchestration of the present day."[33]

If Copland had simply sought a master of orchestration, he could just as easily have claimed Strauss, rather than Mahler, as his preferred ancestor. But praising Strauss as an orchestrator would not have suited Copland's public advocacy for Mahler or for modern music; as we have seen, Copland was excited about studying in Paris, which he specifically placed against Strauss's Berlin. What's more, Rubin Goldmark, whom Copland considered old-fashioned, seemed to value Strauss's music more highly than Mahler's as a representative of newer trends, and Goldmark specifically praised Strauss's orchestration. Speaking in Boston in 1910, Goldmark referred to Strauss's "new style of

Example 3.1b. Honegger, *Pacific 231*, mm. 97–101, selected woodwinds and brass.

Example 3.2a. Honegger, *Pacific 231*, mm. 119–23, selected woodwinds.

Example 3.2b. Mahler, Fourth Symphony, mvt. 4, mm. 46–50 (4-2 to 4+3), first horn and selected woodwinds.

polyphony" as "indescribably fascinating," and he added, "It is mostly through his polyphony that his startlingly novel harmonic effects are obtained, which are heightened by an orchestration that knows no limits as to baldness or ingenuity."[34] To be sure, Copland was selective in his assessment of Strauss and Mahler; opulent and lavish moments can be found in Mahler's orchestration just as more delicate, intricate ones can be found in that of Strauss. By pitting Mahler against Strauss, Copland does not seem to have been saying that Strauss was an unskilled orchestrator; rather, he was drawing a distinction between the "over-rich" quality of Strauss's orchestration and what he generally noticed as Mahler's "economy."

For Copland, promoting Mahler's orchestration as a precursor of Honegger's was therefore a means of forging a broad musical network for musical neoclassicism—one that was wide enough to encompass an Austro-German composer who had been dead for fourteen years and who was best known for long symphonies. Copland's creation of a Mahler–Honegger nexus, ostensibly based on orchestration, was thus a tool for demonstrating that neoclassicism had a historical and international pedigree. Copland happened to encounter Mahler in the right place (Paris) at the right time (the early 1920s) under the supervision of the right person (Nadia Boulanger) to perceive Mahler and neoclassicism in a plausible, convincing musico-historical alliance.

Copland's public advocacy for Mahler continued after 1925 in lectures, short articles, and books—all in ways that reflect his evolving identity as an American composer who embraced romanticism more and more openly. One of the most important venues for this Mahler advocacy was his stint as a lecturer at the New School for Social Research in New York, intermittently from 1927 to 1939. There, Copland taught courses on music history, focusing often (though not entirely) on twentieth-century composers. Ideologically, the New School was an ideal venue in which to highlight Mahler's music in the context of international modernism. Many of the individuals associated with the New School, founded in 1919 as a venue for adult education, partook of the cosmopolitan outlook after World War I that defined Copland's related views on musical modernism in the 1920s.[35] Moreover, it was one of what Carol J. Oja has identified as "alternative spaces" that "generated a counterforce to New York's longstanding musical institutions," like the New York Philharmonic, "which were too busy marketing European warhorses to pay much attention to the creative activity surrounding them."[36] The New School was also, as Sally Bick has discussed, viewed as "subversive and radical," with a "dissenting tradition" that "became an emblem of its intellectual and artistic freedom, an ideal that bred unorthodoxies but also invigorated innovation."[37] This environment gave Copland an appropriate forum in which to promote music like Mahler's—music that, despite Mengelberg's advocacy, still fell outside the mainstream.

The circumstances of Copland's arrival at the New School as an instructor in 1927 reinforce the internationalist context of his Mahler advocacy. It was apparently Copland's connection with the prolific music critic Paul Rosenfeld, a vocal proponent of American modernism and strong believer in the value of European music, that enabled him to join the New School faculty.[38] As Copland recalled of his cash-strapped late 20s, he actually "inherited" the lectures from Rosenfeld, who "had tried lecturing for a winter and hadn't enjoyed it. . . . He asked me whether I would like to take over.[39] Copland did just that, teaching a course on modern music in the fall of 1927. Later, his New School course "What to Listen for in Music" would turn into a bestselling book of the same name; it was first published in 1939.

Copland had a precedent in Rosenfeld for highlighting Mahler in his New School lectures, and he did so frequently. Even though Rosenfeld was highly critical of Mahler in his writings, claiming to doubt Mahler's relevance to the twentieth century (Rosenfeld's views will be explored further in chapter 4), Mahler did figure into Rosenfeld's course on modern music in the spring of 1927; the *New York Times* reported that the course was the institution's first musical offering and would feature a session on Max Reger, Arnold Schoenberg, and Gustav Mahler under the heading "German Modern Music."[40] Rosenfeld returned with a course in the spring of 1933, "Modern Music: From Nationalism to Internationalism," which included the session "A New View of Strauss and Mahler."[41]

The relationship between Mahler's music and both modernism and romanticism infused Copland's lectures—at least according to the fragmentary handwritten notes he preserved for each session. An examination of these notes, housed in the Copland Collection at the Library of Congress, reveals that his ideas about Mahler underwent subtle but significant shifts that mirrored changes in his own broader musical outlook over the course of the 1920s and 1930s. Such shifts are detectable even though the lectures are written in shorthand, and the complete meanings of terms and ideas are not always clear. As we have seen, Copland tied Mahler to counterpoint and orchestration, painting him as a proto-modernist and seeming to reject romanticism in the process ("if one discounts for a moment the banal themes, the old-fashioned romantico-philosophical conceptions so dear to Mahler," he had written in his *New York Times* letter). In the New School lectures, Copland's complex relationship with Austro-German romanticism—including a sense of admiration for it, at times—emerges more clearly.

Beginning with the Fall 1927 course "The Evolution of Modern Music" (labeled, as Sally Bick discovered, "Aesthetics of Modern Music" in Copland's collection), Copland led a session on orchestration that placed Mahler in a decidedly international context, grouping him with Richard Strauss and the French-born American composer Edgard Varèse.[42] After a broad review of orchestration from the sixteenth to the twentieth centuries, Copland addressed Mahler in terms that largely mirrored his *Times* letter from two years earlier, with some expanded comments on the orchestration itself. His lecture notes mention several traits: "Contrapuntal orchestration—every line clear—dry sounding—no muddiness—originality—use of enormous numbers of instruments."[43]

Here, and much more directly than in his *Times* letter from 1925, Copland linked Mahler's orchestration to a French tradition, as opposed to a Germanic one; his lecture notes on Mahler match his comments on nineteenth-century French orchestration: "Harmonic—clear sounding—little or no doubling—contrast in tone color—no filling in—all lines clear." By stark contrast, he described German orchestration in this way: "Harmonic—rich sounding—much doubling—mixture of tone colors—much filling in—only main lines clear."

Copland listed "Der Einsame in Herbst" (the second movement of *Das Lied von der Erde*), as well as "Um Mitternacht" from the *Rückertlieder*, at the bottom of his page of notes on Mahler. Entered in a different color than the lecture's main text but perhaps at around the same time as its original writing (notes for other lectures in the same course include similar additions), this was likely a cue for himself to play excerpts from these works from the keyboard, as the course catalog noted that lectures would be "illustrated at the piano."[44] Both Mahler lieder offer apt keyboard demonstrations of Copland's thesis, even without the benefit of differentiated timbres to illustrate Mahler's "clear sounding" orchestration to his students. "Der Einsame in Herbst" begins with a duet between a wave-like violin passage and a sighing oboe, with horns and clarinets delicately weaving their way into the musical fabric. The lightly textured opening of "Um Mitternacht"—a song that lacks strings and, therefore, a strong connection to lush romanticism—plays on the exchange between a lilting motive and a descending one among a few wind instruments.

As Copland continued to lecture on Mahler, his ideas about Mahler as a romanticist and a modernist shifted, often seeming to contradict earlier positions he had already expressed; indeed, from year to year, Copland was not consistent in how he weighed Mahler's significance as a romantic or a modern. Notes for Copland's Fall 1928 course, "Masterworks of Modern Music," include the session "Post-Romanticism of Mahler," which reveals an expanded view of Mahler's significance, moving well beyond arguments about modern orchestration.[45] In Copland's general introduction to Mahler in this lecture, which focused solely on the composer (instead of having Mahler share time with others), Copland linked him to the "deterioration" of German music, the "rise of French music," and the "end of the Romantic tradition." In this context, though, Mahler stood apart from colleagues like Strauss and Reger as a "modern figure" and a "brilliantly original orchestrator" who wrote "music built contrapuntally" that exhibited "independence of melodic line." Expanding on ideas outlined in the *Times* letter from 1925, and arguing "for a more balanced judgement [*sic*]" of Mahler, Copland took note of the "admiration of Germany, Holland" for Mahler's music. He listed "pros" and "cons," likely more as a summary of prevalent views about Mahler than as Copland's own personal catalog of favorable and critical commentary. The single "pro" on the list was "successor of Beethoven," likely a reference to Mengelberg's assertion that Mahler was the "Beethoven of our time."[46] Copland's "cons" list was more developed; it included "plagiarist, uneven, banal"; "essentially a 'conductor'"; and "tragedy of the Jew—Rosenfeld's view." On the latter point, Copland was referring to Paul Rosenfeld's stunning claim that Mahler tried but failed to reach his true potential as a Jewish artist because of fear of the external consequences of giving voice to that supposed inner propulsion in anti-Semitic Europe (a topic to be taken up further in chapter 4 and that connects to Copland's own identity as a Jewish composer in the United States).

In this 1928 lecture, Copland connected Mahler with neoclassicism—but in contrast to his assertion in the *Times* that Mahler's romantic side should be ignored, his argument here for Mahler's significance tended toward an embrace of romanticism. This change was perhaps a reflection of a certain kind of nostalgia—a sense that, by 1928, "the experimental period of contemporary music was definitely on the wane," as he later wrote.[47] To be sure, Copland included in the lecture what were by now his standard talking points on Mahler's "modern" qualities, in comparison to Richard Strauss—the "independence of melodic line"; the sense that Mahler's music was "built contrapuntally"; and Mahler as a "brilliantly original orchestrator," with adjectives like "no muddiness" and "bare" to drive the point home. But in a section of the lecture on Mahler's "character," Copland dwelt on Mahler's expressive power, referring to "intense emotionalism" and using the adjectives "earnest, passionate, metaphysical, ethical, grandiose" to define Mahler, whom he labeled "a true post-romanticist."

Given that the lecture's title was "Post-Romanticism of Mahler," this side of Mahler seems to have become more important to Copland's estimation of Mahler's significance by the late 1920s. Again pointing to romanticism, Copland referred here to Mahler's "use of folk song to escape to youth." Although such elements did not figure as prominently in the lecture from a year before, at that time Copland had listed "grandiose, naive, folk-quality" as among Mahler's positive attributes, and "bombastic, banal, over-long" as negative ones. Toward the end of the decade, Copland was no longer urging audiences to ignore the "romantico-philosophical conceptions," as he had in his 1925 *Times* letter. Of course, the *Times* letter and the New School lectures served different purposes; an exposition of Mahler as a romanticist was more important in an introduction to Mahler in a course on music than in a polemical piece on Mahler's modernism. But rather than discounting that aspect of Mahler as irrelevant to his appeal, as he had done in the *Times*, now Copland presented it as a special feature. And ultimately, Copland urged his students to excuse Mahler's "weaknesses"—"banal" music (softened by the idea that his "personality shines through others," another echo of the *Times* letter, where Mahler was "never more Mahler than when he was copying Mozart"); "over-long" music; a "lack of taste"; and "bombastic—theatricality." He did so with a statement that recalls Boulanger's own appeal for accepting Mahler in her review of the Amsterdam festival in 1920: "Adorable personality—excuse faults for sake of genius."

The notes for this 1928 lecture, which focus on *Das Lied von der Erde* as the "masterwork" in question, contained significantly more in the way of detailed points on musical specifics than the previous year's lecture, providing one of the clearest windows available into his views on his favorite Mahler work (here he called it Mahler's "most perfect work"). Clarifying the placement of Mahler as a post-romanticist, Copland at once identified the work's romantic, nostalgic aspects, writing, "Breathes spirit of isolation, of weariness of world," "sings of youth and beauty long past," "resigned acceptance of life and death," and "at same time—farewell to romanticism!" His discussion of the first five songs focuses on their textual content, with very little on the music (unfortunately, a page that would have comments on the sixth, "Der Abschied," is missing from the collection of notes). For instance, he described "Der Einsame in Herbst," which Copland mentioned in the previous year's lecture, as a "Lament for the withering of nature in fog and frost," calling it "restrained—contrapuntal—Mahlerish poetry."

The 1928 lecture notes are also remarkable because of Copland's expanded list of composers he believed Mahler influenced. Now, instead of just Honegger (as in the 1925 *Times* letter) or Schoenberg and Honegger (as in the 1927 lecture), Copland placed Milhaud on the list. At some unknown point years later, and in a slightly different color than the main lecture notes, he would write in the names of Britten and Shostakovich, as well as his own initials—thereby explicitly positioning himself as Mahler's musical descendent. Britten, who was born in 1913, was only a teenager when the lecture was initially delivered, so the names of these three figures were clearly added well after 1928. Perhaps Copland felt moved to add these names when reviewing his notes in retrospect while preparing his *Our New Music* (1941), in which Britten and Shostakovich are both listed.[48] As for Copland's initials, their presence may reflect his own recognition of a debt to Mahler in a significant musical project of the period in which the lecture notes were initially composed; around that time, Copland was composing his *Symphonic Ode*, a work he specifically associated with Mahler. In 1931, not long after composing the *Ode*, Copland told the poet Lola Ridge, in comparing the *Ode* with his own recent *Piano Variations* (1930), that it interfaced with an "older" aesthetic than the *Variations*: "You will find a certain relation between the Ode and an occasional movement in the grandiose style by Gustav Mahler but it would be much more difficult to relate the Variations to any of the older composers."[49] Strikingly, in the lectures from 1927 and 1928, Copland pointed to Mahler's "grandiose" side, therefore linking himself, via Mahler, to a sense of romantic expansiveness. This was a change in attitude from his *Times* letter in 1925, where Copland seemed to consider it a flaw that Mahler "has on occasion been grandiloquent."

In his Fall 1929 course "Forms of Modern Music," Copland further developed a transnational context for Mahler, one in which he emphasized a comprehensive view of recent music history in keeping with his sense of an end to the "experimental" period. One of his goals here, he wrote in a syllabus, was "to indicate the outstanding compositions of the past twenty years in each form"; thus works were grouped by genre or performing forces in order "less to concentrate attention on works of prime importance than to plot out main currents so as to promote a sympathetic appreciation of modern music as a whole."[50] "Opera," "Chamber Music," "Ballet," and "String Instruments" were among the session titles, and Copland considered Mahler's Eighth Symphony in a session on oratorio. Copland defined the term oratorio broadly, using it to encompass recent choral symphonies, cantatas, requiems, masses, and more traditional oratorios. Mahler's Eighth Symphony (choral symphony), Honegger's *Le roi David* (traditional oratorio) and Florent Schmitt's *Psalm 47* (cantata) served as the genre's representatives for discussion. (Schmitt's *Psalm 47* apparently replaced Roussel's *Psalm 80*; the catalog advertised a Roussel "Psalm" but not a work by Schmitt.)[51] Other recent choral symphonies in Copland's list included Mahler's Second Symphony, Schoenberg's *Gurrelieder*, Pfitzner's *Von deutscher Seele*, Vaughan Williams's *Sea Symphony*, Holst's *Choral Symphony*, and Kodály's *Psalmus Hungaricus*.

In these lecture notes, Copland returned to a portrayal of Mahler as a proto-modernist, repeating many of the same points from previous lectures but tempering his praise for Mahler's idiom. Here, he defined the "Mahler problem" in terms of "pros" and "cons," and he again referred to Mahler's "loveable personality" (certainly a reference to his "personality" as a composer) and the need to "excuse faults." On the one hand, apparently contradicting his emphasis on romanticism just the year before, he explicitly downplayed that aspect of Mahler's musical importance, declaring that in terms of "Mahler's importance for modern music," he has "no value to us as post-romanticist—passionate, intense emotionalism, metaphysics." He went on to extol Mahler's use of counterpoint, the "independence of melodic line," the "clarity + complexity of counterpoint—that you can hear!" as well as his orchestration ("30 years ahead of his time," and a "love of clean colors"). In his 1925 *Times* letter, Copland had pointed to part 1 of the Eighth Symphony as a shining example of Mahler's contrapuntal artistry; in this lecture, Copland found a specific way to incorporate Mahler's modern "oratorio" into a discussion of recent counterpoint.

A possible hint of Copland's appreciation for Mahler's romantic legacy in this lecture—besides the mere fact of highlighting one of his most enormous works, in terms of length and performance forces—was the addition of a new name to Copland's catalog of Mahler's musical descendants: the Austrian composer Ernst Krenek, whose *Jonny spielt auf* Copland also listed on the syllabus for the first week, in a session on opera. In his notes, Copland pointed to "Mahler's influence on Schoenberg (counterpoint), Honegger (orchestra), and Krenek (sentiment)." Additionally, Copland ended the Mahler portion of the oratorio lesson in 1929 by mentioning "Mahler's place with Berlioz and Liszt," presumably a way of estimating Mahler's position in music history as a significant one, if not at the level of Beethoven. Copland would continue this thread in his book *What to Listen for in Music*, where he wrote that "if one can pick and choose among the separate movements of his nine symphonies, I for one am certain that his eventual position will be equivalent to that of Berlioz."[52]

Six years later, when Copland returned to the New School in the Fall of 1935, his advocacy for Mahler took a sharp turn away from internationalism with the course "Music of Today: Seven concerts of recorded music by contemporary composers with analyses, commentaries, and piano illustrations by Aaron Copland." Here, Copland limited "the illustrations to music available on records" and centered the course "on music of the past ten years" and compositions "seldom heard or never before performed in New York."[53] Unlike in the 1929 lecture, in which Mahler mingled with Honegger and Schmitt in an international session on oratorio, in 1935 Copland grouped composers by nationality, including a session on "Germans: Mahler, Hindemith, and Kurt Weill." This grouping by nationality rather than style or genre was a new choice for Copland in these lectures, perhaps a reflection of a dominant sensibility of musical nationalism in the 1930s that superseded the internationalism of the 1920s.[54] It also adds to Howard Pollack's observation that Copland's interest in contemporary Austro-German composers, including Hindemith and Kurt Weill, has been overshadowed by a tendency to highlight his esteem for French composers.[55] Depicting German music as having been in "collapse" ("music 'sick' with the 19th century"), Copland positioned Hindemith and Weill as "a new start from a different premise." And posing the broad question "Why Mahler?," Copland answered with his usual points about Mahler's modern approach to counterpoint and orchestration.

Although it is tempting to attribute Copland's choice of the tragic *Kindertotenlieder* and the monumental Second Symphony for this lecture to a developed appreciation of Mahler's romanticism, Copland was introducing musical examples via phonograph; his options for the Mahler session were severely restricted in 1935, when most of Mahler's music had not yet been committed to record. A handwritten list of recordings to be used during the course resides in the folder that also contains the lecture notes; it includes baritone Heinrich Rehkemper's 1928 recording of the *Kindertotenlieder* with Jascha Horenstein conducting the Berlin State Opera Orchestra (listed by Copland as Polydor 66693–5), as well as two options for Symphony no. 2: Oskar Fried's 1924 recording with the same group (Polydor 66290–66300), and Eugene Ormandy's January 1935 recording with the Minneapolis Symphony Orchestra (Victor 11753–63, labeled simply "Victor" in Copland's list).

At the same time, and perhaps going hand in hand with his placement of Mahler in a German context, Copland again swung in the direction of romanticism and away from modernism in his estimation of Mahler's value—more consistent with his 1928 lecture than his 1927 or 1929 ones. While in 1929, Copland told his audience that Mahler had "no value to us as post-romanticist," in 1935 he said quite the opposite, writing that Mahler sang "the swan song of the 19th century" and referring to "a farewell to beautiful romanticism" (echoing his comment on *Das Lied* from 1928, but with "beautiful" added). Copland added, "Mahler should be listened to in that spirit," and he continued: "All the elements of Romanticism there in an exaggerated degree." His list of these elements included "love of the grandiose," "intimacy with nature," "use of folk song feeling" (which Copland associated with "escape to youth"), "earnest, passionate," and "metaphysical." Copland went on to say of *Das Lied* that it "breathes the spirit of isolation, of loneliness, of the end of a world" and, strikingly, that Mahler "speaks to the Romanticist in all of us."

Significant aesthetic reorientations around 1930 may help explain Copland's willingness to discuss Mahler's romanticism in such a positive light by 1935—suggesting that, for Copland, modernism and romanticism could coexist. Later, Copland pictured the period from 1890 to 1930 as one of musical experimentation, with an opportunity in 1930 to reflect with admiration on the past: "By 1930," Copland wrote, "composers everywhere began to sense the necessity for consolidating the gains made for their art through so many years of experimentation. Like Hindemith, they wanted to 'cash in' on the discoveries of the pioneers, to take stock of all the new musical resources that were now at their disposal." Copland added, with a telling nod to the nineteenth century, "Moreover, from the aesthetic standpoint, there was no longer anything to fear from Romanticism; it had been firmly established that new music, in whatever style, was to be objective in attitude, clearly conceived, and contained in emotional expression."[56] This was hardly a ringing endorsement of romanticism; Copland seemed to be suggesting not a return to romantic musical ideals, but instead a recognition that in the 1930s, new music no longer needed to be explicitly positioned as a reaction to romanticism.

The sense of an aesthetic shift around 1930 was strongly felt at the time. As Carol J. Oja points out in her commentary on Copland's *Piano Variations*, in the late 1920s "the rage against historical traditions that had inflamed early-twentieth century modernists had been spent, as the past and present began to fuse productively once again."[57] And Elizabeth B. Crist has traced the impulse toward accessibility to late-1920s progressivism as well as the Popular Front, to which she connected Copland's developing interest in folk tunes and a sense of musical naiveté.[58] This attitude helps account for the shades of a pro-romantic view of Mahler that began turning up in Copland's Mahler lectures from the late 1920s but that are much more evident in 1935.

In addition to leaving the door open for romanticism in modern music, Copland—by positioning Mahler as a predecessor of Hindemith and Weill in 1935—drew an implicit link between Mahler's romanticism and the populist-tinged *Gebrauchsmusik* of the Weimar Republic, perhaps from the standpoint of the audience–composer relationships that Copland concerned himself with in the 1930s. In the Mahler lecture from 1935, Copland did not argue directly that Mahler's music prefigured Hindemith and Weill in any specific way, although Copland did mention Hindemith's "Contrapuntal texture" and "emotional" component, as well as the "cheap, banal tunes" in Weill's music—suggesting connections to Mahler's aesthetic. (Earlier, in 1930, Copland drew a direct association between Mahler and Hindemith, writing in a review of Egon Wellesz's *Die neue Instrumentation*, "No matter what we may think of this last-of-the-romantics as composer, he was indubitably an orchestrator of genius," and he made a specific reference to Hindemith's Concerto Grosso, op. 36, and Honegger's *Pacific 231* as works Mahler influenced.)[59] Nor did Copland suggest that Mahler's romanticism bore a specific musical relationship with *Gebrauchsmusik*. Copland was certainly ambivalent toward both *Gebrauchsmusik* and romanticism.[60] But both aesthetic approaches at least shared an emphasis on accessibility and the potential to reach wide audiences, making Mahler, Hindemith, and Weill an intriguing grouping.

Four years after "Music of Today," and in the clearest gesture toward the music of the past in any of his New School courses of this period, Copland taught the course "Symphonic Masterpieces" in early 1939.[61] The catalog entry advertised works by Haydn, Mozart, Beethoven, Berlioz, Brahms, Franck, Mahler, Sibelius, Stravinsky, and

Roussel.[62] Here, Mahler stood in a line of symphonists extending back to the eighteenth century. Returning to the Second Symphony—the same work he highlighted in his letter to the *New York Times* back in 1925—Copland again foregrounded Mahler's romanticism, as he did in the 1935 lecture, even as he seemed to distance himself from it, writing, "We are no longer involved—'no relative of ours.'" Here, Copland made his standard comments about Mahler's counterpoint and clarity, this time with the addition of "harmonic freedom (daring)" that derived from the "independence of melodic lines." But just as he did in 1935, Copland also conceded that Mahler "speaks to the romanticist in all of us"; he gave over much of the lecture to the goal of connecting Mahler to the nineteenth century, itemizing his romantic qualities ("essentially a naif spirit," an "intensely emotional figure," "earnest, passionate, turbulent," with a "love of the grandiose, apocalyptic," "love of nature," "love of folk song," "filled with sense of farewell to life & beauty = romanticism to Mahler"). Copland also painted Mahler as a successor of Beethoven by addressing the "great length" of Mahler's symphonies and the "originality of the form," particularly in his employment of the human voice in several symphonies.

The timing of Copland's turn toward "symphonic masterpieces" in the 1930s is revealing of his own priorities as a composer. In the context of World War II, as Elizabeth B. Crist has discussed, Copland was attuned to a sense of accessibility and social resonance; the same year, Copland wrote "A Composer from Brooklyn," an autobiographical piece in which he pointed out that concert audiences gravitated toward esteemed masterpieces, putting composers in a dangerous position if they were to write music "in a vacuum."[63] And Annegret Fauser has recently written of the prestige the symphony held in America during the war years.[64] In the 1940s, Copland would go on to write his own Third Symphony, his most grandiose work to date and, with its four-movement structure, his clearest effort at a "symphonic masterpiece" along the lines of those found in his 1939 lectures.[65] The catalog entry for this course read, "The symphonic field is chosen as the archetype of present-day music making."[66] By monumentalizing Mahler's Second Symphony as a model of symphonic greatness (and not simply of "modern" greatness, as he had done earlier with *Das Lied* by placing it in the lecture series "Masterworks of Modern Music"), Copland was perhaps offering up the Second Symphony as a new classic—not only one that he viewed as having neoclassical characteristics but also one that audiences could connect with Beethoven, Brahms, and other standard names in orchestral composition.

Copland's shifting priorities in the 1920s and 1930s thus throw into relief the broader significance of his time as an educator at the

New School, where he was sharing the music of Mahler and other composers with a wider audience than those who would have simply been impressed by counterpoint and orchestration. These new audiences were likely not composers or even music experts; rather, they were members of the general public who, by attending lectures at the New School, hoped to gain enrichment in the humanities. Moreover, women and Jews made up a large proportion of those who enrolled in New School courses, at least according to data from before Copland's time there, as reported by Peter M. Rutkoff and William B. Scott.[67] Indeed, Jewish students may have been particularly interested in what Copland had to say about Mahler and Jewish identity. Of course, Copland's audiences for these lectures were certainly smaller than the readership of his *New York Times* letter to the editor. In 1927, he told Nadia Boulanger that he spoke to 125 people weekly.[68] Later, he recalled "talking to perhaps fifty people," and interestingly, given his increasing focus on accessibility in his own music, he added that "the audience tripled when I announced my subject as Music rather than Modern Music."[69] His lectures enabled him to enact, through pedagogy, his growing interest in reaching a broad audience, with Mahler's profile changing along the way.

To bring the public aspect of Copland's engagement with Mahler full circle, a close look at his first detailed comments to appear in print on the subject since the 1925 *Times* letter—a section on post-romanticism in *Our New Music* from 1941—demonstrates the fifteen-year evolution of Copland's ideas about Mahler's significance. It also helps fill in the gaps where Copland's New School lecture notes remain sketchy, revealing even more of what he likely told his audiences in those sessions. In the book, Copland made his usual points in highlighting Mahler as a precedent for neoclassicism. He again viewed "the curiously contrapuntal fabric of the musical texture" and the "strikingly original instrumentation" as Mahler's contributions that "were years in advance of their time." He even made the connection to neoclassicism explicit, writing that Mahler's "use of the orchestra as a many-voiced body . . . was typical of the age of Bach and Handel. Thus, as far as orchestral practice is concerned, Mahler bridges the gap between the composers of the early eighteenth century and the neoclassicists of our own time."[70] In a later chapter, Copland linked the "hard, dry, crackling sonority" of Igor Stravinsky's orchestra to Mahler's music.[71]

But just as in his lecture for the course "Symphonic Masterpieces," Copland softened the technical discussion of Mahler's musical procedures by couching it firmly in terms of his broader appeal as a composer; in *Our New Music*, he offered a more detailed case for Mahler's larger significance: "The irascible scherzos, the heaven-storming calls in the brass, the special quality of his communings with nature, the gentle melancholy of a transitional passage, the gargantuan *ländler,* the pages of an incredible loneliness—all these, combined with the above-mentioned histrionics, an inner warmth, and the will to evoke the largest forms and the grandest musical thoughts, add up to one of the most fascinating composer-personalities of modern times."[72] Further, Copland wrote admiringly that *Das Lied,* Mahler's "greatest work," is the "swan song of the entire romantic movement," that Mahler "was saying a final farewell to the nineteenth century," and that "all his music reinvokes the past glories of that golden age, but with an added note of regret from a wonderful epoch that was gone without hope of recall."[73] All this would have been out of place in the 1925 *Times* letter, where Copland downplayed Mahler's "romantico-philosophical" essence as worth forgetting. But in the early 1940s, Copland—fully committed not only to accessibility and direct communication with audiences, but also to reconciling modernism with past traditions—perhaps found in Mahler's romantic essence an avenue by which to engage new audiences for Mahler's music.

That Copland adjusted his views of Mahler's significance to fit his contemporary ideas shows the extent to which Europe continued to loom for American modernist composers in the 1930s, even at a time when Copland shifted away from transatlantic cosmopolitanism and toward a pan-American focus.[74] This focus is indeed clear in Copland's correspondence with the Mexican composer Carlos Chávez, in which the two musicians demonstrated what Howard Pollack has called "a certain Pan-American resistance and solidarity in the face of European cultural domination."[75] At the same time, Copland's discussions of Mahler's significance suggest a complex narrative in which a European musical past—and even the Austro-German wing of that past—continued to have much to offer contemporary American art music, in terms not just of technical features but also of sensibility.

Olin Downes, in his review of *Our New Music* in the *New York Times,* was astute to question Copland's proposed division between romanticism and what Downes called "classicism." Downes, no admirer of Mahler's music, objected to Copland's tethering of Mahler to the eighteenth century, writing that Copland "does not seem to mind Mahler's inflated rhetoric, his exhibitionism, and the turgid orchestration of his symphonies," despite the fact that Copland himself "is constantly exclaiming against music of huge proportions and pretentious utterance." In reality, Copland's evolving comments on Mahler support Downes's skepticism about musical categories; as Downes wrote, "so-called 'classicism' and so-called 'romanticism' are constantly present, in varying proportions, in all art, and . . . through the centuries the esthetic pendulum has swung backward and forward."[76] Indeed, the pendulum swung even in Copland's own estimation of Mahler's music, in which Copland found much to praise in its apparent classicism at first and, over time, in its romanticism. The fact that Copland was never consistent, from year to year, in placing Mahler more on the side of romanticism or modernism belies a sense that Copland himself must have held that the dichotomy was a false one.

One final lecture, from the late 1950s, demonstrates how Copland's estimation of Mahler's importance to twentieth-century music continued to develop along with changes in his musical outlook after World War II—and particularly in 1957, when Copland completed his twelve-tone *Piano Fantasy*. Indeed, Copland's advocacy for Mahler in the public sphere continued after these New School lectures and *Our New Music*, especially in the late 1950s, when the growth of his conducting career gave him an opportunity to engage with Mahler's works from the podium. Detailed commentary on *Das Lied von der Erde* survives in notes for a lecture on Mahler for the Canadian Broadcasting Company's *20th Century Masterpieces* series, broadcast January 27, 1957, for which a recording has not yet surfaced.[77] Here, Copland argued that the end of *Das Lied* exerted a "great influence on Schoenberg and his school," citing its "silvery, bell-like sounds—achieved thru use of celesta, 2 harps, mandolin, sustained strings."[78]

Of course, this was not the first time Copland mentioned Schoenberg or other members of the Second Viennese School in a lecture on Mahler; in the "Symphonic Masterpieces" lecture on Mahler from 1939, Copland referred to the "admiration of Schoenberg, Berg, Webern" for Mahler. Nor was it the first time Copland referred to the style of orchestration at the close of *Das Lied* as it relates to those figures; in *Our New Music*, from 1941, he noted that "characteristic of one small corner of [Schoenberg's] orchestration is the love of a magical, bell-like sonority that is somehow extracted from harp, celesta, glockenspiel, mandolin, and so forth. Alban Berg took full advantage of that hint in his last orchestral works."[79] His description of that "bell-like" orchestration matches what he later said, in 1957, about *Das Lied*—firming up a link between Schoenberg and Mahler. It is likely no coincidence that his claim that Mahler "had great influence on Schoenberg and his school" came in the same month in which Copland completed the *Piano Fantasy*, about which he wrote that he made "liberal use of devices associated with" twelve-tone writing.[80] And it was the next year, in 1958, that Copland led the Ojai Festival Symphony Orchestra in California in a program that included Mahler's *Kindertotenlieder* (sung by Grace Bumbry) and his own *Short Symphony*, an especially notable concert in that it was his work's West Coast premiere.[81] Thus, Copland placed his own music in a network that extended back to Mahler and the Second Viennese School.

Copland claimed in the 1957 lecture notes that Mahler, as a post-romantic, was one of several composers, including Richard Strauss and Jean Sibelius, whose "esthetic was old—mostly," but whose "methods," which were "sometimes new," were "able to be disengaged" from their context. In reality, though, Copland could never finalize the divorce between Mahler's "methods" and "esthetic"; his admiration for Mahler's particular brand of romanticism, as we have seen, inflected the commentary that was ostensibly meant to place Mahler outside that realm. As Copland himself said at the end of his 1957 lecture notes, "the fascination of Mahler" is "what looked toward the past and what toward the future." This relationship between past and future—between Mahler's "esthetic" and his "method"—becomes even clearer in an examination of Copland's relationship with his Jewish identity, and of Mahler's place in that identity.

Chapter Four

MAHLER IN COPLAND'S JEWISH ROMANTICISM

This chapter takes as its starting point a remarkable comment Aaron Copland made late in his career about an apparent disconnect between his identities as both a Jewish and an American musician. In an interview from 1972, Ralph P. Locke asked Copland if he thought that "being Jewish has influenced your music." Copland's striking reply suggested that he saw his Jewishness as a potential artistic liability and even a foil for a sense of American identity: "It's never been a problem," he said. Although the "grandiosity in some of my larger works, like the *Symphonic Ode* . . . might be thought Jewish in origin," Copland continued, "it hasn't been a preoccupation, certainly not to the extent that being American has." Expanding on this implicit disconnect between Jewishness and Americanness, Copland invoked the idea of the "Jewish problem," saying that it "never presented itself to me in any form or caused me any trouble, mostly because I wasn't brought up in a Jewish neighborhood, so I wasn't aware of Jewishness at the time, everyday [*sic*], from morning till night." In the interview, Copland conceded that his own "so-called 'American' music" perhaps has "some Jewish characteristics," but he could not identify them specifically. He noted the "relatively minor role" that Jewishness played in his music relative to Leonard Bernstein's, remarking that the younger figure had "a kind of patriotic fervor" about the subject.[1] Copland's chamber work *Vitebsk* (1929) for violin, cello, and piano offers one of the only overt examples of a Jewish presence in his music, based as it is on a Hasidic song Copland heard at a production of S. Ansky's play *The Dybbuk* in 1925.[2] Drawing a connection to his heritage as a child of Jewish immigrants from Eastern Europe (his parents came from what is today Lithuania), his goal for *Vitebsk*, he stated in his autobiography, was to "reflect the harshness and drama of Jewish life in White Russia."[3]

The fact that Copland answered a general question about Jewish influence in his work with a somewhat defensive reply about the "Jewish problem" (to which Locke did not refer in his question) helps situate his self-identification as a Jew and an American within the larger cultural environment of twentieth-century America—an environment in which, for a considerable period of time, Jews were seen with suspicion. The "Jewish problem" as a construct refers to a longstanding debate about the position of Jews in society. In the United States after World War I, as the historian Eric Goldstein has discussed, "white Americans . . . were increasingly convinced that Jews represented a distinct 'problem' in American life." As Goldstein argued, Jews—"because they remained a minority and were concentrated in pursuits that had such a great impact on American values and perceptions"—emerged more and more as "a target for those nervous about the direction of modern American culture." This was especially an issue after World War I, which "represented to many native-born whites a final break with the idealized, community-based culture of their past." Thus, "many white Americans"—including prominent voices like the industrialist Henry Ford—"cast the Jewish 'race' as an infiltrating force, one that was powerful enough to penetrate the central institutions of American life but dedicated to its own selfish interests."[4]

Many observers of the musical scene seemed to feel that a separate, ingrained Jewish racial identity prevented Jewish composers from participating in the development of a distinctly American tradition of art music—a view that helps explain why Copland did not position his own Jewishness as part of that larger project in his answer to Locke's question, even many decades after World War I. Indeed, as Beth Levy has put it, Copland did not disclaim his Jewishness so much as he "sidestepped it so completely that audiences today are often unaware that Copland did not begin his career as a 'common man." As Levy has discussed, Jews as musicians faced criticism in terms of authenticity, originality, assimilation, racism, and xenophobia.[5] One appalling example of this attitude comes from 1920, when the New England composer and critic Daniel Gregory Mason wrote that the "insidiousness of the Jewish menace to our artistic integrity" endangered "the vital nucleus of the American temper," which Mason viewed as "Anglo-Saxon reticence."[6]

The perception of a Jewish threat to American musical identity—a perception Copland's comments on the "Jewish problem" show he was keenly aware of throughout his life—suggests a fruitful lens through which to view his relationship with the music of Mahler as a fellow Jewish composer. A central goal of this book is to argue that Copland sought inspiration in the Austro-German romantic tradition, with Mahler's romanticism serving as a proxy, of sorts, for a romanticism of Copland's own that he did not proclaim overtly. In this chapter, I argue that Copland's advocacy of Mahler as a Jewish composer intersects closely with his own interest in romanticism. Evidence for this comes from his relationship with the writings of yet another Jewish figure, the prominent critic Paul Rosenfeld. Rosenfeld repeatedly criticized Mahler for supposedly suppressing his creative impulses as a Jewish artist and instead emulating his Austro-German predecessors. Copland responded to this criticism by wrestling with the question of how a composer could simultaneously express a sense of originality and draw successfully on a musical past. Of course, this was a central challenge American composers faced in negotiating their relationship with the Austro-German tradition, and it was the precise challenge that Rosenfeld claimed Mahler, as a Jewish composer in Austria, had failed to meet. By defending Mahler in Rosenfeld's terms, Copland reconciled his own Jewishness not only with an aspiration to be recognized as a fresh compositional voice in America, but with his own affinity for the Austro-German tradition.

While Copland advocated repeatedly for Mahler in print, he rarely commented on Mahler's Jewishness in any direct way; on the other hand, he praised Darius Milhaud of *Les Six* for successfully navigating a sense of Jewish identity. Copland was certainly aware of Mahler's position as a Jew in fin-de-siècle Vienna, albeit one who converted to Roman Catholicism for professional reasons; in *Our New Music* from 1941, Copland referred to Mahler as an especially "racial" composer, in contrast to Milhaud. Taking note of a "deeply nostalgic" sensibility in Milhaud's music, Copland wrote,

> Since this nostalgia is shared by none of his French confreres, I take it to be a sign of Milhaud's Jewish inheritance. That he is not so racial a composer as [Ernest] Bloch or Mahler seems natural if we remember that his ancestors settled in Provence in the fifteenth century so that his Jewishness has long been tempered by the French point of view. Nevertheless his subjectivism, his violence, and his strong sense of logic (as displayed by his strict use of polytonality) are indications that the Jewish spirit is still alive in him.[7]

Copland later wrote in a review of Peter Gradenwitz's *The Music of Israel* (1949) that Milhaud demonstrated how a composer could "remain profoundly national and at the same time profoundly Jewish."[8] As Howard Pollack has discussed in detail, Copland thus revealed Milhaud as a possible model for his own work—a Jewish composer who, in Copland's view, successfully wrote music that could be perceived in terms of his nationality but one who also expressed his Jewishness as a core part of his identity.[9] Copland's statement on Milhaud also sheds light on his invocation of the "Jewish problem" in his response to Locke's question; he was positioning his restrained form of musical Jewishness as compatible with his strong personal identification as an American composer.

Copland's linkage of nostalgia in Milhaud with Jewishness also suggests that Copland perhaps found in his own Jewishness an opportunity to reconcile his artistic heritage in Austro-German romanticism with a sense of musical Americanness. As Pollack has also pointed out, Copland tied tragedy, drama, and grandiosity—all traits readily squared with Mahlerian romanticism—to a specifically Jewish expressiveness.[10] And in a frequently quoted letter to Leonard Bernstein from 1939, Copland cautioned his protégé about the Jewish flavor of a draft of what would become the third movement of Bernstein's Symphony no. 1, "Jeremiah": "As far as I can judge, you are hopelessly romantic as a composer. It was clever to have adopted the 'Jewish' manner in this piece and thereby justify the romanticism of the piece. (I don't mean to imply that this was more than sub-conscious.) But somehow, someday, that richness of feeling that I call romantic will have to be metamorphosed so that it comes out more new-sounding, more fresh."[11] That Copland acknowledged the connection between romanticism and Jewishness amounts to an admission of the importance of romanticism in his own musical heritage. At the same time, he was skeptical of emulating Bloch, perhaps because Bloch's music so overtly proclaimed its composer's Jewishness. And it apparently did so without, from Copland's perspective, leaving enough room for a different sense of national identification—in Copland's case, an American one.

Copland did not expand on why he thought both Mahler and Bloch were especially "racial" in contrast to Milhaud, but by using the term "racial" to describe a kind of essential Jewishness, Copland was drawing on a typical understanding of Jewish identity in the early twentieth century. The debate as to whether Jews constituted a race, religion, nation, or some combination was a complex one. After World War I, it was common for Eastern European Jews in America to consider themselves as members of a distinct race, due to a "minority consciousness" that developed as a result of their increased integration into American society.[12] But this began to shift in the late 1930s toward a more cultural and less racial definition of Jewishness; the significant role many Jews began to play in American political life meant "a greater willingness to redefine American nationalism in ways that did not question the status of Jews and other immigrant groups as a stable part of white society," as Goldstein put it.[13]

Copland's ambivalent mentions of Bloch, along with his reference to Mahler as "racial," invite a closer look at the writings of Paul Rosenfeld, who critiqued Mahler and others in specifically racial terms. Copland wrote in his memorial tribute to Rosenfeld in 1947 that he could "very well remember the excitement of reading his first articles about the young Stravinsky and the young Ernest Bloch. That must have been around 1919 or 1920."[14] Indeed, Rosenfeld was a crucial figure in Copland's development as a musical thinker, and Copland engaged closely with his writings, though he certainly did not agree with everything Rosenfeld wrote. In his autobiography, Copland recalled having read Rosenfeld's commentary on music in *The Dial* around 1919, before he departed for Paris. At that time, Rosenfeld "was considered the one to read for the most recent developments." And despite the fact that Rosenfeld's "prose may have been too lush at times," Copland noted that Rosenfeld "wrote perceptively about controversial figures such as Schoenberg, Stravinsky, Ornstein, Mahler, and Sibelius."[15] Leaving room for disagreement with Rosenfeld's ideas, Copland wrote in the same memorial statement quoted above that he had admired Rosenfeld more for "the sharpness of his sensitivity to music" than for the "exactitude of his judgments."[16]

One of Rosenfeld's judgments was great admiration for Bloch's music, which Rosenfeld regularly praised by connecting it with Jewishness. The compilation *Musical Portraits: Interpretations of Twenty Modern Composers*, published in 1920, contains articles Rosenfeld wrote for *The Dial*, *The New Republic*, and *The Seven Arts*, and it is likely that Copland had taken in these writings. The book's final chapter, on Bloch, shows the depth of Rosenfeld's esteem for Bloch as a significant figure in modern music at the time—perhaps the most significant. It begins with a sweeping, evocative, and literary description of the relationship between Eastern and Western culture and culminates in the statement that "in the music of no composer" was the then-recent "fusion" of East and West "as plainly evident as it is in that of Ernest Bloch." Referring specifically to Bloch's suite for viola and piano, Rosenfeld wrote, "Here, the West has advanced furthest east, the East furthest west," and the "organizing power of Europe is married to the sensuousness of Asia."[17]

It was Bloch's embrace of his own deep-seated Jewishness, Rosenfeld posited, that made this blend possible. He wrote that "no composer was better fitted by nature to receive the stimulus of the onrushing East. . . . As a Jew, Bloch carried within himself a fragment of the Orient; was in himself an outpost of the mother of continents. And he is one of the few Jewish composers really, fundamentally self-expressive. He is one of the few that have fully accepted themselves, fully accepted the fate that made them Jewish and stigmatized them."[18] He praised Bloch for what Rosenfeld considered "racial" characteristics, writing that he composed music that was "a large, a poignant, an authentic expression of what is racial in the Jew" and noting in particular the "harsh and haughty accents of the Hebrew tongue," the "abrupt gestures of the Hebrew soul," and the "titanic burst of energy that created the race and carried it intact across lands and times, out of the eternal Egypt, through the eternal Red Sea."[19] At the same time, Rosenfeld observed a balance between Bloch's Jewishness and what he saw as Bloch's position in the ancestry of Western art music—that "he rests quite as heavily on the great European traditions of music as he does on his own hereditary strain."[20]

On the other hand, Jewishness was central to Rosenfeld's scathing view of Mahler's place in music history—a view that reflected contemporary ideas about the relationship between Jewishness and other kinds of identities. According to Rosenfeld, Mahler denied his own Jewishness by stymieing the expression of an essential component of his character and subjugating himself, instead, to his Austrian setting. In a lengthy discussion of Mahler in *Musical Portraits,* Rosenfeld suggested that his music was "pre-eminently a reflection of Beethoven's" and argued that

> if he never spoke in authentic accents, if out of his vast dreams of a great modern popular symphonic art, out of his honesty, his sincerity, his industry, his undeniably noble and magnificent traits, there resulted only the unhappy boring colossi that are his nine symphonies, it is indubitably, to a great extent, the consequence of the fact that he, the Jew, was born in a society that made Judaism, Jewish descent and Jewish traits, a curse to those that inherited them. The destiny that made him a Jew decreed that, did he speak out fully, he would have to employ an idiom that would recall the harsh accents of the Hebrew language quite as much as that of any tongue spoken by the peoples of Europe.

His Austrian environment, Rosenfeld continued, allowed Mahler "to participate in its activities only on the condition that he did not remind it continually of his alienhood, of his racial consciousness." As long as Mahler could "suppress within himself all awareness of his descent and character and peculiarities, and attempt to identify himself with [Austrian society's] members, and try to feel just as they felt and spoke just as they spoke," then he could feel "the sense of equality, of fraternity, of citizenship."[21]

Ultimately, for Rosenfeld, Mahler was torn between a natural desire to create music as a Jewish artist and a fear of the consequences for doing so:

> In the place of the united self, there came to exist within him two men. For while one part of him demanded the free complete expression necessary to the artist, another sought to block it for fear that in the free flow the hated racial traits would appear. For Mahler would have been the first to have been repelled by the sound of his own harsh, haughty, guttural, abrupt Hebrew inflection. He would have been the first to turn in contempt from his own gestures. There was in him the frenetic unconscious desire to rid himself of the thing he had come to believe inferior. And rather than express it, rather than speak in his proper idiom, he made, unaware to himself, perhaps, the choice of speaking through the voices of other men, of the great German composers; of imitating them instead of developing his own personality; of accepting sterility and banality and impotence rather than achieving a power of speech.[22]

The thrust of this commentary was that Mahler was, for the most part, irrelevant, as one more passage sums up: "There is not one of poor Mahler's nine symphonies, honest and dignified as some of them are, that exists as fresh, new-minted, vivid music."[23]

Rosenfeld continued to explore these themes in "The Tragedy of Gustav Mahler," published in the collection *Musical Chronicle* and dated March 1922 (not to be confused with another article by Rosenfeld with the same title, from the *New Republic* in 1916). For Mahler to have been a successful composer, Rosenfeld argued here, he would have needed to find a way to overcome an almost impossible situation. Mahler, he wrote, "was born a Jew. And to be born a Jew, particularly in the Austria of the 1860's, was not intensely conducive to the sustainment of that fresh faith in life, that relaxed love of men, from which great song springs. It was, on the contrary, a circumstance full of baleful encouragement to those who had been hurt, to button tighter and hug ever closer to themselves the ancient gray overcoat of fear."[24] And Mahler was not the only Jewish figure that Rosenfeld viewed this way; Jewishness figured into his critiques of several figures.[25] Specifically on Giacomo Meyerbeer and Felix Mendelssohn, two giants of the early-to-middle nineteenth century, Rosenfeld said that they, in contrast to Bloch,

> refused to accept themselves for what they were. The weakness of their art is to be understood only as the result of the spiritual warfare that threatens to divide every Jew against himself. There was operative in them, whether they were aware of it or no, a secret desire to escape their stigmata. They were deliberately deaf to the promptings of the beings that were so firmly planted in the racial soil. They were fugitive from the national consciousness. The bourn of impulse was half stopped.[26]

Copland was certainly familiar with Rosenfeld's commentary on Mahler. In addition to his general comments about admiring Rosenfeld's writings, he referred in notes for his New School lectures to Rosenfeld's views on Mahler's Jewish identity—even though Copland's direct reaction to those views never turned up in his published writings on Mahler. In the Mahler lecture for the 1928 course "Masterworks of Modern Music," he referred vaguely to the "tragedy of the Jew—Rosenfeld's view." Although Copland's precise take on "Rosenfeld's view" is unknown, it is not surprising that Rosenfeld's ideas would have surfaced for Copland while he was preparing his New School lectures. As discussed in chapter 3, Copland took over the lectures for Rosenfeld himself, and Jewish students were an important segment of the New School's clientele.

Notes from a later lecture by Copland provide some clues about his approach to the "tragedy" Rosenfeld identified in Mahler's music. On April 15, 1951, Copland spoke in Jerusalem on "Jewish Composers in the Western World"; in his notes he referred to the "Paul Rosenfeld 'accusation,'" seemingly in the context of a discussion of Mahler as the "assimilated Jew par excellence."[27] It is unclear whether Copland meant that he or Rosenfeld saw Mahler as the supreme example of the "assimilated Jew." Perhaps Copland meant that while Rosenfeld believed Mahler failed to express his Jewish identity, Copland thought of him as a composer who successfully melded his Jewish and Austrian identities. Or perhaps Copland was simply referring to Rosenfeld's claim that Mahler blended into his environment so thoroughly that he completely quashed his inner voice as a result—with "par excellence" thus taking on a sarcastic edge.

Whatever the case, Copland made other notes in the same lecture that suggest he disagreed with Rosenfeld; given Copland's advocacy of Mahler's music, it seems likely that Copland referred here and elsewhere to Rosenfeld's view primarily to reframe or even refute his conclusions—ultimately positioning Mahler as a Jewish composer for whom Jewishness was not a liability. Indeed, Copland seemed to frame his whole lecture as a rejection of Rosenfeld's belief that a recognition of Jewishness must be a central part of a Jewish composer's musical art. In the introduction to the lecture, he wrote that "I know what the audience wishes to hear: The artist of Jewish race, who has affirmed his Jewishness in his art, comes out best." This, of course, was precisely Rosenfeld's thesis about Bloch. But Copland advanced his own theory: that "the truly Jewish composer need not worry about his Jewishness—it will be evident in his work." The degree of Jewishness, in this view, depended on "temperament" and "environment," but Copland made no value judgment about the extent to which temperament ought to give way to environment, or vice versa; he simply noted, "If by temperament he is deeply racial art will come out Jewish," and "if by environment, non-Jewish, that will mix with temperament."

Copland did not elaborate on what he heard as particularly Jewish or "racial" in Mahler's oeuvre, but it is likely that he had in mind the very elements he associated with romanticism; by implication, then, Mahler's rather non-Jewish (Austro-German) environment happened to accord well with what Copland seemed to view as Mahler's Jewish temperament. Referring to Milhaud's music, Copland wrote in *Our New Music* that its "nostalgia," "subjectivism," and "violence" reflected its composer's Jewish background. In the same text, as seen in chapter 3, Copland referred similarly to Mahler's "irascible scherzos, the heaving-storming calls in the brass, the special quality of his communings with nature, the gentle melancholy of a transitional passage, the gargantuan *ländler*, the pages of an incredible loneliness—all these, combined with the above-mentioned histrionics, an inner warmth, and the will to evoke the largest forms and the grandest musical thoughts, add up to one of the most fascinating composer-personalities of modern times."[28] Again, Copland did not explicitly link these qualities to Jewishness in Mahler's case, but the parallel between Milhaud's specifically Jewish romanticism and Mahler's not-specifically-Jewish romanticism through these traits—given Copland's identification of Mahler as "racial," also in the same text—is striking.

Copland did not specify where, exactly, in Mahler's music these characteristics might be found, but his descriptions are apt for several of Mahler's works. By "irascible scherzos" he may well have had in mind the Rondo-Burleske movement of the Ninth Symphony and the scherzo of the Second Symphony, and "heaven-storming calls in the brass" points to several moments in the finale of the Second Symphony. "Gargantuan ländler" suggests the expansive second movement of the Ninth Symphony," and pages of incredible loneliness" call to mind the conclusions of both *Das Lied von der Erde* and the Ninth Symphony, with their transparent and spacious textures. Mahler's works are considered in more depth in chapter 5 as models for Copland's own music, but for the purposes of the present discussion, Copland's reference to such a wide range of musical characteristics reveals that his vision of Mahler's Jewishness was a broad one that left much room for multiple stylistic elements in Mahler's works. Rather than claiming that Jewish musical elements were incompatible with Austro-German ones, or that they stood out from the musical fabric, Copland seemed to be suggesting that such elements could and did operate within an Austro-German context—and, what's more, that they were not incompatible with Mahler's originality.

This was quite different from how Rosenfeld heard Mahler. Whereas Copland seemed to appreciate what Rosenfeld called Mahler's "sheer brute force" as a sign of his distinct personality, for Rosenfeld this "brute force"—in the vast forces required for the Eighth Symphony, and evident from the beginning of the work, for instance—was ultimately a way of trying to imitate Beethoven, even to write what Rosenfeld called Beethoven's Tenth Symphony.[29] Copland, on the other hand, rejected the pairing of Beethoven and Mahler, suggesting that resemblances in his music to Beethoven were a self-conscious part of Mahler's artistic persona; he wrote, "One is always being told that Mahler was no Beethoven. Quite so. The difference between Beethoven and Mahler is the difference between watching a great man walk down the street and watching a great actor act the part of a great man walking down the street. The two experiences can be equally impressive, though in different ways."[30]

As both Copland and Rosenfeld were vague about how specific musical details connected to their larger arguments, the opening of Mahler's Eighth Symphony, seen in example 4.1, offers a potential—if quite conjectural—avenue into the differing perspectives on Mahler of these two figures. It sets the medieval Latin hymn "Veni, Creator Spiritus" (Come, Creator Spirit), and Rosenfeld, for his part, disparaged the "brassy, pompous theme that opens the Eighth" and called it "platitudinous."[31] He further wrote, "For a moment, a work like the Eighth Symphony stuns the auditor with its sheer physical bulk. After all, one does not hear a thousand voices singing together every day, and the brass and the percussion are very brilliant. Soon, nevertheless, there insinuates itself the realization that there is in this work neither the all-creating spirit the composer so magniloquently evokes, nor the heaven he strives so ardently to attain."[32] In this work, Mahler indeed immediately confronts the listener with *fortissimo* entrances in various instruments, followed by the choirs themselves. But where Rosenfeld (in a review from 1916) identified in this symphony a "vast flood of sound,"[33] Copland may well have heard, in the trumpets and trombones, a more positive example of Mahler's distinctive "heaven-storming calls in the brass"—one that perhaps prefigures moments in his own *Symphonic Ode* (1929) and *Fanfare for the Common Man* (1942). And while the two critics may well have agreed that Mahler's initial theme itself is banal, the imitative texture between trumpets and trombones may have elicited Copland's admiration of Mahler's counterpoint and a sense, expressed in his 1925 *Times* letter, that "no matter how ordinary the melody may be, there is always somewhere, either in the beginning or end, one note, one harmony, one slight change which gives the Mahler touch." Rosenfeld, on the other hand, may well have

Example 4.1. Mahler, Eighth Symphony, part 1, mm. 1–8.

seen this as an example of "agonizedly straining, pushing and laboring, trying to manufacture his banal thematic material into music by the application of all the little contrapuntal formulas."[34] Moreover, Mahler's careful selection of instruments—bass clarinet, bassoons, and low strings that punctuate the opening organ pedal sonority but disappear at the entry of the choirs—shows the nuanced attention to details of orchestration that Copland also appreciated (and that Rosenfeld, as will be seen below, also acknowledged).

That Copland invoked romantic—even Jewish—characteristics as a way of defining Mahler as an original composer is crucial evidence that his formulation of Mahler's overall importance was linked to Jewishness itself. In *Our New Music*, he seemed to place those characteristics in the service of Mahler's originality, writing that despite claims that "he plagiarizes unblushingly, filching material from Schubert, Mozart, Bruckner, or any other of a half dozen of his favorites," his work is "Mahlerlike in every detail"; he went on immediately to mention the "irascible scherzos," "heaven-storming calls in the brass," and other features that resonate with romanticism and are listed above, and that "add up to one of the most fascinating composer-personalities of modern times."[35] Here Copland was elaborating on an argument he made about Mahler in his letter to the *New York Times* from 1925, that he "was never more Mahler than when he was copying Mozart." But pointing to Mahler's (Jewish) romanticism to demonstrate his originality was a stunning about-face from the apparent anti-romanticism of the *Times* letter.

An important component of Mahler's originality for Copland, then, seems to have been that he could express his individual Jewish voice even though he had assimilated into the Western art music tradition—and that he could do so by evoking romanticism. To be sure, Rosenfeld also acknowledged that some aspects of Mahler's music could be considered original, commenting that "in general plan, his symphonies are original enough," and that he "oftentimes employed an instrumental palette distinctly his own."[36] Rosenfeld also wrote that "sharp vestiges of originality pierce through the billowing rubble," and he spoke of Mahler's "prodigious orchestral technique."[37] But on the whole, Copland's view of Mahler's originality was the opposite of that of Rosenfeld, who wrote that Mahler's "genius never took musical flesh" and that his later symphonies "throw into cruelest relief Mahler's essential sterility."[38] For Rosenfeld, any unique voice Mahler hoped to cultivate—a voice that in Rosenfeld's view, given Mahler's cultural heritage, had to have been Jewish—was crushed under the weight of the Austro-German tradition. For Copland, on the other hand, Mahler's Jewish voice was precisely what made his music his own.

Copland's stance on Mahler's originality, along with his own position as a Jewish composer in America, invites a rereading of his 1925 *Times* letter through the lens of his engagement with Rosenfeld's writings on Mahler's Jewishness. Indeed, striking parallels in Copland's word choice suggest that his argument for Mahler's originality was in many ways a direct reply to Rosenfeld's writings. Prior to Copland's letter in the *Times*, Rosenfeld wrote of Mahler that "the living stuff is lost in the great unfilled voids of the canvasses."[39] Copland's argument that Mahler's works "have in them the stuff of living music" and exerted "living influence" takes up the same discourse of fertility and sterility that drove so much of Rosenfeld's own writing on music. Rosenfeld had also declared that Mahler simply imitated his German forbears "instead of developing his own personality."[40] Copland's comment that Mahler "was never more Mahler than when he was copying Mozart" counters this claim. For Rosenfeld, Mahler was "helpless on nearly every page."[41] For Copland, "Every page he wrote has that individual quality that we demand from every great composer." And for Rosenfeld, although he did praise Mahler's orchestration, "his orchestration is not revolutionary, and is often commonplace enough."[42] For Copland, as we have seen, that category—orchestration—was where Mahler's relationship to modernism manifested itself most fully.

And more than simply responding to Rosenfeld, Copland also built on Rosenfeld's ideas. Rosenfeld prefigured Copland in crediting Mahler for vibrant orchestration that, he claimed, contrasted with that of Richard Strauss. Rosenfeld wrote, "Sometimes, it is nothing more than his miraculous gift of instrumentation that is green among the charred ruins," and—hinting at the terminology of neoclassicism—that Mahler's "usage of the modern orchestra" was "so much more simple and reserved and sharp than Strauss.'"[43] In the *Times* letter and elsewhere, as we have seen, Copland seized on this comparison, writing that Mahler's orchestration was superior to that of Strauss.

Rosenfeld's framing of Mahler's Jewishness in reproductive terms—calling him a "sterile" composer—is also a precedent for Copland's vision of Mahler's importance. Drawing on Richard Wagner's virulent nineteenth-century attack on Jewish creative figures, Rosenfeld wrote, "If there is anything visible behind the music of Mahler, it is the Jew as Wagner, say, describes him in 'Das Judentum in der Musik,' the Jew who through the superficial assimilation of the people among whom he is condemned to live, and through the suppression of his own nature, becomes sterile."[44] And Rosenfeld applied this discourse to some American composers. With an edge of sarcasm, he called such figures as George Whitefield Chadwick and Frederick Converse "highly respectable and sterile 'American' composers."[45] On the face of it,

Rosenfeld's description of Mahler as "sterile" is a claim that Mahler was unable to create vibrant musical compositions. But it may also be read as undercutting a sense that Mahler could be considered an ancestor of recent musical trends. If Mahler was indeed "sterile," then Copland could not serve as his self-declared musical descendant.

For Copland, then, disputing what Rosenfeld saw as Mahler's musical sterility meant placing Mahler in a complex aesthetic network in which neoclassicism, romanticism, and Jewishness intersected. Copland's use of Mahler to connect these concepts is remarkable because, as Carol J. Oja has shown, neoclassicism was sometimes linked to a sense of impotence and femininity—especially in comparison to more experimentalist strains of modernism in America. And this discourse was related to the fact that Copland and others associated with American neoclassicism studied with a woman, Nadia Boulanger.[46] Because it was Boulanger who introduced Mahler's music to Copland, his defense of Mahler emerges as a defense of his own musical education. By disputing Mahler's supposed "sterility"—a critique that, for Rosenfeld, was rooted in Mahler's status as a Jew—Copland bolstered his case for the relevance of American neoclassicism.

But romanticism remained important, and the invocation of Mahlerian grandiosity may have been one of the key avenues by which Copland communicated his Jewish identity in his music. Copland did write that the *Symphonic Ode* contained "reflections of a Jewish heritage, remnants of Paris (Boulanger's *la grand ligne*), influences of Mahler (the orchestration) and Stravinsky (motor rhythms)."[47] And as we have seen, Copland also referred to a "relation between the Ode and an occasional movement in the grandiose style by Gustav Mahler."[48] In one additional comment from 1968, about forty years after the *Ode*'s composition, Copland said, "In addition to a sense of Americanness . . . I also had a—shall we say, Hebraic—idea of the grandiose, of the dramatic and the tragic, which was expressed . . . very much in the *Symphonic Ode*."[49]

Such adjectives—"grandiose," "dramatic," and "tragic"—point directly to Austro-German romanticism and to the qualities Copland admired in Mahler. Howard Pollack has pointed out not only Copland's general association of Jewishness with romanticism but the more specific fact that for Copland, the "grandiose" was closely tethered to a sense of Jewishness and that it was similar to the more negative "bombast" that Copland connected to German music (and which, we have seen, Copland also ascribed to Mahler).[50] Going further, Copland's description of the *Ode* suggests that a sense of the Jewish "grandiose" forged a pathway for incorporating the Austro-German tradition into his music without giving explicit credit to it—and therefore without sinking the project of defining American music as distinct from the Austro-German tradition. Unlike Austro-German romanticism, Jewishness—which Copland himself agreed was a fundamental, if peripheral, part of his musical persona—*could* find a place in the discourse of American modernism, controversial as it sometimes was. Pollack has suggested that Copland's detection of "bare grandiosity" in another work, the *Piano Variations*, reflected a jointly American and Jewish musical perspective—American in its bareness, Jewish in its grandiosity.[51] By rejecting Rosenfeld's claim that Mahler failed to express his authentic nature, Copland made room for himself to express his own Jewish, romantic, and American voice.

Chapter Five

MAHLER'S IDIOM IN COPLAND'S "AMERICAN" SOUND

That Aaron Copland, as a composer, owed a musical debt of some kind to Mahler is widely acknowledged. But the nature of that debt is only marginally understood. Commentators have long pointed out in general, and occasionally with some specificity, instances in which Copland seemed to draw on examples in Mahler's music for his own. Copland himself acknowledged such instances, noting, for example, that "Heart, We Will Forget Him" from the *Dickinson Songs* (1950)—which he called, strikingly, "the romantic fifth song"—"has been likened to Mahler." (That piece is not discussed in detail in this study, but indeed its walking rhythm recalls "Nun will die Sonn' so hell aufgeh'n" from Mahler's *Kindertotenlieder*, while its melody is strongly suggestive of both "Liebst du um Schönheit" and "Ich bin der Welt abhanden gekommen" from the *Rückertlieder*.) Copland's acknowledgment of Mahler here came despite his claim of "no direct influence" from Mahler in the *Dickinson Songs*; Copland granted that Mahler (along with Ives and Fauré in that collection) may have been "part of my working apparatus."[1]

As we have seen thus far, and as Copland's comment further attests, his advocacy of Mahler suggests that he had developed a complex musical relationship with Mahler's output, one that might manifest in his own music in profound ways. That relationship included ambivalent and often admiring commentary about Mahler as a romanticist or post-romanticist, suggesting that as a composer Copland was not interested in borrowing techniques to create an anti-romantic sound divorced from those techniques' romantic context; on the contrary, he was using them, in part, to create his own aesthetic links with romanticism.

In fact, Copland adopted elements from Mahler that helped him define America musically, both in terms of romanticism and modernism. Ultimately, his personal response to Mahler shows the significant extent to which Mahler—whom Copland himself recognized as deeply tied to Austro-German romanticism—informed the same music that audiences continue to identify as quintessentially American.

The concluding section of Mahler's *Das Lied von der Erde* provides the clearest and most striking point of reference for Copland's own idiom from multiple standpoints, including orchestration, melody, harmony, and musical meaning. Copland described the passage (the final page of the score; see ex. 5.1) in detail in his 1957 lecture on Mahler for the CBC, where in his lecture notes he made a point of its "magical effect." He attributed the effect of this passage partly to the "silvery, bell-like sounds" of the celesta, sustained strings, mandolin, and two harps—a "translucent, other-worldly sonority"—but also to the fact that the vocal line "never cadences." Indeed, the work's conclusion centers on the contralto (or baritone, depending on the performance) repeating "ewig," (forever) on the notes E and D (the third and second scale degrees in C major), over an extended C major chord; the contralto stops singing after measure 566. Copland did not specifically mention the sustained nonchord tones that shade that concluding sonority. But the noncadencing D as well as the added A in the flute and oboe support what Copland considered to be Mahler's aesthetic position here: that "symbolically," Mahler "seems to be clinging to life, not wanting to let go" and that he "seems unable to take leave of that beautiful period—the romantic period." Copland added that "the whole work takes on the aspect of a swan song of romanticism," and that "by identifying the spirit of the romantic world with the world itself—it becomes a farewell to a world." Ultimately, according to Copland, "it is a farewell and an end," but one that also "contains within itself the birth pangs of a new world."[2] Here Copland was quoting the English music critic Wilfrid Mellers, who wrote in a 1941 article on Mahler that the "mournful fragmentariness" of Mahler's late works represents "the end of a world" as well as "the birth-pangs of a new."[3]

This idea—that, as Copland continued, "the fascination of Mahler" is "what looked toward the past and what to the future"—was long a crucial part of his view of Mahler's significance. In his 1935 lecture series "Music of Today," Copland wrote that Mahler sang the "swan song of the 19th century."[4] In the 1941 book *Our New Music*, which appeared the same year as Mellers's article, Copland considered *Das Lied* "in many respects the swan song of the entire romantic movement," noting (as already quoted in chapter 3),

Example 5.1. Mahler, *Das Lied von der Erde*, “Der Abschied,” mm. 562–72 (69-6 to 69+5).

> something symbolic in the reluctance of the composer to touch the final chord in the concluding movement of both this work and of his *Ninth Symphony*. It is as if the composer knew, deep down inside himself, that he was saying a final farewell to the nineteenth century. All his music reinvokes the past glories of that golden age, but with an added note of regret for a wonderful epoch that was gone without hope of recall.[5]

Other evidence points to Copland's longstanding interest in these musical passages and its possible relationship to his own music; his friend and colleague Michael Tilson Thomas wrote that Copland "spoke often of Mahler's music, especially the spare and slowly moving passages of the 9th and 10th Symphony and *Das Lied von der Erde*," and he suggested a link between such passages and Copland's *Appalachian Spring*.[6]

What Copland identified as Mahler's "reluctance . . . to touch the final chord" in *Das Lied*—letting nonchord tones hang over C major—generates a striking effect of motionlessness, or what Stuart Feder aptly called an "aesthetic statement of endlessness."[7] Mahler's Ninth Symphony contains similar gestures; Julian Johnson has observed "a kind of harmonic stasis based on the saturation of the diatonic field" in that symphony's opening and conclusion.[8] Indeed, one of the first melodic gestures of the Ninth Symphony is the repeated descending F♯–E over D major in the second violins, and this gesture has been heard as an echo of the descending E–D over C major that concludes *Das Lied*.[9] (Although Copland only mentioned the finale of the Ninth Symphony in *Our New Music*, he apparently considered Mahler's Ninth to be his "favorite orchestral symphony" by Mahler, and the first movement his "favorite among Mahler's instrumental movements," as the music critic Jack Diether put it in a 1957 article.)[10] Johnson has also noted the contrapuntal nature of what we might call Mahler's static manner, writing that the "moments of stasis are created by a deliberate freezing of the counterpoint, an elision of lines that should move contrapuntally in time against each other," especially at cadences. Ultimately, the Ninth's conclusion, seen in example 5.2, with its "cadential voice leading left merely suspended in the containment of a saturated vertical complex . . . projects a vision of infinite desire for resolution without any resolution actually occurring."[11] What Johnson refers to as "vertical simultaneities"—for instance, what seems at the end of *Das Lied* (which Johnson also mentions in his discussion) to be a C-major chord with an added sixth and the remnant of an added second—actually emerges from Mahler's contrapuntal practice; as Johnson put it, such simultaneities "are the result of contrapuntal lines overlapping and eliding

Example 5.2. Mahler, Ninth Symphony, mvt. 4, mm. 177–85.

in a way that equivocates their normal function."[12] (Debussy is also a reference point for this sound; the pentatonic sonority that concludes "Pagodes," noted in chapter 2, furnishes that moment with a sense of harmonic stasis.)[13]

The inconclusive conclusions of Mahler's *Das Lied* and his Ninth Symphony offered Copland a special musical model for his own ambivalent relationship with romanticism. The most striking instance of this musical modeling appears in Copland's *Music for the Theatre,* one of his most successful early works. This five-movement composition marked an important moment in Copland's career as a young American modernist. It arose from a commission by the League of Composers; Copland wrote most of it at the MacDowell Colony in New Hampshire in the summer of 1925, finishing the work in September. All this composition took place in the months following the letter on Mahler that he published in the *New York Times* in April of that year. The work marked Copland's most overt use of jazz in an orchestral composition up to that point. As he put it, "My aim was to write a work that would be recognizably American within a serious musical idiom," with jazz providing "a native product from which to explore rhythm."[14]

Resemblances and even direct references to *Das Lied* and Mahler's Ninth permeate *Music for the Theatre.* For one, the "music seemed to suggest," as Copland put it, "a certain theatrical atmosphere" without being tied to a specific scenario.[15] This description offers a tantalizing parallel with much of Mahler's practice as a composer who, as Copland later put it in his 1957 CBC lecture notes, "never wrote operas (strangely)."[16] The bold eclecticism of *Music for the Theatre*—combining, as it does, popular idioms with an orchestral palette and a symphonic shape—mirrors that of Mahler's works. Zooming in on the Prologue of *Music for the Theatre,* we find a descending three-note motive that Copland acknowledged unintentionally "resembles the nursery tune 'Three Blind Mice.'"[17] His contemporaneous praise for *Das Lied* calls attention to the similarity of this descending gesture to the "ewig" passage in *Das Lied,* as well as to the initial descents in the Ninth Symphony.[18] Heightening the resonance of this comparison is that when the "Three Blind Mice" gesture appears, as seen in example 5.3, Copland deprives it of a sense of arrival when it reaches the third note. Here, the repeated B–A–G in the trumpet might suggest G major, but the strings reveal the final G as merely an F𝄪, the start of a new three-note progression in D-sharp major that ends, stunningly, on B major, seamlessly setting up a repeat of the progression. This continual snubbing of resolution serves as an enlargement of Mahler's technique of avoiding cadences, as seen in *Das Lied* and the Ninth Symphony. Moreover, descending scalar passages pervade the entire Ninth Symphony, which offers a point of contact with *Music for the Theatre* in the latter work's fourth movement, Burlesque. According to Copland, this movement reflected the spirit of the 1920s; it was "partly inspired by the popular comedienne Fanny Brice" and illustrated a "love of grotesquerie achieved by a liberal use of harmonic dissonance."[19] The work's American inspirations do not detract from a link to the similarly motoric, hard-edged, and dissonant (and comparably titled) Rondo-Burleske movement of Mahler's Ninth, which Copland highlighted in his 1925 *Times* letter; aside from their shared sensibility, both the Burlesque and the Rondo-Burleske contain central episodes that contrast sharply with the energetic opening sections that precede them.

The most striking parallel between *Music for the Theatre* and Mahler's idiom, though, takes place at the end of the Epilogue. Here appears an effect powerfully reminiscent of the corresponding portion of *Das Lied.* As Copland's work closes, the sense of a firm arrival on the apparent tonic of B major is undermined. In example 5.4, F♯ in the piano and a downward leap in the solo violin establish B as a central pitch, and the solo violin descends, eventually, to its final B; at the moment it reaches that pitch, though, the entrance of a solo bassoon

Example 5.3. Copland, *Music for the Theatre*, “Prologue,” 2-1 to 2+2.

on D♯ conceals the cadential thrust of the solo violin line, as does the bassoon’s eventual touchdown on G♯, the sixth scale degree. This concluding moment suggests that Copland borrowed from Mahler the contrapuntally frozen sense of harmonic “saturation” that Julian Johnson observed. Copland’s counterpoint helps generate what sounds, in the context of the jazz-inflected work as a whole, like a jazzy major chord with an added sixth. In addition to evoking the inconclusiveness of the “ewig” vocal line from *Das Lied*, the bassoon, as the conspicuous carrier of the added sixth, serves a timbral and harmonic function similar to that of the flute and oboe in *Das Lied*.

That Copland seems to have drawn on *Das Lied* for this concluding gesture is especially tantalizing, given the significance of that gesture as it pertains to the “Americanness” of *Music for the Theatre* and American music that followed it. Copland specifically identified *Music for the Theatre* as a work that “*sounded* American” and “could not have been written by a European” because of its place in his “jazz period”—“precisely what I intended at the time, just as I consciously hoped to

Example 5.4. Copland, *Music for the Theatre*, "Epilogue" 59+4 to 59+15.

forward the cause of contemporary American music by my activities and writings."[20] Indeed, Larry Starr noted that *Music for the Theatre* "is typically cited as the work in which the composer revealed fully, for the first time, his authentic, personal, 'American' voice."[21] Starr then turned his attention to the work's conclusion, labeling the bassoon line—as well as other moments in Copland's output with the "sound of a solo wind instrument playing a spare, gently arcing, melodic line over a hushed accompaniment"—as the "voice of solitary contemplation." It is a voice that Starr also located in *Appalachian Spring* and *Billy the Kid,* which are more typically associated with Copland's musical evocations of Americana. Although Starr linked the solitary voice in *Music for the Theatre* with the urban experience of "standing alone in a crowd," he also noted its naturalistic resonances, writing that the bassoon passage sounds "perhaps more pastoral than truly urban."[22]

The fact that the ending of *Das Lied* encapsulates this same sort of solitary contemplation—in a distinctly pastoral setting—lends support to Starr's interpretation of the Epilogue of *Music for the Theatre* as Copland's musical manifestation of the interchangeably urban or rural solitary voice and, in turn, of Copland's own musical romanticism. Suggesting a clear connection between *Das Lied* and Copland's romanticist interest in nature, and in turn to his own *Music for the Theatre,* Copland in his CBC broadcast notes from 1957 called "Der Abschied" from *Das Lied* "Mahler at his most characteristic: It is Landscape painting as only he does it." Copland also made note of the recitative-like passages and the "lonely" quality of the voice in such passages. (Starr does steer clear of the term "lonely" in describing Copland's own "solitary" utterance in order to "avoid . . . connotations of darkness of tragedy that might be attached to this condition.")[23] Indeed, the text at the conclusion of *Das Lied* explores the parting of two friends and the loneliness that follows, with the line "Ich suche Ruhe für mein einsam Herz" (I seek rest for my lonely heart) preceding an image of an earth that will blossom forever—the harmonically motionless conclusion with the repeated "ewig" passage. In *Music for the Theatre,* Starr located the "voice of solitary contemplation" as early as the extended descending oboe line in the Prologue shortly after [3], which returns in the solo violin at the end of the Epilogue; not only does this line echo throughout *Music for the Theatre,* but it bears a conspicuous resemblance to the recurring descent of "ewig" in *Das Lied.* Thus for Copland, "Der Abschied" served as a model not just for a striking harmonic effect or a delicate approach to orchestration, but for a specific depiction of solitude.

These links to Mahler—orchestral techniques and concepts that resonate with romanticism, like solitude and nature—belie Copland's argument in the *New York Times,* written the same year in which he composed *Music for the Theatre,* that Mahler was to be considered "a composer of today" only if his "romantico-philosophical conceptions" were divorced from his orchestral technique. Indeed, the *Das Lied*-derived conclusion of *Music for the Theatre* points up the later piece's connection with romanticism. Granting Copland his interpretation of the end of *Das Lied*—that its avoidance of a cadence symbolizes Mahler's desire to maintain a tenuous grip on romanticism simply by never really completing its final gesture of farewell—one can't help but note that Copland's conclusion to *Music for the Theatre* draws heavily on the example of *Das Lied,* with a plaintive voice that avoids finality and emphasizes solitude.

Copland's Mahler-informed "voice of solitary contemplation" turns up again, as Starr pointed out, twenty years later in *Appalachian Spring* (in my discussion I refer to the orchestral suite Copland created in 1945). Here, some of the signature aspects of Copland's style—the stacked triads and open intervals—merge with a contrapuntally-derived diatonic sonic flood that is, again, reminiscent of Mahler's late works. Here though, it is not just the "sound of a solo wind instrument playing a spare, gently arcing, melodic line over a hushed accompaniment," as Starr put it, that binds it to *Music for the Theatre*; it is the interplay of these solo lines, which layer to create a similar harmonic ambiguity. Elizabeth B. Crist observed in the opening of *Appalachian Spring* a "sonic depiction of a pastoral landscape" created through the "pandiatonic stasis" that emerges from the collision of A-major and E-major triads, and she has called this stasis a marker of "unsentimental nostalgia" because of its "finely honed" dissonance.[24] But the similarity to the solitude of *Music for the Theatre,* accessed by way of Mahler's pandiatonicism and landscape painting, shows that the line between "unsentimental nostalgia" and a more romantic, or sentimental, sensibility is hazy at best.

The conclusion of the ballet suite heightens the sense of a direct relationship between the diatonic stasis in *Appalachian Spring* and *Das Lied.*[25] In *Appalachian Spring,* the prayerful coda (which in some ways recapitulates the work's introduction) teems with three-note descending motives that are redolent of *Music for the Theatre* in their withholding of the tonic (C) when the melody does reach that note, as in the sixth and eighth measures of example 5.5. And in the final measures of the suite (ex. 5.6), it is only after the flute makes its final descent to C that the clarinet firmly establishes C major as the tonic (the same key as the conclusion of *Das Lied*) by arpeggiating a C-major triad; at first, when the flute reaches C, the sustained strings merely play the pitch C and avoid the triad itself, slightly weakening a sense of settling on C major. Eventually, the cellos and violas do outline C major, but the

Example 5.5. Copland, *Appalachian Spring* (orchestral suite), 67+1 to 67+9, strings.

violins soon interrupt with the pitches of G major, leaving the glockenspiel and harp to reinforce the tonic. Although it lacks the added sixths of both the end of *Music for the Theatre* and *Das Lied*, it does bear a strong connection with Mahler's idiom through the gentle obscuring of the final C-major arrival, the "silvery, bell-like sounds" (how Copland described the end of *Das Lied*), and the "saturation of the diatonic field" (to borrow the phrase Julian Johnson employed to describe Mahler's Ninth).

A stunning musical precedent for the conclusion of *Appalachian Spring*, and one that also contains strong roots in *Das Lied*, is the "Sunset" movement from Ferde Grofé's *Grand Canyon Suite* (1931). Grofé positioned his music as distinctly American, despite its strong Austro-German underpinnings. In an article that focuses mostly on the *Grand Canyon Suite*, Grofé wrote that "once the idea to compose had me in its grip," the music he hoped to write (and here he was referring not to this work in particular, but to any work), "seemed to call for a tonal

Example 5.6. Copland, *Appalachian Spring* (orchestral suite), 73-4 to 73+10.

language not that of Bach, Beethoven, Brahms, or even symphonic moderns, but for a truly American idiom, falling easily on the average ear and completely understandable by ordinary Mr. and Mrs. John Q. Citizen and even their adolescent offspring." As for a critic who complained about Grofé's orchestration and wrote that only the greatest symphony composers could sufficiently capture the Grand Canyon through music, Grofé responded, "The greatest of symphony writers

Example 5.6.—*(concluded)*

were Mozart, Haydn, Beethoven, and Brahms, and as none of them ever was in Arizona, I do not quite see how they could have done musical justice to Arizona."[26] It is not at all surprising that Grofé attempted to carve out a musical space distinct from Austro-German romanticism, but his insistence that this work reflects a "truly American idiom" invites skepticism. As Brooks Toliver wrote, recalling Larry Starr's blending of pastoral and urban in his analysis of *Music for the Theatre*, the *Grand Canyon Suite*'s "sunrise, sunset, and storm could just as well have been observed from an alpine meadow, a bank overlooking the Rhine, or a rooftop in the city of the suite's premiere, Chicago."[27]

Although "Sunset" from the *Grand Canyon Suite* is readily heard as a musical version of a southwestern American panorama in the moments before nightfall, *Das Lied*—and by implication a European landscape—inhabits the movement's conclusion (ex. 5.7). The program published with the score in 1943 sets the scene vividly: "Now the shades of night sweep over the golden hues of the day. As evening envelops the desert in a cloak of darkness, there is a suggestion of animal calls coming from the distant rim of the canyon."[28] Celesta and bells cascade downward, perhaps imitating the receding sunshine. Descending seconds on the third and second scale degrees of D major (F♯–E), highlighted by the first violins and sounded over a descending bass line, suggest the seemingly endless glide of the sun as it sinks beneath the canyon wall in the distance. The harp's repeated D, A, B, and F♯ evoke the appearance, and twinkling, of the night's first stars; the vibraphone's C♯ conjures up the howling of a lone wolf; the brief call-and-response in the French horn descends from the romantic European gesture of a *ranz des vaches*, with a motive that concludes on A; and sustained strings establish D major with an added second (the E that does not resolve in the first violins). The final sonority is thus yet another "saturated vertical complex," this time a pandiatonic D major in which various melodic fragments cease their forward motion.

This digression into the work of Grofé points up the aspects of Copland's music—so often placed in the service of a narrative that downplays its Austro-German heritage—that also found their way into American orchestral music by composers other than Copland toward the middle of the twentieth century. This method of evoking nostalgia through diatonic saturation and through a resistance to settling securely on a tonic parallels Copland's view of Mahler's romanticist (or, as Copland put it, post-romanticist) tendencies; it suggests, as Copland wrote about Mahler, a "note of regret from a wonderful epoch that was gone without hope of recall." Rather than landing firmly in the twentieth century himself, Copland seemed to be rehearsing, through his own music, what he viewed as Mahler's romantic swan song—continually finding ways to capture, sonically, an aching sense of farewell.

Matthew Riley and Anthony D. Smith, in their study of musical nationalism, placed aspects of *Appalachian Spring* in the "tradition of European musical landscape with pedal points and sustained string notes as 'background' and woodwind snatches as 'foreground'

Example 5.7. Grofé, *Grand Canyon Suite*, “Sunset,” 6+2 to 6+11.

Example 5.7.—*(concluded)*

figures or nature calls." Pointing to the beginning of the work, but in a description that applies equally to the conclusion, "A major triad is arpeggiated and a dissonant seventh on top is left unresolved, indicating a sense of timelessness and 'pure' sonority requiring no 'in-time' resolution." They write that in general, Copland "places his textural bearings from Stravinsky in avoiding the vocal-expressive idiom typical of the orchestral strings and favouring bell-like sonorities," thus creating some distance between Copland's American "frontier" and certain "European" (and by implication, Austro-German) "musical homelands."[29] Nonetheless, it is really Mahler whose textural and harmonic techniques seem to inform the "note of nostalgia" that they observe in this very music.[30]

Remaining on the subject of nostalgia, Samuel Barber—more typically than Copland labeled a twentieth-century romantic—employed a strikingly similar sound in his nostalgia-infused *Knoxville: Summer of 1915* (1947), which sets a text by James Agee and which is, like *Das Lied*, a work that blends voice and orchestra. Noting its nostalgic resonances, Riley and Smith characterized this work as "one of the best-known evocations of the American homeland" in its gesture toward a pre-World War I "state of pastoral innocence."[31] Riley and Smith discerningly point to the conclusion's extended major triad as an echo of *Appalachian Spring*. But in light of Copland's own debt to Mahler, *Knoxville*'s roots in *Das Lied* emerge in what Riley and Smith have identified as its "rocking" motif (seen in the harp and violins in ex. 5.8) and pentatonic quality.[32] These generate a sense of suspended motion, or "timelessness" (as Riley and Smith put it in describing *Appalachian Spring*) that is again quite similar to that found at the end of Mahler's symphonic song cycle.

Returning to Copland's own works, the same descending second that turns up in *Music for the Theatre* and Grofé's "Sunset" is used in its most obviously Mahlerian sense in the *Clarinet Concerto* (1947–48), another work in which Starr identified the "voice of solitary contemplation."[33] The opening of the concerto is strongly reminiscent of the beginning of Mahler's Ninth Symphony; both feature harp and pizzicato strings, the familiar descending seconds, gently unfolding arc-like melodies, and rich string passages over a harmonic center that is mostly static (C major in the concerto, D major in the symphony).[34] But it is later in the concerto's first movement that Copland combines the stepwise descending gesture with the stacked tonic and dominant triads of *Appalachian Spring*. As seen in example 5.9, it is just before the cadenza that sustained strings provide the pitches of C major and G major, with a G-major arpeggio in the harp hinting at the bell-like timbre found in both *Das Lied* and *Appalachian Spring*. This hazy

Example 5.8. Barber, *Knoxville: Summer of 1915*, 28+5 to 28+11.

Example 5.8.—*(concluded)*

Example 5.9. Copland, *Clarinet Concerto,* 114+1 to 115+7.

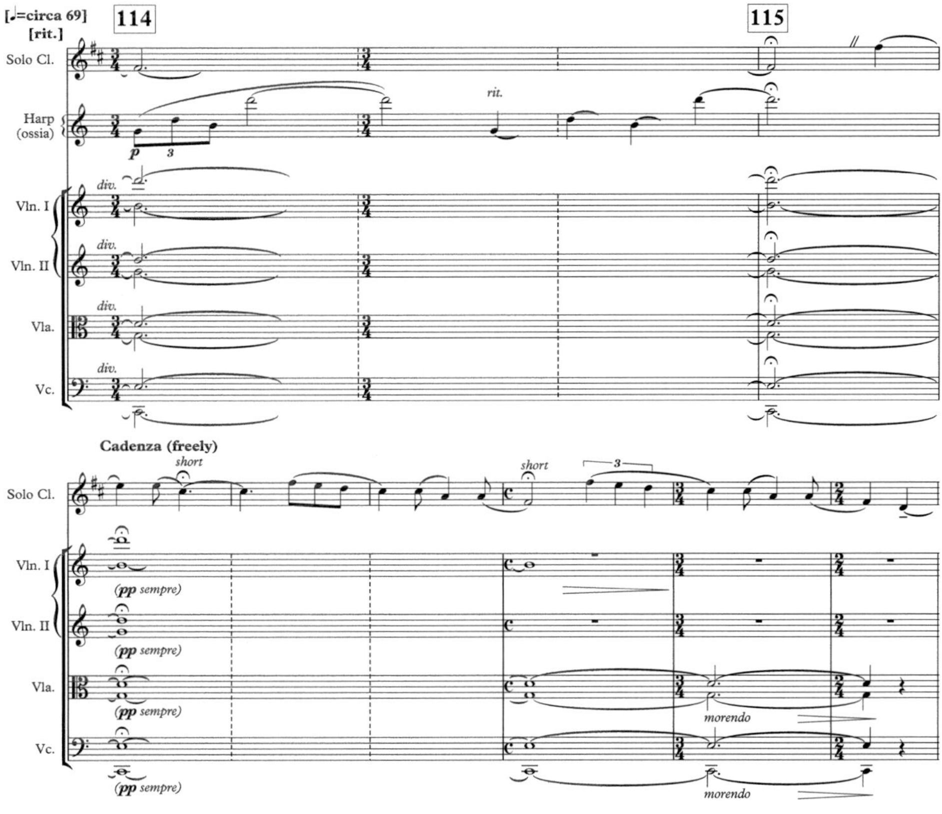

composite sonority, another powerful example of diatonic saturation, takes on structural significance, substituting for the classical six-four as a preparatory harmony for the cadenza. And it is in this cadenza that the solo clarinet moves from E to D and then B, conspicuously side-stepping the tonic of C—another gesture toward the descending and tonic-avoiding figures in *Das Lied.*

By avoiding the tonic in a pandiatonic context, the *Clarinet Concerto* joins the network of other compositions discussed thus far that are tinged with Mahlerian nostalgia, and shows that romanticism in Copland's music was not a short-lived phenomenon. Robin Holloway observed that "Mahler's sweetness and nostalgia . . . flowers in the first movement of that work."[35] A decade later, a sense of tonic avoidance similar to the end of *Das Lied* appears in Copland's twelve-tone *Piano Fantasy* (1957) in the "Very slow and expressive" section toward the work's close. In this exquisite passage, seen in example 5.10, the

Example 5.10. Copland, *Piano Fantasy*, mm. 953–70 (pp. 43–44).

repeated B–G♯ in the lower register undergirds the delicate dance of the main melodic line (shown in the upper staff) around E—often landing on that pitch but just as often dodging it. The *Piano Fantasy* has a strong heritage in romanticism; Howard Pollack noted its "pastoral and nostalgic side," and Lawrence Morton described the piece as "tragic."[36] The fact that Mahlerian gestures similar to the ones in the *Clarinet Concerto* and *Piano Fantasy* also appear in works like *Music for the Theatre* and iconic compositions of Americana like *Appalachian Spring* bolsters the link among Copland's recurring "voice of solitary contemplation" and a romantic, even sentimental sense of nostalgia drawn from Mahler's idiom and operative across Copland's career.

Looking to other dimensions of romanticism, such as the "folk-quality" that Copland mentioned as early as his 1927 New School lecture on Mahler, Copland's famous use of the Shaker hymn "Simple Gifts" in *Appalachian Spring* may have some roots in Mahler's First Symphony. Composed as it was by Joseph Brackett in the nineteenth century, "Simple Gifts" is not, strictly speaking, a folk song, but it does possess a folk-like simplicity and straightforwardness that attracted Copland. In *Appalachian Spring*, Copland recalls the second movement of Mahler's First Symphony in his juxtaposition of dominant and tonic. In the suite (see ex. 5.11a, which shows woodwinds and brass only), at [58]+1, oboes and clarinets share the G-flat-major melody while flutes and horns regularly punctuate the texture with a bell-like D♭, the dominant, which injects some irregularity into the passage's harmonic profile. In Mahler's First Symphony, at the beginning of the scherzo's B section (see ex. 5.11b), the woodwinds carry the E-major melody (which foreshadows in shape, range, and diatonicism the Shaker melody Copland would later use), while the trumpets sound a thirdless B major, the dominant, in measures 47 and 49, where the woodwinds clearly imply the tonic. This bell-like sonority clashes with the melody, much as in *Appalachian Spring*.

Perhaps Copland indeed drew on Mahler for this effect. Later, he would select Mahler's First Symphony, along with just four other Mahler works (including *Das Lied* and the Ninth Symphony) to recommend to record collectors.[37] And as a musician who valued Mahler's "folk-quality," Copland may well have had in mind a particularly folk-like section of Mahler's dance movement when setting the dance-infused Shaker hymn.

Another important component of Copland's idiom, also with prior examples in Mahler, is his evocation of the wide-open spaces typically associated with the American West. Copland's use of open intervals to suggest such spaces continues a long tradition in art music. Michael V. Pisani has pointed out that the "pastoral simplicity based on the

Example 5.11a. Copland, *Appalachian Spring* (orchestral suite), 58+1 to 58+7, woodwinds and brass.

pentatonicism of folk tunes and the spaciousness of parallel chords and open fifths" often linked to "Americanism" had precedents in the work of earlier composers who generated sonic depictions of American Indians—precedents Copland would likely have disavowed as important to his musical development.[38] Neil Lerner connected Copland's "famous 'open' sound, the disjunct melodies and widely spaced voicings" to the "pastoral tradition," and to melancholy and nostalgia.[39] Elizabeth B. Crist has noted that the open fifths that begin *Billy the Kid* (1938), though they have "become sonic hallmarks of the West," actually "evolved only over a long period of time and in relation to pieces without Western connotations" within Copland's own oeuvre.[40]

These kinds of sounds have a strong basis in Copland's study of Mahler. Lerner has linked the pedal points and frequent fourths in the opening of *Appalachian Spring* specifically to the beginning of Mahler's First Symphony.[41] David Schiff observed that Mahler "influenced the bucolic scenery of 'Appalachian Spring,' which, even though it has become emblematically American, leans heavily on the finale of Mahler's Fifth Symphony."[42] It might well be said that it also leans on

Example 5.11b. Mahler, First Symphony, mvt. 2, mm. 45–49 ([5]+2 to [5]+6), trumpets and selected woodwinds.

Mahler's First Symphony; passages in *Appalachian Spring* and the opening of the First Symphony are similar in their rhythmic flexibility and the use of sustained strings and harp as a backdrop for motifs that alternate in solo wind instruments. Moreover, both Mahler and Copland employed melodic intervals other than fourths; the chain of leaps in the solo oboe passage at [5]+1of the *Appalachian Spring* suite, which includes a sixth at the start of the excerpt, might be heard as an elaboration of a moment toward the beginning of Mahler's First Symphony that features ascending sixths in the oboes followed by a chain of leaps in oboe, piccolo, and English horn, descending in the Mahler passage (see exx. 5.12a and 5.12b, which show only the oboe passages).

Copland also emulated aspects of Mahler's First Symphony in his Third Symphony (1946), in particular a sensitive use of register in the strings, to create eerie, spacious effects. That he would turn to Mahler for inspiration while composing a symphony should come as no surprise; in *What to Listen for in Music,* he pointed specifically to Mahler

Example 5.12a. Copland, *Appalachian Spring* (orchestral suite), 5+1 to 5+5, oboe.

Example 5.12b. Mahler, First Symphony, mvt. 1, mm. 15–21 (1-3 to 1+4), oboes.

when considering the sound of the twentieth-century symphony: "We can find the derivation of new contrapuntal textures and new orchestral colors in [Mahler's] work, without which the modern symphony would be inconceivable."[43] As Copland said of his own Third Symphony (similar to his comments about the *Dickinson Songs* from the beginning of this chapter), "It is an ambitious score, often compared to Mahler and to Shostakovich and sometimes Prokofiev, particularly the second movement. As a longtime admirer of Mahler, some of my music may show his influence in a general way, but I was not aware of being directly influenced by other composers when writing the work."[44] Copland's debt to Mahler is revealed pointedly in the concluding moments of the Third Symphony's first movement. At 18+1, the combination of sustained E in the lower strings, harmonics on B in the upper strings, and woodwind fragments (ex. 5.13a) unleashes a sonority quite similar to that of the sweeping introduction of Mahler's First Symphony (ex. 5.13b), which is marked "Wie ein naturlaut" (Like a sound of nature). The final measures of Copland's movement expand on Mahler's practice of delicately variegating the role of strings at the beginning of his First Symphony, as seen in examples 5.14a and 5.14b. Along with highlighting the same descending fourths that permeate Mahler's introduction, Copland, like Mahler, divides string sections internally, and he even goes a step further by creating three solo violin parts.

Copland also seems to have turned to Mahler to evoke birdsong. Of course, Mahler and Copland were not alone among composers to simulate such sounds, but Mahler did set a special precedent for

Example 5.13a. Copland, Third Symphony, mvt. 1, 18+1 to 18+6, bassoons and horn omitted.

Copland in alternating brief motifs for solo wind instruments—an effect that is audible throughout the development section of the first movement of Mahler's First Symphony. A striking passage of Mahler-related birdsong appears at 29+1 in the second movement of Copland's Third Symphony, where the frantic, almost ametrical birdsong ideas (ex. 5.15a) suggest the alternating flute and piccolo at measure 439 of the finale of Mahler's First Symphony (ex. 5.15b). And the last movement of Copland's symphony provides yet another reference point for Mahlerian birdsong. Following the movement's opening section is a passage that suggests birdsong; this section is reprised at 118+1 (ex. 5.16a). There, the piccolo, as Howard Pollack has observed, is strongly suggestive of Mahler's Second Symphony, recalling the passage that leads to the climactic chorus of "Aufersteh'n" (ex. 5.16b).[45] Similar material, again highly reminiscent of the introduction of Mahler's First Symphony, can also be heard in the opening section of

Example 5.13b. Mahler, First Symphony, mvt. 1, mm. 1–8.

Example 5.14a. Copland, Third Symphony, mvt. 1, 19+6 to 19+12, strings.

Copland's score for the film *The Red Pony* (1948), a depiction of dawn on a ranch in Central California—appropriate for a sense of an awakening of nature.

One more side of Mahler's compositional framework that seems to have appealed to Copland was that of the massive scale of Mahler's orchestra and the outsize effects it could create—especially when its resources were unleashed toward singular moments of climax, rather than carefully divided up as in the examples above. In Copland's output, such sheer power is most evident in the *Symphonic Ode*, where, toward the work's conclusion, Copland's unleashing of the orchestra's full sonic potential recalls many similar moments in Mahler's oeuvre. Indeed, an association between the *Symphonic Ode* and Mahler's style has long been noted; as seen above, Copland himself all but declared that he drew on Mahler in composing the work, referring to its "influences of Mahler (the orchestration)."[46] In 1931, he wrote of a "relation between the Ode and an occasional movement in the grandiose style by Gustav Mahler."[47] And in his New School lecture from 1927 Copland used "grandiose" in a positive sense, listing it as one of Mahler's "qualities" as opposed to "faults." Nor has notice of this aspect of the

Example 5.14b. Mahler, First Symphony, mvt. 1, mm. 28–30 (2-8 to 2-6), strings.

Ode's relationship with Mahler escaped more recent commentators; Howard Pollack suggested that the work's "grandeur and perhaps, too, its bell-like tollings" connect to Mahler.[48]

All these cases of strong precedent in Mahler for Copland's signature sonorities over a large portion of his career thus demonstrate their romantic underpinnings. As the lectures from the New School have already shown, Copland—particularly toward the 1940s—wrestled with and sometimes even embraced Mahler's romanticism. And as we have also seen, Copland (as well as others, like Grofé, who also strove to depict a sense of musical Americana) employed Mahlerian sonorities, particularly as heard in Mahler's First Symphony, *Das Lied von der Erde*, and the Ninth Symphony. In works such as *Music for the Theatre*, *Appalachian Spring*, and the Third Symphony, Copland seems to have done so in ways that connect deeply with romanticism.

In his 1957 CBC lecture notes on Mahler, Copland jotted down that his "first contact" with *Das Lied* was with "NB in Paris," and that it was a "pleasure to be talking about it 35 years later."[49] For much of that thirty-five-year period, engaging directly with Mahler mostly meant

Example 5.15a. Copland, Third Symphony, mvt. 2, [29]+1 to [29]+7, selected woodwinds.

Example 5.15b. Mahler, First Symphony, mvt. 4, mm. 440–43 ([39]+5 to [40]-5), woodwinds.

Example 5.16a. Copland, Third Symphony, mvt. 4, [118]+1 to [118]+8, piccolo and flute.

Example 5.16b. Mahler, Second Symphony, mvt. 5, mm. 459–471 ([30]+5 to [31]-1), piccolo and flute.

studying scores and playing them on the piano. In turn it also meant craving the aural experience of Mahler's music—particularly in a live setting. He wrote in a letter to Natalie Koussevitzky on October 29, 1931, just under two weeks after Natalie's husband, Serge, conducted the work's American premiere, that he "felt terrible when I read of the performance of Mahler's Ninth Symphony. How could it go on without me?"[50] It was four years earlier, in 1927, that Copland had written to Nadia Boulanger that he "would go a long ways to hear" the Eighth Symphony.[51] Two years before that, in 1925, while informing Boulanger of his plan to publish a letter in the *New York Times* on Mahler's Second Symphony, Copland wrote, "How I wish I could hear all the others, especially the 'Seventh.'"[52] For a composer who gushed about Mahler's orchestration and admired his counterpoint, translating Mahler's kaleidoscopic textures from the complex sound of the full orchestra to the relatively uniform timbre of the piano—his main avenue for hearing Mahler's music in Paris and the United States in the 1920s—could have been satisfying only up to a point.

When Copland borrowed from Mahler in his own music over the following decades, he did so in part, perhaps, as an avenue through which to "hear" Mahler's music—not by attending performances but through the creative act of recomposing aspects of it in his music. Mahler—as a romanticist and a proto-modernist—inhabited Copland's music and, in turn, his American sound. What we might consider Copland's continual recomposition of Mahler in various works, and particularly his reimagining of the end of *Das Lied von der Erde,* adds a new dimension to his interpretation of that work as Mahler's inability "to take leave of that beautiful period—the Romantic period." It seems that Copland himself found, in Mahler, one avenue for holding on tightly to musical romanticism.

Chapter Six

COPLAND, KOUSSEVITZKY, MAHLER, AND THE CANON

Although New York is the American locale most closely identified with Gustav Mahler, the city of Boston played a crucial role in broadening his impact in the United States. During his time in New York that began in 1907, Mahler—by then a famous conductor and composer—nearly moved north to become conductor of the Boston Symphony Orchestra, whose founder, Henry Lee Higginson, seems to have recruited him and even offered him a position in 1908.[1] Mahler also conducted the Metropolitan Opera (in 1908) and the New York Philharmonic (in 1910) in Boston.[2] He did not perform his own music in Boston on those trips, but even before Mahler's arrival in the United States, audiences in Boston had some opportunities to hear his music. In February of 1906, the conductor Wilhelm Gericke led the Boston Symphony Orchestra in the first performances of Mahler's Fifth Symphony on the East Coast, performing it in Boston and on tour in New York, Philadelphia, and Baltimore.[3] During this tour, what was perhaps the first performance of the Adagietto as a stand-alone movement was heard in Baltimore on February 14, 1906.[4] (The first performance of the Adagietto detached from the other movements was previously thought to have occurred on April 1, 1906, with Mengelberg conducting the Royal Concertgebouw Orchestra.)[5]

Despite these inroads, Mahler's music did not find a firm place in Boston's repertory after the first years of the twentieth century. That city's most important Mahler champion after his death was the German conductor Karl Muck, who conducted the Fifth Symphony in 1913 and 1914 and the Second Symphony in 1918—the only times the BSO performed Mahler symphonies in that decade.[6] In New York, as we saw above, the public presence of Mahler's music blossomed, with Willem Mengelberg conducting Mahler symphonies for New York audiences regularly from 1921 onward. But in Boston, Mahler remained absent from the BSO's programs. With the exceptions of Pierre Monteux's 1923 performances of Mahler's First Symphony and a selection of songs from *Des Knaben Wunderhorn* in 1924, the BSO did not perform Mahler's music between 1918 and 1927.

Mahler reappeared on the Symphony Hall stage during the tenure of the Russian-born, internationally renowned conductor and double-bass virtuoso Serge Koussevitzky. Koussevitzky took over as conductor of the BSO beginning in the 1924–25 season, and his tenure lasted twenty-five years. On December 7, 1928, Koussevitzky conducted the BSO in the Boston premiere of *Das Lied von der Erde*, and he went on to perform it several more times in the 1930s.[7] On October 16, 1931, he led the American premiere of Mahler's Ninth Symphony in Boston and also performed it in New York that season; as with *Das Lied*, he repeated the Ninth several times in the following decade.[8] Koussevitzky added the Fifth Symphony to his repertory in the 1937–38 season.[9] The BSO's longtime concertmaster Richard Burgin—who, like Koussevitzky, hailed from Russia—also conducted the BSO in Mahler's music during Koussevitzky's tenure, as did Dimitri Mitropoulos and Bruno Walter as guest conductors.[10] And Koussevitzky's conducting protégé, Leonard Bernstein, conducted Mahler's Second Symphony in the late 1940s in Symphony Hall and at Tanglewood.[11] Although Koussevitzky's programming of Mahler symphonies declined in the 1940s for unknown reasons, he returned to Mahler's music toward the end of the decade, leading Mahler's Seventh in his final season, in 1948, and *Das Lied* in the summer of 1949.[12]

It is tempting to view this flourishing of Mahler activity at the BSO from the late 1920s through the 1940s simply as part of a larger trend toward the recognition of Mahler's music across the country. Indeed, Boston was not alone in seeing an increase in performances of Mahler's works in the late 1920s; a number of important European conductors with ties to Mahler—including Mengelberg, Walter, and Otto Klemperer—moved to the United States and led major orchestras in Mahler's compositions.[13] Moreover, it was a time of increased public advocacy for Mahler beyond the realm of the concert hall. The Bruckner Society of America formed in 1931 to encourage performances of the music of Mahler and Bruckner in the United States.[14] Starting in 1932, this organization published a journal, *Chord and Discord*, which featured listings and reviews of concerts of those composers' music as well as longer articles on their work. The society also recognized conductors for performing Mahler and Bruckner by handing out medals of honor, and Koussevitzky was among the recipients.

But Boston's Mahler revival, in particular, was more than the product of a broader awakening of interest in Mahler in the United States;

it was closely connected to Aaron Copland's musical activism. In what follows, I situate Koussevitzky's interest in Mahler—little-known today despite its importance in the 1930s and 1940s—within the context of his championing of modernism in the concert hall and the promotion of American composers like Copland. Specifically, I consider correspondence, reviews, and scores to argue that Mahler's music served a special purpose for Koussevitzky as a concert programmer—that by performing Mahler, he found a way to balance his own artistic priorities and the expectations of concert hall audiences to hear the standard Austro-German symphonic repertory. Richard Crawford, in his discussion of orchestra conductors in twentieth-century America, aptly summarized these contrasting interests, writing that conductors negotiated the needs and expectations of composers and publics: "An art that excluded the new *did* risk its connection to present-day life; and concerts that left audiences baffled *did* put public support at risk."[15] As we shall see, Mahler's music served an important purpose for Koussevitzky because it simultaneously fit into and defied both pathbreaking modernism and established Austro-German repertories—aligning closely with Copland's own multifaceted vision of Mahler as both a modern and a romantic.

Koussevitzky's goal of providing space for both modernism and the canonical Austro-German repertoire in the concert hall intersected with his, and Copland's, position in a transatlantic modernist network. Koussevitzky has long been viewed as a champion of American, Russian, and French composers. But in his time, he was also recognized as a premier Mahler conductor in the United States, on a par with Mengelberg, Mitropoulos, and Walter—a role that has since been mostly forgotten.[16] An article about Mahler's American reputation that appeared in 1941 in *American Music Lover*, the predecessor to *American Record Guide*, had as its epigraph a quotation attributed to Koussevitzky that "to make [Mahler's] art better known should be the desire of every artist."[17] The original source of that quotation, as we will see, was a handwritten note that Aaron Copland provided to Koussevitzky. In light of Koussevitzky's close ties to Copland and Boulanger, his decision to perform Mahler emerges as a key aspect of his broader musical outlook.

Koussevitzky did not come to the United States with a history of performing Mahler or with the intention of making Mahler more widely heard. Mahler, in fact, does not seem to have been part of Koussevitzky's repertory until 1928, four years into his tenure at the BSO and twenty years after his first major conducting venture, which took place with the Berlin Philharmonic in 1908.[18] According to the biography by Koussevitzky's friend, the Russian composer Arthur Lourié,

Mahler himself was among the prominent conductors whom Koussevitzky saw and heard conduct, and it was supposedly through such firsthand experiences, rather than formal training, that Koussevitzky learned to lead orchestras.[19] In 1911, as the Boston music critic Moses Smith wrote in another biography, Koussevitzky's New Symphony Concert Union made its debut in Moscow, and the orchestra presented works by Mahler in its first two seasons—though it was not Koussevitzky but rather Artur Bodanzky, the Austrian-born conductor who later worked at the Metropolitan Opera in New York, who led Mahler's Fourth and Seventh symphonies as guest conductor.[20]

Koussevitzky's time in Paris in the early 1920s, during which he became known as a conductor of modernist music, brought him into contact, through Nadia Boulanger, with Aaron Copland. As Copland later recalled, Boulanger correctly surmised that Koussevitzky would be interested in meeting a young American composer, since Koussevitzky would be preparing to take over the Boston Symphony Orchestra in 1924.[21] Getting to know Koussevitzky presented a vital opportunity for Copland; he went on to compose the *Symphony for Organ and Orchestra*, of which Koussevitzky conducted an early performance with Boulanger as soloist in February 1925 with the Boston Symphony Orchestra.[22] Koussevitzky's reputation for programming works by young American composers continued through his entire BSO tenure; he conducted new music by Copland, George Gershwin, Walter Piston, William Schuman, Samuel Barber, and others.[23]

By no means did Koussevitzky's fondness for new music give him a smooth ride in Boston. One challenge that would come to define Koussevitzky's tenure there—a challenge that emerged even before his physical arrival in 1924—was an overarching concern that he would emphasize modern works at the expense of the classic Austro-German canon that BSO audiences had come to expect and enjoy. In September of 1923, on announcing that Koussevitzky's term would begin the following season, the *Boston Globe* reported his "great reputation in Europe as a vivid interpreter of modern and ancient music" and added that the conductor would "need all his courage if he intends, as he doubtless does, to make Boston audiences sit through programs featuring works of Honegger, Milhaud, Prokofiev, Stravinsky, Bartók."[24] When Koussevitzky arrived in the United States in 1924, the *Globe* suggested that he would turn Boston into "the world center for modern music."[25] Koussevitzky's predecessor, Pierre Monteux, had already set the stage for such a transformation; the musician who had led the infamous premiere of the *Rite of Spring* in Paris in 1913 led the BSO from 1919 to 1923 and introduced the United States to works by Stravinsky, Honegger, Ravel, Malipiero, and others.[26] But unlike Monteux, who conducted the Metropolitan Opera in New York before he took over the Boston position, Koussevitzky came to the BSO directly from the modernist nucleus of Paris.

As soon as Koussevitzky arrived in Boston in the fall of 1924, he addressed the concern over his interest in modernism and acknowledged the need to balance the classic and modern. (In this context, the terms *classic* and *classical* appear to refer to the so-called masters from the baroque to the late romantic eras.) In one article, he was quoted as saying, "I am neither modernist nor classicist in my musical preferences. The works of the great classical masters are absolutely indispensable to me. But music is not a static art."[27] Drawing a distinction between his plans for America and his reputation in Paris, Koussevitzky said that in Paris, "It was my purpose to present a new musical art. Here it is entirely different. I am here for an entire season, so my programs will contain both the old and the new."[28]

As Koussevitzky's tenure began, opinions differed on the extent to which he achieved that balance. On his first two programs, the *Globe* reported that his decision to perform works by Vivaldi, Weber, Wagner, Honegger, Scriabin, Debussy, and de Falla meant that "standard orchestral music gets its due on both programs, as is right and proper."[29] In January of 1925, in remarking on plans for separate all-Stravinsky and all-Beethoven programs, Penfield Roberts wrote that Koussevitzky "is holding the balance between ancients and moderns even, and trying to satisfy both those to whom the history of music ended with Brahms and those for whom it began with Debussy and has culminated in Stravinsky."[30]

Despite such early reports that would seem to have confirmed Koussevitzky's commitment to the established repertory, parity between so-called modern and classic (including romantic) works in programs remained an issue well into his time at the BSO. In October 1927, at the beginning of his fourth season, the *Globe* ran an article with the headline, "'Traditions—Who Makes Them!' Scoffs Mr Koussevitzky." There, Koussevitzky was quoted as saying, "Future conductors will find themselves compelled to follow my lead in making the programs a living record of the progress of modern music, as well as a gallery of masterpieces of the past."[31] Some agreed with him. A *Globe* article looking back at that season in the spring of 1928 argued that Koussevitzky's practice of including new works was necessary for the future of art music, since "on every program Mr Koussevitzky has put a modern piece, let outraged conservatives wail as they might. In this he is right. . . . If the novelties go unheard there can be no new classics, since our classics were all once hotly debated and often harshly condemned novelties."[32] The next season, in October 1929, the *Globe* reported, "it is said that Dr Koussevitzky and the trustees receive many letters of protest. Yet modern pieces are played in the face of hostility, silent and vocal." Nevertheless "even the people who dislike modern pieces cannot give up their season tickets without losing their chance of hearing the classics, which, quite rightly, make up the bulk of the programs."[33] At the end of that season, in April, Roberts commented that a program of works by Beethoven "delighted the lovers of the classics. It must have consoled some of them for the many occasions when moderns have predominated on Dr Koussevitzky's programs."[34] Given this discourse, Koussevitzky must have been keenly aware of a need to meet the diverse expectations of Boston's musical stakeholders.

Besides monitoring Koussevitzky's potential to over-program modern compositions, some critics raised doubts about his commitment to providing Boston's audiences with satisfactory renderings of classic orchestral fare. In the same review from 1925 in which he praised Koussevitzky's balance of new and old, Roberts specifically criticized his treatment of that repertory: "Koussevitzky as usual did not conduct according to what passes for the tradition. He was not successful with the introduction and first movement of the Seventh Symphony, which he misconceived as akin to the 'Eroica' and Fifth in mood. Elsewhere his interpretations were vivid and deeply moving, though not always according to the directions in the orchestral score about tempi, dynamics, etc."[35] In his biography of Koussevitzky, Moses Smith—who covered BSO concerts for the *American*—corroborated such early concerns, writing that "in the conductor's readings of many standard compositions the knowing musician, with the best will in the world, recognized arbitrary, irritating departures from sound practice, lapses from good taste and repeated examples of poor orchestral balance." According to Smith, such issues related to a sense that Koussevitzky was simply unfamiliar with some portions of the standard repertory. As he wrote, some "charged that Koussevitzky's neglect of the German classics and his waywardness with them when he did play them were due to the same cause: he didn't really know them." Smith also suggested that in Europe Koussevitzky was used to short seasons and the ability to follow his own artistic whims, but in Boston, he simply lacked time to study scores and thus faced a significant learning curve.[36]

Perhaps related to questions about Koussevitzky's familiarity with standard scores were concerns about his musicianship, as allegations that he struggled to read orchestral scores apparently held some currency; although they may not seem immediately relevant to issues of his commitment to balancing classic and modern repertoire, it is conceivable that such allegations would have suggested to some onlookers that Koussevitzky was musically unfit to present standard masterpieces.

In 1928, Olin Downes of the *New York Times* tried to ease such attacks—and, as Smith suggested, likely ended up exacerbating them—by discussing reports that Koussevitzky hired assistants to play scores for him at the piano.[37] According to Downes, it was Koussevitzky's "faculty of the most amazing and instantaneous assimilation" that mattered and that made him successful, regardless of his technical abilities, which Downes assured his readers were more than adequate.[38] And in a diary entry from April 26, 1931, H. L. Mencken recalled speaking with Koussevitzky about the issue, which the conductor apparently attributed "to a misunderstanding of his method of preparing for conducting" that would make it appear as though he "was being taught the music, à la Caruso." For Mencken, such a claim of incompetence, given Koussevitzky's vast experience, was "nonsense"; nonetheless, "it is seriously believed by many persons that he is unable to read a score."[39] Koussevitzky's awareness of popular beliefs about his musicianship might well have spurred him to continue programming previously unheard works, as audiences' lack of familiarity with such works would have insulated him from any complaints that his performances contained mistakes.[40]

The issue of maintaining the standard repertory remained central to the discourse surrounding the Boston Symphony Orchestra even by the time Koussevitzky was solidly established in his role at the helm of the BSO. A reprint of a *Boston Evening Transcript* article from June 22, 1935, appeared among the BSO's promotional materials for the following season. The article, by George Henry Lovett Smith, compared Koussevitzky's choice of repertory in his first eleven seasons as conductor with the previous eleven seasons and concluded that Koussevitzky actually conducted more performances of "standard" composers' works (by which the author meant "composers standard enough to be heard through twenty-two seasons"). "The result of the investigation," he wrote, "makes one wonder how controversy can continue when the figures are so even—the classics being played as often as ever, the moderns more significantly chosen."[41] Imperfect though these measures may be—the author was not clear about exactly how he counted the "number of performances" for each composer—the article, and its presence in promotional materials, shows the extent to which Koussevitzky's relationship with the so-called classics was under constant surveillance.

Moreover, perceptions of an imbalance between modern and classic repertories spanned Koussevitzky's tenure at the BSO and were included in retrospective assessments of his career. Looking back in 1947 on Koussevitzky's inaugural season from 1924 to 1925, Moses Smith reported that thirty-one of the 110 pieces (or 28.2 percent) performed by the BSO during Koussevitzky's first season were by Wagner, Beethoven, Mozart, Handel, Brahms, Schubert, Mendelssohn, Schumann, or Weber—a proportion small enough for Smith to label as neglect of the standard repertory.[42] If this counts as neglect, then Koussevitzky's predecessor was also guilty; by one count at the end of Monteux's final season in 1923–24, twenty-seven out of 104 works (or 26 percent) were by the same composers—actually a smaller proportion than in Koussevitzky's first season.[43] The conclusions depend partly on the arbitrary decision of which composers are considered to be standard ones, and, within that list, whether all works receive the same weight. Koussevitzky's reputation for playing modern works probably affected Smith's claim about neglect more than the actual numbers did.

The above discussion of ideas about Koussevitzky's commitment to (and ability in) the standard repertoire illuminates the challenges he faced in coping with the delicate, constantly judged balance between new and old on his programs—a balance that Mahler's music, as filtered through Copland's perspective of it as simultaneously romantic and modern, turned out to be a useful to tool for navigating. Around the time that Koussevitzky introduced Mahler's Ninth Symphony to the United States, on October 16, 1931, this balance was at the forefront of public discourse around the BSO. Ahead of the 1930–31 season, newspapers announced that Koussevitzky and the BSO would celebrate the organization's fiftieth anniversary with concerts of new works by composers such as Hindemith, Prokofiev, Roussel, and Stravinsky.[44] But at the beginning of the 1931–32 season, the *Boston Post* reported on a shift—that Koussevitzky planned on "fewer actual novelties than usual" and a "considerable emphasis on standard works that had been unduly neglected."[45]

Perhaps to gain wider acceptance for new works and to bridge the uncomfortable modern-classic divide, Koussevitzky at this time broadened the definition of classic repertory to include works by certain contemporary composers. At the beginning of the 1931–32 season, the *New York Times* quoted Koussevitzky as saying,

> I think the period of experimentation is no more. During the past seven years I have devoted much of my time and energy to new compositions. Now . . . our outlook is much clearer . . . a great number of works highly appreciated a few years ago have completely disappeared. It seems to me we have reached a definite stage in the twentieth century music. A slow but definite selection is becoming apparent and I feel it is our duty to cooperate toward its achievement to the best of our ability, for the sake of the art of music. I do not wish to say that we must not play new compositions, but it is necessary to

> appreciate what we must play and what we must not. Composers like Stravinsky, Prokofieff, Hindemith, and Honegger are already 'classified'; their works can not any longer be considered new music; they are almost classics for us.[46]

By claiming that these composers wrote "classics"—and seeming to imply that even their new compositions were not really "new"—Koussevitzky was strategically opening up the definition of *classic* (which included Austro-German romantics) to include works by these composers. The more composers under that umbrella, the less Koussevitzky could be accused of neglecting classic figures.

It is unclear if Koussevitzky meant that even unheard works by those more recent composers were "classics," but he also granted an unheard work by Mahler a place in that pantheon. In season previews, Mahler's Ninth Symphony emerged as part of Koussevitzky's large category of so-called classic works, at least as critics understood the category. In the *Boston Post* preview cited above, Mahler's Ninth was listed among the "standard" but "neglected" compositions that Koussevitzky planned to introduce to Boston. One brief season preview reported that works by Mahler and Anton Bruckner would come as part of Koussevitzky's two-pronged plan to perform, on the one hand, music by established living composers and, on the other hand, "great music of the past not often played."[47] Here, Bruckner's and Mahler's symphonies, both of which Koussevitzky planned to conduct, were specifically named in the latter group.

The coupling of Mahler and Bruckner added to this sense that Koussevitzky revived a neglected nineteenth-century master by performing Mahler. The proposed association between the two composers was certainly not new with these season previews. One letter to the *New York Times* in the summer of 1930 suggested that with regular performances of Bruckner and Mahler symphonies, "audiences would gradually become familiar with their works and could not help but admire the divine and romantic beauties of these masters."[48] Four years earlier, in 1926, Olin Downes had compared Bruckner and Mahler and concluded that both "are properly relegated to the position of by-products of the Wagnerian epoch and the time immediately following it in Germany."[49] A strong relationship between these two composers' music is certainly not a given, but the facts that both were born in the nineteenth century and wrote long symphonies for large orchestras made their work obvious subjects for pairing.

The supposed kinship between the two composers was the official stance of the Bruckner Society of America. And the group's linking of Bruckner to Mahler actually suggests an attempt to make Bruckner appear relevant to contemporary music as an ancestor of Mahler, with Mahler known to have meant much to members of the Second Viennese School. Schoenberg, Webern, and Berg, in turn, admired both Mahler and, quite literally, discord in music, which may help explain the title of the Society's journal, *Chord and Discord*.[50] At the same time, the popular linkage between Mahler and Bruckner situated Mahler firmly in a nineteenth-century context, placing him alongside a composer of an earlier generation who died before the turn of the twentieth century.

Koussevitzky was indeed involved with this group, at least nominally; his name appears in the first issue of *Chord and Discord* (February 1932) as an honorary member of the organization. He received one of the Society's medals of honor in January 1932, when he conducted Mahler's Ninth Symphony in New York just a few months after leading the American premiere in Boston.[51] What is more, prominent conductors of other major American orchestras did indeed perform Mahler's music during the same year that Koussevitzky gave the American premiere of Mahler's Ninth (1931), leading to the reasonable conclusion that there was some connection between these performances and the Bruckner Society's advocacy.[52] In July, Howard Taubman of the *New York Times* reported that calls for hearing the works of Sibelius, Bruckner, and Mahler at Lewisohn Stadium, the New York Philharmonic's summer home, "have become increasingly articulate during the last year."[53]

Although Koussevitzky was involved with the organization on at least a superficial level, and although performances of Mahler's works by other conductors may well have influenced his programming decisions, pressure or incentives from the Bruckner Society of America apparently played no direct role in his decision to introduce Mahler's Ninth Symphony to the United States in 1931. As it happens, at least one of the Bruckner Society's senior members was surprised about Koussevitzky's interest in Mahler. In his 1932 book *Gustav Mahler, Song-Symphonist*—published by the Bruckner Society—Gabriel Engel, who seems to have founded the organization and was listed in the first issue of *Chord and Discord* as the journal's editor, called it "curious that Dr. Koussevitzky of the Boston Symphony has most recently displayed a tremendous interest in just this neglected work."[54] If the Bruckner Society had successfully encouraged Koussevitzky in his Mahler explorations, Engel likely would have known about it and indicated that achievement in his book.

Perhaps, then, Koussevitzky's clustering of Mahler's Ninth Symphony with the classics provided cover for him to present a work he actually viewed as significant to modernism. The most striking of those details is a brief statement, "Dr. Serge Koussevitzky on Mahler," that appeared in the first issue of *Chord and Discord* alongside other testimonials about Mahler and Bruckner:

> Gustav Mahler in my estimation belongs on a par with the greatest masters of symphonic art. He is not yet fully accorded the appreciation which is his due. Twenty years have passed since his death, and we can better understand this remarkable man who was able to sing with profound and pathetic accents the final song of the romantic era, using a technic—both contrapuntal and orchestral—which was thirty years in advance of his time. Once Mahler's significance is grasped, the world will make light of his apparent weaknesses, his banalities, his longeurs [*sic*]. To make his art better known should be the desire of every artist.[55]

This statement captures Mahler's potential to serve the need to balance new and old music—a need that, as we have seen, defined Koussevitzky's tenure with the BSO. On the one hand, two decades since Mahler's death were considered enough time for a retrospective glance at the composer's achievements. Following a canonizing impulse, Mahler is here labeled one of the "masters of symphonic art," along with, presumably, Haydn, Mozart, Beethoven, and Brahms. At the same time, according to this statement, Mahler was a contemporary, having used counterpoint and orchestration in ways that ultimately served as a precedent for music composed more recently.

If this view of Mahler as modern with respect to texture and scoring seems to echo Aaron Copland's modernist defense of Mahler from his *New York Times* letter from 1925, that is because Copland, not Koussevitzky, almost assuredly wrote Koussevitzky's statement for him. In a folder of Copland's correspondence in the Serge Koussevitzky Archive at the Library of Congress, virtually the same passage appears on a sheet of paper in Copland's handwriting.[56] It is likely that representatives of the Bruckner Society of America, rather than urging Koussevitzky to perform Mahler's music in the first place, took note of his interest and asked him for a statement on Mahler's significance, for which Koussevitzky turned to Copland. Incidentally, by having Copland compose this statement, Koussevitzky provided him with an unlikely venue for expressing his views about music—a journal that focused on deceased Austro-German composers. Copland certainly did not consider Bruckner to have been Mahler's equal; so it is ironic that Copland's words were published in the official organ of an organization named for a composer whom Copland had called "just plain bad" (carrément mauvais).[57] And in engaging Copland as his ghostwriter, Koussevitzky showed his alignment with Copland's appreciation of both Mahler's late-romantic idiom and his connection to the modernist composers Koussevitzky favored, including Honegger, Hindemith, Stravinsky, and Copland himself.

Ultimately, the fact that Koussevitzky turned to Copland to write his statement is not at all surprising, given that Copland may well have played a major role in Koussevitzky's decision to perform Mahler in the first place, with *Das Lied von der Erde* on December 7, 1928. About one week before that concert, Koussevitzky wrote to Copland, in French, that *Das Lied* "fills me with enthusiasm and admiration" (me remplit d'enthousiasme et d'admiration!).[58] It is of course a matter of speculation, but this brief passage suggests that the two had already had conversations about *Das Lied*—raising the distinct possibility that Copland, with his partiality toward that particular work, was the one who had introduced it to Koussevitzky. Copland's reply to Koussevitzky—"I am thinking of you and of Mahler" (Je pense à vous et à Mahler!)—also ties Copland to the event and, perhaps, to Koussevitzky's decision to perform *Das Lied*.[59] Copland indeed mentioned that he would travel from New York to Boston on Saturday, December 8, so that he could hear *Das Lied* and remain in town early the following week to help with rehearsals for the premiere of his own *Two Pieces for String Orchestra*.[60] Also, his lecture series at the New School for Social Research shows that Mahler and *Das Lied* were certainly on Copland's musical radar that season; as we have seen, in that season's "Masterworks of Modern Music" course, Copland included a session on *Das Lied von der Erde*. Perhaps it was no coincidence that Koussevitzky chose to introduce Boston to *Das Lied* during the same season, in what was apparently his first foray into Mahler's music.

Koussevitzky's decision to lead the American premiere of Mahler's Ninth Symphony three years later, on October 16, 1931, also suggests Copland's programming advice. Two weeks after the American premiere, Copland, as we saw in chapter 5, wrote to Natalie Koussevitzky, "I felt terrible when I read of the performance of Mahler's Ninth Symphony. How could it go on without me?" In light of the earlier letters between Copland and Koussevitzky on Mahler, Copland's hyperbolic statement again raises the distinct possibility that he was referring to more than simply his admiration for the work itself—that he considered himself deeply connected to and perhaps even partly responsible for the BSO's performance of the Ninth Symphony.

The reprinting of Copland's *Times* letter from 1925 in the program for the American premiere of the Ninth Symphony in 1931 also points to Copland as one of Koussevitzky's sources of information about the music of Mahler and other European composers.[61] In fact, Koussevitzky seems at times to have solicited Copland for material on compositions. On February 14, 1928, Natalie Koussevitzky wrote Copland, asking him for a copy of Copland's lecture on Stravinsky's *Oedipus Rex* in advance of her husband's leading of the American premiere of that work, which took place on February 24.[62] She wrote again the next day, asking him for his program from a Paris performance; she told Copland that this program would "be very useful for the Bostonian programs."[63] Later in 1928, Koussevitzky again turned to Copland concerning a European composer; in the same letter from November 29, 1928, in which Koussevitzky praised *Das Lied*, he asked Copland for his thoughts on the piano score of Mussorgsky's opera *Boris Godunov*.[64] This was likely because Koussevitzky was planning on conducting the work at the Paris Opéra in 1929.[65] Copland, for his part, also lectured on that opera in the fall of 1928.[66] And *Boris Godunov* had been an early favorite of Copland's. It was a work he witnessed at the Metropolitan Opera in New York before even departing for Paris.[67]

Another striking piece of evidence linking Copland to Koussevitzky's performances of Mahler's Ninth Symphony came from the Canadian-born American composer Henry Brant, for whom Copland served as an important mentor in the early 1930s. Many years later, Brant recalled an early meeting with Copland in which the latter had a score of Mahler's Ninth Symphony open at his piano. According to Brant, Copland told him that he had convinced Koussevitzky to conduct Mahler's symphonies and turned the conductor into a Mahler champion.[68] Given the correspondence and other materials linking Copland with Koussevitzky, Copland's claim to Brant that he pointed Koussevitzky toward Mahler seems to have been no exaggeration.

That Koussevitzky's interest in Mahler was tied to Copland's influence is significant in that it expands our view of Copland as a symphonic advisor to Koussevitzky. Specifically, encouraging Koussevitzky to highlight certain composers reveals Copland as a conduit for the transatlantic flow of ideas and repertories spanning the modern/romantic divide, not simply an advocate of American composers. As Howard Pollack has discussed, Copland is known to have had clout in suggesting American music for Koussevitzky to perform with the BSO.[69] Around the time of the *Das Lied* performances in December of 1928, Copland certainly had a direct line to Koussevitzky in terms of suggesting music by non-European composers to conduct; in October, Copland told the Mexican composer Carlos Chávez that he would give Koussevitzky a copy of one of his scores.[70] Koussevitzky still made his own decisions on what to perform, and Copland was not always successful in persuading Koussevitzky to program any given work; in one case, Copland recommended a work by Elliott Carter that Koussevitzky did not play.[71]

Given Copland's background, and his desire to hear more of Mahler's music, it is perhaps to be expected that Copland would have suggested Mahler's music to Koussevitzky—and specifically *Das Lied von der Erde* and the Ninth Symphony. Koussevitzky's concerts were a major reason that Paris served as a center of modern music for Copland during his time there from 1921 to 1924, and Copland's interest in Mahler—especially *Das Lied*—first emerged, of course, in Nadia Boulanger's studio. Moreover, it was Boulanger who introduced Copland and Koussevitzky to each other during that time, an event that helped set Copland on the path toward American recognition, thanks partly to Koussevitzky's advocacy of his work. And that recognition was tied closely to Mahler. Copland's *Music for the Theatre,* whose premiere Koussevitzky conducted with the BSO in 1925 during his second season, was seen in chapter 5 to have strong musical relationships with *Das Lied.*

That Koussevitzky took Copland's advice to perform Mahler sharpens the focus on Koussevitzky's framing of Mahler as a classic, standard, and romantic composer. Such framing might have satisfied trustees and musically conservative ticketholders who yearned for Koussevitzky to embrace works of the standard repertory, just as the rhetorical turn of calling modern favorites like Stravinsky, Prokofiev, and Honegger "classified" suddenly made Koussevitzky a defender of the classics rather than simply an explorer of modernism. But Koussevitzky's comment, ghostwritten by Copland, that Mahler was "thirty years in advance of his time" reveals an alternate place for Mahler within Koussevitzky's longstanding project to promote modernist music. By conducting Mahler's *Das Lied von der Erde* and Ninth Symphony, Koussevitzky was not merely presenting the music of a neglected nineteenth-century master. He was folding Mahler's works into his broader musical agenda—and he was doing so under the cover of the hazy division between modernism and romanticism that Copland himself cultivated.

The evolving reception of Koussevitzky's Mahler concerts shows that Mahler met his need to create—or, at least, to appear to create—balance in his programs between the modern, on the one hand, and the classic and romantic, on the other. Critics tended to connect Koussevitzky's first foray into Mahler, with *Das Lied* in 1928, to romanticism. At the same time, their discussions revealed potential for distancing Mahler from his predecessors. Moses Smith, in his review of the Boston premiere of *Das Lied,* contrasted Mahler's music with that of new composers, writing that "there is more music in this one symphony . . . than in nine-tenths of the modernists' output." Smith also claimed, "The ultra-moderns jeer at [Mahler] as 'old-hat,' writing for a swollen orchestra instead of employing what they call economy of means."[72]

Similarly, Penfield Roberts wrote in the *Globe* that the composition's "imaginative affinities are with Brahms and Wagner, not with Stravinsky or Hindemith, from whose work it is far removed as is a Schubert song from a Mozart air."[73] Leslie A. Sloper of the *Christian Science Monitor* wrote that Mahler "owes a rather patent debt to some of his predecessors, in particular Wagner," but that the "musical material, like the emotion, is controlled."[74] And Moses Smith, despite detaching Mahler from the "ultra-moderns" and their idea of "economy of means" (for that writer in this context, a negative term that implied a "paucity of ideas"), credited Mahler with that very characteristic in the same review, writing, "Two instruments are not used where one could suffice."[75]

As Boston's audiences became more familiar with Mahler's music, critics began to attach Mahler more overtly to recent trends in modernism and to the terminology connected to neoclassicism. At the same time, they continued to consider Mahler a nineteenth-century figure, echoing Copland's own ambivalence on the matter. In his review of a performance of *Das Lied* by Koussevitzky in 1930, Alfred H. Meyer articulated the same dual placement of Mahler's music—straddling romantic and modernist sensibilities—that Copland had already expressed:

> Though not of the innovators he nevertheless eschews the rhetoric of the romantics—in his day all the world other than that part which had gone into the Debussy camp. Economical, clear and clean as a whistle, his style is strangely prophetic of the stripped and spare manner of the later modernists. Now and again it approaches the tenuous outlines of chamber music. Of the trappings of Wagnerianisms only one item remains: a single motif runs through the entire six pieces.

In the same review, Meyer also distanced Mahler from the "innovating movement" of Debussy and Stravinsky, writing, "Mahler is no modernist, though he wrote when the innovations of Debussy had all been made."[76] Meyer's ambivalence about Mahler's aesthetic position served Koussevitzky's practical needs as a conductor. Because Mahler was "no modernist," Koussevitzky could not be accused of neglecting the classics by playing his music. At the same time, Mahler's "economical" style suggested that his music was similar to that of the modernist composers whose promotion Koussevitzky also valued.

Linkages of Mahler to neoclassicism continued to develop in the Boston press after the American premiere of his Ninth Symphony at the beginning of the orchestra's fifty-first season, on October 16, 1931. Moses Smith—who had previously contrasted Mahler's *Das Lied* with the works of the "ultramoderns"—now wrote that the Rondo-Burleske movement contained a "brilliant unexpected" conclusion that "foreshadows the ultra-moderns." Smith's positive response to the third movement, he wrote, "was to be expected from advance report."[77] Here, Smith may have been referring to Copland's *New York Times* letter from 1925, which, as noted above, was printed in the concert's program book. Penfield Roberts, who earlier had called Mahler's *Das Lied* "far removed" from Hindemith and Stravinsky, now wrote—in what seems, remarkably, to have been a recitation of Copland's rhetoric—that Mahler "was far ahead of his time. His harmonies, his instrumentation, his essentially polyphonic idiom all belong to the past decade, not to his lifetime." At the same time, Roberts considered Mahler "a genius to be classed with Brahms, possibly in some ways above him"—cementing Mahler's position as, simultaneously, a master and a contemporary.[78] Similarly, Warren Storey Smith linked Mahler's Ninth Symphony to the modernist favorites of Koussevitzky and Copland, writing that "if its idiom seems transparent to listeners accustomed to the music of Stravinsky, Honegger, Hindemith, and their fellows, it might easily have baffled the audiences of Dr. Muck's time, who received cordially the more obvious Fifth Symphony."[79] Here, Warren Storey Smith was drawing an implicit link between Koussevitzky's advocacy for recent European modernists and his audiences' preparedness for a Mahler work that was actually composed two decades earlier. In other words, for observers like Roberts and Warren Storey Smith, Koussevitzky had successfully connected Mahler to his modernist project and, at the same time, developed Mahler's connection to the BSO's standard repertory.

For some critics, pairing Mahler's Ninth Symphony, in its American premiere, with Wagner's *Siegfried Idyll* and the *Tannhäuser* overture allowed Koussevitzky to create a well-balanced program that offset the newness of the Mahler work. According to a review by Philip Hale, the BSO's program annotator, the *Tannhäuser* overture "furnished the needed balance," presumably with a long, newly heard symphony by a composer whose music was relatively unknown and that (in Hale's formulation) sounded distant from Wagner's shorter, older work.[80] Similarly, as another reviewer wrote, "No more severe test could perhaps be put to a comparatively untried musical work than to place it on the program with such staunch and standard fare" as Wagner's works.[81] On the other hand, Moses Smith called the program "oddly balanced" and drew a connection between the Mahler symphony and the *Siegfried Idyll*: "Perhaps Mr. Koussevitzky had his tongue in his cheek when he set the lovely Idyl [*sic*] after the Mahler Symphony," Smith wrote, "for the last movement of the latter resembled in mood and expression Wagner's little masterpiece."[82]

Ultimately, Koussevitzky's reputation as a conductor who balanced modern and classic—and Copland's project to position Mahler across those lines—stood to gain much from a complex discourse in which Mahler crossed the border between old and new, with no one quite agreeing on how to define those categories. The more that critics mused about Mahler's historical position, the more Koussevitzky could claim to be both a supporter of romanticism and classicism and a booster of modernism. Leslie A. Sloper's 1931 review of Mahler's Ninth captures how Koussevitzky enacted Copland's dual vision of Mahler as both a romantic and a modern. "If the nineteenth century ended, as some insist, in 1914, this symphony may perhaps be described as the swan song of a period as well as of Mahler's completed symphonic writings," Sloper wrote, adding, "Although there is a twentieth century air about some of its gestures, its heart belongs to the neo-romantic age. It peers into a future of greater instrumental freedom and harmonic and contrapuntal transparency, but its feet are planted on ground that was first trod by Beethoven."[83]

If performing Mahler had been merely about the novelty of rarely heard works, Koussevitzky would not have continued to develop a reputation as one of the most active performers of Mahler's music in the United States throughout the 1930s by repeating these works. His first concerts of *Das Lied* in 1928 seem to have marked a turning point. In addition to leading it again in 1930, he conducted it in 1936 and 1937 and then again much later, at Tanglewood over the summer after his final season as the BSO's conductor, in 1949. And the Ninth was a mainstay of Koussevitzky's mobile profile. He and the BSO performed it at Carnegie Hall in two programs during the season of the premiere, and then played the fourth movement there in 1936 and the whole symphony again in 1941.

One of Koussevitzky's additions to his Mahler repertoire in 1937—the Fifth Symphony—may also be viewed in terms of the tension between modern and classic that Koussevitzky cultivated at the BSO. It was an intriguing choice because Koussevitzky had already been credited with providing a vision of Mahler that was quite distinct from the "more obvious" side of Mahler's aesthetic, as Warren Storey Smith had put it, that the Fifth Symphony—already familiar to Boston from Muck's time—supposedly represented. By conducting this work after having introduced Mahler's Ninth and *Das Lied* to Boston, Koussevitzky reminded his audiences that Mahler had been one of the classics all along.

Koussevitzky's stature as one of the chief Mahler conductors of his era—strongly in place by the late 1930s—confirms the importance of his positioning of Mahler's music. In 1936, *Globe* critic Cyrus Durgin singled out his performances of *Das Lied* for special recognition: "In all his dozen years as conductor of the Boston Symphony Orchestra," Durgin wrote, "Dr Serge Koussevitzky has accomplished nothing for which we could be placed more in his debt than the first performances here, and subsequent repetition," of Mahler's song cycle.[84] Given Koussevitzky's tireless advocacy of new works by American and European composers, this was a stunning evaluation. That same year, the Bruckner Society of America announced that Koussevitzky had received another medal for his support of Mahler's music.[85] And the 1941 article in *American Music Lover*—which quoted his ghostwritten passage on Mahler's significance—implied that Koussevitzky was a leading Mahler advocate in the United States.

Despite Koussevitzky's active role in performing Mahler's work and shaping its reception, there are no extant recordings of his Mahler performances.[86] Nonetheless, some tantalizing evidence survives in the form of scores and orchestral parts to document one striking aspect of Koussevitzky's performance practice: abridgments that Koussevitzky made in his performances of Mahler's Ninth Symphony. These abridgments may be profitably viewed as part of Koussevitzky's balancing act between advocating for modernism and dedicating himself to the Austro-German canon.

In the first half of the twentieth century, it was common and even expected for conductors to make cuts in symphonic works. In his *Dictators of the Baton* (1943), David Ewen wrote that Koussevitzky "does not hesitate to change tempi, to make deletions, to revise scoring or to alter dynamics if he feels that the music profits by such a treatment."[87] Indeed, reviews revealed that Koussevitzky made cuts in other works, such as Liszt's *Faust Symphony*.[88] Ewen linked Koussevitzky's manipulation of scores to the precedent set by other major conductors in America, including Mahler himself. "The very great interpreter whose taste and judgment are discerning can afford such indulgences," Ewen wrote, "with which lesser artists can only spell ruin. [Hans] Von Bülow, Mahler, and [Arthur] Nikisch more often than not brought about new, brilliant, and eloquent qualities in the music they conducted as a result of their discriminating revisions. And Koussevitzky has done so too."[89]

It is clear through newspaper reviews and other archival material that abridging Mahler's symphonies was once a common practice. For instance, Ernst Kunwald shortened the Third Symphony when he led the first American performance in 1914, and Frederick Stock did the same with Mahler's Seventh in its American premiere in 1921.[90] In 1942, the Hungarian-born conductor Erno Rapee abridged the Eighth Symphony in a highly anticipated concert with the Radio City Music Hall Symphony Orchestra, which was broadcast to Latin America.[91]

And in 1943, when the future Mahler advocate Leonard Bernstein was assistant conductor of the New York Philharmonic, Artur Rodzinski led the group in an abridged performance of the Second Symphony.[92]

Koussevitzky justified making changes to compositions on the grounds that conductors had an obligation to identify and communicate a score's vibrancy. He claimed to value interpretive freedom as a means of bringing out a work's living essence. "Today we often hear 'musical authorities' declare, when discussing a performance: 'Let music speak for itself.' That up-to-date motto is dangerous, because it paves the way for mediocre performers to come and accurately play over a composition from beginning to end, claiming that they 'let the music speak for itself.'" He continued,

> A perfect interpretation may have two different aspects, equally faithful to the score of the composer. One may be called mechanically perfect, the other organically perfect. The first gives the beauty of mathematical balance, symmetry, and clarity; the second is the indivisible, living, pulsating élan vital of the composition. One aims to present a beautified surface or reflection of the composition. In the other, the composition—its central idea—lives as a reality. . . . Like a mystic experience, the organic interpretation puts the listener in direct touch with the absolute reality hidden in the great work.[93]

Although Koussevitzky did not specifically mention making deletions, his idea of going beyond a "beautified surface or reflection of the composition" implies that such alterations were an acceptable way of unearthing some deeper meaning and remaining, as he put it, "faithful to the score of the composer."

The claim that a composition contains a living essence—one whose emergence depends on an interpretive hand—connects to the ideas Copland and Paul Rosenfeld expressed about Mahler's significance. For Copland in his 1925 *Times* letter, as we have seen, certain movements of Mahler's symphonies "have in them the stuff of living music"—implying what he later suggested more directly, that conductors ought to select individual movements from Mahler's symphonies rather than presenting the works as complete entities.[94] Similarly, after hearing Koussevitzky perform Mahler's Ninth Symphony in New York in January 1932, Rosenfeld asserted of Mahler's symphonies that some "will have to be edited, and the Mahlerites will have to choose between half the loaf or none at all"; he also wrote that "the time when conductors will have the wit to detach the living pages from the sick trunk of the whole cannot be remote."[95] Although these examples (especially Copland's) refer to the related practice of performing individual movements instead of whole works, Rosenfeld's belief in a conductor's freedom to reduce a Mahler symphony to its so-called "living" essence accords with Koussevitzky's claims that his adjustments to others' works unearthed deeper musical truths than if scores were treated as fixed texts.

Koussevitzky's precise deletions in Mahler's Ninth are preserved in three sources: his full score of the Ninth Symphony and the four-hand piano arrangement by J. V. Wöss, both held in the Koussevitzky Collection of the Boston Public Library, and an incomplete set of parts, located in the Boston Symphony Orchestra's library. The full and piano scores contain marks in blue pencil (and lead pencil, in the case of the piano score) as well as corner folds that at one time yoked pages together, all indicating passages Koussevitzky skipped or considered omitting. The parts preserve Koussevitzky's deletions with marks in blue, red, and lead pencil. The orchestra used these same parts again in the 1951–52 season, when BSO concertmaster Richard Burgin conducted the work. (Burgin appears to have made his own deletions; some were the same as Koussevitzky's, but some were Burgin's own.) Figure 6.1 shows one cut in the third movement as labeled in Koussevitzky's piano score (with marks in blue and lead pencil), and figure 6.2 shows the end of the same cut as labeled in the full score (in blue pencil).

By considering the markings from the various scores that document Koussevitzky's performances, one may identify specific sections that he eliminated in the Ninth Symphony. Deletions Koussevitzky made or considered making are listed in table 6.1; some of these deletions overlap, and most are in the third movement. The table includes deletions that are indicated in the full score, and it designates if evidence exists for those cuts in the piano reduction or the parts; omitted here are other passages that markings in parts suggest Koussevitzky may have deleted, but for which there is no clear evidence in the full score. In addition to the measure numbers drawn from the critical edition, I indicate these cuts' locations in terms of distance from rehearsal figures, and the numbers are inclusive; measure numbers are also provided.

Koussevitzky's several performances of Mahler's Ninth took place between October 16, 1931, and March 13, 1941. It is impossible to match the notated cuts with specific performances. Performance dates recorded by the musicians on some of the part books indicate that at least some of these books were used in Koussevitzky's performances of the Ninth as early as December 8, 1933 and as late as February 28, 1941; it is possible that the musicians even used the same books for the American premiere on October 16, 1931, but simply did not write down that particular date. Furthermore, in Koussevitzky's full score,

Figure 6.1. Deletion marked in Mahler, Ninth Symphony, Koussevitzky's piano score (Universal Edition, no. 3397). Photo courtesy of the Boston Public Library, Kous.M209.M22 no. 9 1912x.

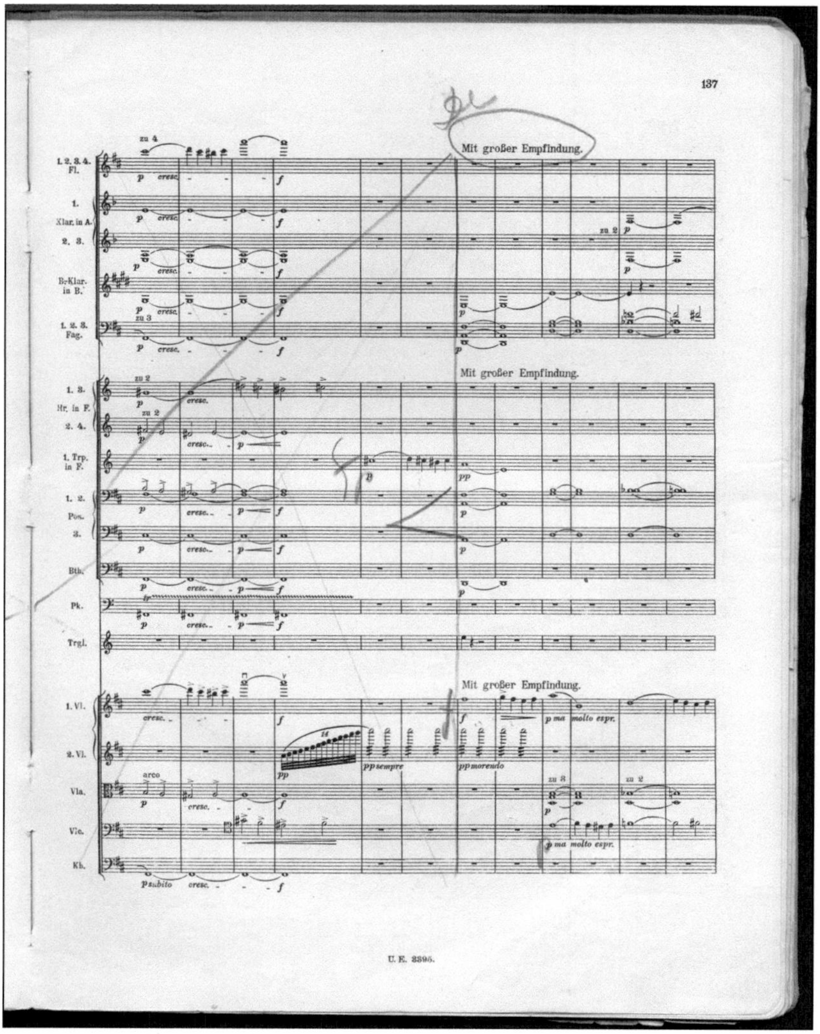

Figure 6.2. Deletion marked in Mahler, Ninth Symphony, Koussevitzky's full score (Universal Edition, no. 3395). Photo courtesy of the Boston Public Library, Kous.M1001.M29 no. 9 1912bx folio.

Table 6.1. Deletions in Serge Koussevitzky's full score of Mahler's Ninth Symphony

Movement	First measure of cut	Last measure of cut	Length of cut (measures)	Also indicated in piano score (P); orchestral parts (O)
1	16+1 (m. 356)	16+52 (m. 407)	52	P; O
2	21+32 (m. 218)	22+50 (m. 332)	115	P; O
2	26–2 (m. 540)	27+12 (m. 577)	38	O
3	33–29 (m. 180)	35+15 (m. 310)	131	P; O
3	36+26 (m. 354)	39+12 (m. 457)	104	P; O
3	37–6 (m. 374)	38–11 (m. 393)	20	P
3	37+1 (m. 380)	38–11 (m. 393)	14	O
3	38+21 (m. 424)	39+12 (m. 457)	34	P; O
3	39+3 (m. 448)	39+12 (m. 457)	10	P
3	40–23 (m. 471)	40–13 (m. 481)	11	P; O
3	42–7 (m. 569)	43+21 (m. 612)	44	P; O

some of the marks for cuts are themselves struck through or partially erased, showing that he did not always perform the work with the same omissions. Similarly, assorted conducting marks even appear within sections that were, at one time or another, slated for deletion.

A few details offer clues into the chronology of some of the abridgments. One of the part books is a handwritten copy of the third French horn part, dated March 25, 1936, two days before Koussevitzky conducted it that season. In this copy, presumably made in time for the 1936 performances, no signs exist of the large, 104-measure cut of nearly the entire D-major episode in the third movement, from [36]+26 to [39]+12 (mm. 354–457). But there are markings for the shorter deletions within that section, from [37]+1 to [38]-11 (mm. 380–93) and [38]+21 to [39]+12 (mm. 424–457). Meanwhile, other part books include the longer cut (although the markings for it are only barely visible, having been faintly erased), suggesting that this cut was applied in at least some of Koussevitzky's performances before 1936, but not that year or afterward.

Far from indiscriminately slashing passages to make the Ninth Symphony shorter, then, Koussevitzky continually wrestled with decisions about precisely which portions to remove from the symphony. He could have simply retained the same cuts through all his performances of the work, but as table 6.1 shows, he reevaluated and shifted them, especially in the Rondo-Burleske; the cut ending at [39]+12 had three different possible starting points. Adding or subtracting time alone does not appear to have motivated these evolving decisions about where to make omissions in the score, as the timings of the complete symphony from year to year were relatively consistent; the first page of Koussevitzky's full score lists 63 minutes for performances in 1931 to 1932 and 64 ½ minutes for 1936; a first violin part reported 64 minutes on February 28, 1941, while another reported 63 minutes for the previous day (probably in a rehearsal, as the official concert dates were February 28 and March 1). These minor differences could be accounted for by silences between movements, or even inaccuracies in measurement. But Koussevitzky may also have revisited the cuts each season he programmed the Ninth. He might well have even made adjustments between consecutive performances within one program, as he apparently did later with Mahler's Seventh Symphony, which he performed in 1948; a list of timings recorded in a blank page at the beginning of the score of that work in the Boston Symphony Orchestra's library explicitly states that Koussevitzky did not make a cut in the finale on October 15, 1948, but that he did abridge the movement for the next day's performance.[96]

Rather than viewing these deletions as assaults on Mahler's music, one might instead consider what they accomplished for Koussevitzky and his audiences. Some of Koussevitzky's elisions actually lent more consistency to individual movements; in the first and third movements, the deleted sections contain music that stands out as strikingly different from the surrounding material. Koussevitzky's first abridgment includes the *Misterioso* passage in the first movement; that digressive section contains some of the movement's sparsest scoring and most melodically and rhythmically unstable music. Later in the symphony, the wistful, tonally transparent D-major episode in the Rondo-Burleske contrasts sharply with the intense polyphonic profile of the rest of that movement. In his survey of the symphonies, Constantin Floros wrote that this D-major episode "seems like a foreign body" in the movement.[97] Indeed, it is closer in orchestration and tempo to the final *Adagio* than to the rest of the movement. And by removing nearly the entire episode in some performances, Koussevitzky made it possible for the similar turn figures in the following (and completely unabridged) *Adagio* to seem fresher when they first appeared. Moreover, by omitting repeated material, Koussevitzky tightened the work's structure in ways that actually suggest a closer engagement with the music than the analogous decision many conductors have made to leave out the verbatim repeats in Mahler's First and Sixth symphonies.[98] The 131-measure portion that Koussevitzky removed from the Rondo Burleske was a varied repetition of what Floros identified as the movement's first three sections—A, fugato, and B.[99] Similarly, but on a smaller scale, the eleven measures Koussevitzky removed from 40-23 to 40-13 are a varied repeat of the previous eleven.

Koussevitzky also made deletions in Mahler's Ninth by finding repeated figures and simply skipping to the second iterations of those figures, thus rendering unnoticeable the act of deleting material for first-time listeners and, as a consequence, creating the illusion that the work was shorter. In the 115-measure deletion in the second movement, Koussevitzky jumped directly to the second statement of the *Ländler*, which begins almost identically to the first statement. (Paul Kletzki removed the same passage in his 1955 recording with the Israel Philharmonic Orchestra). The other cut in the movement was similarly imperceptible in that Koussevitzky merely skipped from one descending passage in the horns to the next one, which is identical. Not all of Koussevitzky's cuts were so graceful; the large deletion in the third movement from 36+26 to 39+12, of nearly the entire D-major episode, bluntly interrupts the trumpet phrase that inaugurates the episode. In a critical environment that supported abridgment, and in which Mahler was frequently viewed as "appallingly long-winded" (as the Boston critic and program annotator Philip Hale put it in the *Boston Herald* the day after the American premiere of the Ninth in 1931), subtle tightening likely helped Mahler's symphonies match audience expectations to hear shorter works.[100]

Koussevitzky's shifting decisions about deletions in the Rondo-Burleske may be understood in light of the broader discourse of modern and standard in which Koussevitzky was engaged as BSO conductor. It was this section of the work with which Koussevitzky clearly struggled most, as the contradictory and overlapping marks in the scores and parts clearly suggest. Koussevitzky might have found this section to be distended, sprawling, and overly sentimental, especially in the context of a movement that otherwise boasted much dissonance and vigorous counterpoint. While Koussevitzky also reduced portions of the rest of the movement, the sheer length, and uniqueness, of the central episode makes its removal conspicuous. As it was this very movement that Copland apparently singled out in his *Times* letter as the most modern, the lusher middle section perhaps challenged that evaluation.

By the end of his career at the BSO, Koussevitzky had established a reputation as a successful performer of a range of music, both new and old. Although hardly a disinterested bystander, Copland summed up his own attitude toward Koussevitzky's programming in 1952, the year after his death, writing that Koussevitzky and his counterpart in Chicago, Frederick Stock, "demonstrated how it was possible to mix judiciously the old and new without losing public support."[101] At the same time, ideas about new music were undergoing a significant shift as Koussevitzky's tenure was coming to an end in the late 1940s. Although Koussevitzky favored tonal music by living composers, the stature of atonal and twelve-tone works was growing in the middle of the century.[102] The effect of this shift on orchestras was not a direct one; atonal and twelve-tone music by Schoenberg, Webern, Berg, Boulez, and Stockhausen did not suddenly flood orchestra canons. But the post–World War II emphasis on such music posed a challenge to a new generation of conductors who, like Koussevitzky before them, needed to balance their drive for widespread acceptance with their interest in new artistic trends. Leonard Bernstein would carry on the legacy of Koussevitzky and Copland—folding Mahler into a grand plan of marrying accessibility and modernism in American music.

Chapter Seven

COPLAND'S ROLE IN BERNSTEIN'S MAHLER ADVOCACY

To many music lovers, the mere mention of Gustav Mahler conjures up an image of Leonard Bernstein poised at the conductor's podium to lead an impassioned performance of an hour-long symphony. As a conductor, Bernstein garnered most of the credit for having popularized Mahler's music in the twentieth century.[1] From 1960, he was the driving force behind a significant initiative to bring Mahler to a prominent place in the canon of Western art music. As the recently minted music director of the New York Philharmonic and one of the most celebrated musicians in the United States, Bernstein that year presided over the orchestra in a celebration of Mahler's hundredth birthday, conducting several of Mahler's works and starring in the national CBS broadcast of the Young People's Concert "Who Is Gustav Mahler?" He went on to conduct and record all of Mahler's symphonies multiple times with major orchestras, and he continued to bolster his reputation as the world's leading Mahler interpreter.

In establishing the genesis of Bernstein's lifelong relationship with Mahler's music, scholars have, with good reason, highlighted his position in a lineage of conductors. Such figures were certainly the most visible and readily noticed Mahler proponents. It has been tempting to conclude that, in the generation after Mahler, it was Bernstein's conducting mentors who eventually prompted him to follow in their footsteps and perform Mahler's works. In a 2008 article, James M. Keller explained Bernstein's Mahler encounter in just these terms; Keller wrote that Bernstein's "formative years as a musician had placed him in the orbits of numerous figures who qualified as Mahler champions," and he named specifically Artur Rodzinski, Bruno Walter, Fritz Reiner, Serge Koussevitzky, and Dimitri Mitropoulos—all conductors—as Bernstein's predecessors in this realm.[2] In a detailed dissertation on Bernstein and Mahler, Christopher Jarrett Page aligned performance dates to argue that Bernstein's decision to perform Mahler, specifically the Second Symphony (in 1947) and *Das Lied von der Erde* (in 1950), emerged as "a direct result of watching one of his mentors [Rodzinski for the Second Symphony, Koussevitzky for *Das Lied*] rehearse and conduct the work before him."[3] In his 2009 book on Bernstein's political life, Barry Seldes linked Bernstein's interest in Mahler to the fact that he had an early success in substituting for Walter, who had previously served as assistant to Mahler himself in Hamburg, to conduct the New York Philharmonic on November 14, 1943; Seldes speculated that Mahler "had a symbolic if not mythic place in Bernstein's heart, given that Bernstein had been handed the baton by Mahler's protégé."[4] And both Joan Peyser and Nadine Hubbs pointed to Mitropoulos as Bernstein's predecessor in the realm of Mahler advocacy.[5]

Bernstein's links to conductors of an older generation certainly played an important role in his relationship with the music of Mahler. To focus solely on these connections, however, is to overlook Aaron Copland, who was not primarily a conductor but who was one of the most important figures in Bernstein's wide-ranging musical network. Although widely recognized as one of Bernstein's principal mentors in the sphere of composing, Copland has remained noticeably absent from the story of Bernstein's engagement as a conductor with Mahler's music. Scholars have, though, remarked on Copland's influence on Bernstein's compositions, as well as the fact that Copland helped propel Bernstein toward a conducting career and that Bernstein performed Copland's own music regularly and effectively.[6]

But Copland's engagement with Mahler's oeuvre had much to do with Bernstein's success. When Copland does appear in the story of Bernstein's commitment to Mahler, he is usually depicted as a foil for Bernstein the Mahler devotee; well-circulated reports have the older figure expressing frustration that Bernstein's fervid interest in Mahler supposedly interfered with his ability to perform Copland's own music adequately. In 1955, Copland apparently objected to the fact that Bernstein limited rehearsal time for *Canticle of Freedom* to allot more to Mahler's Second Symphony.[7] Copland was also said to have complained that the way Bernstein conducted Mahler caused him to shape warped interpretations of Copland's *Inscape*.[8] And in an even more extreme example of the tendency to portray Copland as being at variance with Bernstein on the subject of Mahler's music, Seldes decontextualized one of Copland's negative comments on Mahler to throw Bernstein's Mahler advocacy into relief. In the Copland quotation, Mahler was "long-winded, trite, bombastic; he lacks taste, and sometimes he plagiarizes unblushingly."[9] Howard Pollack, in his review of Seldes's study, regarded the lack of context for Copland's statement as a major oversight, given the significant extent to which Copland affected Bernstein's musical outlook; in making that point, Pollack was essentially calling for further scrutiny of the Bernstein–Copland relationship with regard to Mahler.[10] Other recent commentary also shows the need for investigating such a connection; in an article about Bernstein and Mahler, David Schiff noted both Copland's personal relationship with Bernstein and his positive views about Mahler that "prefigured" Bernstein's.[11] In fact, as we shall see, the Copland passage that Seldes quoted was one that Bernstein himself later paraphrased when lecturing on Mahler.

I contend here that Bernstein employed Copland's language in order to establish a historical lineage, extending from Mahler to Copland—one that justified the continued use of tonality by modern composers. Bernstein's initial encounters with Mahler date back to his time as Copland's protégé in the late 1930s. Ongoing correspondence in the years that followed indicates that Copland actually encouraged Bernstein's budding interest in Mahler and that, further, Copland encouraged Bernstein to associate Mahler with new music by American composers. Moreover, an examination of a surviving script for a lecture Bernstein delivered during the 1960 Mahler festival suggests that he borrowed content and even phraseology from Copland's 1941 book *Our New Music* in formulating a case for Mahler's significance.

The multiple activities of musicians whose work crosses professional categories, like Bernstein as both a conductor and composer, are typically viewed separately in music history. However, Michael Meckna has shown that Copland and his colleagues, including Elliott Carter, Roger Sessions, and Virgil Thomson, were composer-critics for whom each sphere of professional activity shaped the other.[12] As Meckna pointed out, this was by no means a new phenomenon; in the nineteenth century, Weber, Berlioz, and Robert Schumann had also developed careers as composers and critics.[13] Like these figures, Bernstein destabilizes customary boundaries between professional roles in music history, in his case between composing and conducting. This makes him one among many musicians throughout history—including Beethoven, Berlioz, Weber, Mendelssohn, Wagner, Mahler, Copland, Milhaud, Boulez, and Webern—whose work in one realm certainly informed that in another.

But adequately treating such multifaceted figures as composer-conductors is no easy task, as conducting and composing have long been established as separate professions, so that musicians engaging in both tend to be viewed primarily as one or the other. Even though Bernstein is today recognized equally as conductor and composer, those separate identities are still often compartmentalized, linked only in general terms and in discussions of professional and logistical balance.[14] Nadine Hubbs recently suggested that one of the barriers to serious scholarly study of Bernstein has been the fact that his artistic identity does not fit into musicological classification schemes.[15] Indeed, scholarly discussions tend to address the Mahler–Bernstein connection mostly in terms of Bernstein's career as a conductor, while the Copland–Bernstein connection is seen as having been more important in his career as a composer.[16] It has been especially tempting for commentators to view Bernstein's Mahler project strictly in terms of his conducting because he considered Mahler to be a historical model for negotiating the supposedly insurmountable composer-conductor dichotomy—a dichotomy that, according to Bernstein, left those two activities in deep tension with each other.[17] Moving past this compartmentalizing tendency and toward approaching Bernstein's association with Mahler's music as the enterprise of a whole musician—and not simply of Bernstein the conductor—illuminates the pathways by which ideas about music circulated in the twentieth century.

Bernstein would have experienced Copland's appreciation of Mahler not only through Copland's published work and lectures, but also, most likely, as his (albeit unofficial) student, in private teaching settings. Another private student, Henry Brant, recalled having first encountered Mahler's music in the early 1930s under Copland's auspices; as Brant remembered, Mahler's Ninth Symphony sat open on Copland's piano at one of their early meetings, and the two discussed Mahler's orchestration.[18] Correspondence between the two musicians indicates that Mahler's counterpoint also emerged as a topic in their discussions. In the postscript of a letter to Copland from 1930, Brant included a two-voice passage of music and asked Copland, presumably in reference to an instructive moment from Copland, "Is this Mahler-like?"[19] The memory of another Copland student, the composer Samuel Adler, confirms that Copland continued to use Mahler in private pedagogical settings beyond the 1930s. Adler, who studied with Copland at Tanglewood in 1949 and 1950, specifically recalled speaking with him about Mahler's use of the orchestra in the orchestral songs and in *Das Lied von der Erde*.[20] In *The Study of Orchestration*, Adler recommended Mahler's *Lieder eines fahrenden Gesellen*, *Kindertotenlieder*, and *Das Lied von der Erde* for study, and examples of Mahler's orchestration appear throughout Adler's book.[21] This is not to suggest that Adler selected examples because of any specific remarks by Copland about Mahler's orchestration. Rather, the presence of examples from Mahler's music in Adler's book begins to reveal a shared appreciation of Mahler's orchestration, and of its particular value, within a network of American composers.

Copland's use of Mahler in pedagogical contexts, combined with other documentary evidence, suggests that Mahler was a familiar topic in Copland's discussions with Bernstein beginning from the late 1930s, when Copland essentially served as Bernstein's composition teacher. The two musicians first met in 1937; the next year, while working on his senior thesis at Harvard ("The Absorption of Race Elements into American Music"), Bernstein sought and received Copland's opinion on the question of what caused certain American music, specifically the *Piano Variations* (a Bernstein favorite), to sound, as he called it, "fresh and vital and not stale and European and dry."[22] As Bernstein later recalled in discussing the summer of 1939, after he graduated from Harvard, "Whatever I wrote, I showed Aaron. And that's the closest I ever came to studying composition with anyone."[23]

A letter from Copland to Bernstein the following year, probably from November 1940, establishes that Bernstein examined Mahler's music under Copland's guidance around that time and, further, that Copland encouraged Bernstein to explore Mahler while Bernstein was studying conducting with Fritz Reiner at the Curtis Institute in Philadelphia. This letter, written in New York, reveals that Bernstein's earliest documented encounter with Mahler's music took place with Copland: "Amazing coincidence: Those two Mahler slow movements we played from his 7th are on a program with Billy the Kid—both of them being broadcast Saturday the 9th at 10 P.M. by the NBC under Steinberg. Listen in, huh?"[24] Although the letter is undated, a review in the *New York Times* from November 10, 1940, indicates that the broadcast took place on November 9, when William Steinberg led a program at Radio City Music Hall that included the two Nachtmusik movements of Mahler's Seventh as well as the premiere of the concert version of Copland's ballet.[25] Thus it was the second and fourth movements of Mahler's Seventh Symphony that Copland and Bernstein had reviewed together at a meeting before the letter was written. Copland's opened his letter with the words, "Nothing much to say. Just want to hold hands for a moment by mail." Copland's affectionate statement here points to the romantic relationship the two likely shared in the late 1930s and early 1940s, which perhaps lent emotional weight to Bernstein's early experience of Mahler's music.[26]

The wording of Copland's note points to the mode in which he and Bernstein probably experienced the two Mahler movements before the broadcast: reading through orchestral scores at the piano. No recordings of the Seventh Symphony existed in 1940, and Copland's comment that he and Bernstein "played" the movements recalls the manner in which Copland himself first encountered Mahler's compositions as Nadia Boulanger's student in Paris in the early 1920s.[27]

There, as discussed in chapter 2, Copland was instructed to play through orchestra scores of Mahler compositions at the piano. When it was Bernstein's turn to learn Mahler's music under Copland's guidance in 1940, they certainly could have used Alfredo Casella's four-hand piano transcription of Mahler's Seventh. But Copland's own special interest in Mahler's orchestration, along with his experience of working from Mahler orchestral scores in pedagogical contexts, suggests that he used an orchestral score at this meeting and others. Adding support to this is Bernstein's recollection in 1970 that at some of their sessions Copland would reveal one of his own new works and the two "would play it, four-hand, from the score"—suggesting not that a four-hand arrangement already existed but that the two musicians worked together to realize orchestra scores at the piano.[28]

In light of the firm evidence that Copland guided Bernstein and others toward Mahler, earlier correspondence raises the possibility that Mahler's orchestration in particular figured in Bernstein's informal composition lessons with Copland. In one letter from September 1939, Copland critiqued this aspect of Bernstein's *Lamentation*, which became the third movement of his Symphony no. 1, "Jeremiah": "Your orchestration, which is excellent in spots, nevertheless remains spotty. It doesn't seem particularly, as if you had conceived it as a whole. That is, it doesn't flow smoothly—the contrasts from very thick to very thin don't look to me as if they would come off. . . . But we can talk about the orchestration in more detail when I see you."[29] In the letter, Copland did not name any composers to whom Bernstein ought to have turned as a model for orchestration. And without reference to a specific musical passage, it is impossible to tell whether they discussed Mahler in this particular context—if, for instance, Copland meant that Bernstein had attempted but failed to emulate Mahler in transitioning from thick to thin orchestration. At the very least, however, given Copland's admiration for Mahler's orchestration and his use of Mahler scores with Bernstein, the fact that orchestration turned up in their correspondence at all raises the possibility that Mahler's music surfaced at some point in face-to-face meetings about Bernstein's own compositions.

Another letter, this one from Bernstein to Copland in early 1942, shows that the two had developed a shared discourse that included Mahler; remarkably, it also provides the earliest documentation of Bernstein having heard Mahler in concert. Writing from Boston, Bernstein began his letter, "Liebchen, Aaronchen, Ungeduldes, (I just hoid Mahler)" (Darling, little Aaron, impatient one, [I just heard Mahler]).[30] This was a particularly florid opening even for Bernstein, though their greetings to each other in letters were often playful and intimate.[31] Bernstein's justification for the ornate German was the contrastingly casual New York inflection in "I just hoid Mahler," which suggests that Mahler was also part of their common New York-based vernacular. The other pieces to which Bernstein alluded in the letter (Copland's *Billy the Kid* and an unnamed one by Walter Piston), along with the Friday heading, reveal that Bernstein was referring to a concert that featured Richard Burgin conducting the Boston Symphony Orchestra in the final two movements of Mahler's Fourth Symphony, as well as Copland's *Billy the Kid*, Piston's *Sinfonietta*, and Maurice Ravel's *Alborada del gracioso* on January 30, 1942.[32] If Bernstein did attend a concert that featured Mahler's music before this event, there is not yet any evidence for it. Dimitri Mitropoulos conducted Mahler's First Symphony with the Boston Symphony Orchestra in early 1936, when Bernstein was a student at Harvard, but Joan Peyser reported that he did not attend this concert. [33] During the 1930s, when Serge Koussevitzky led the same group in Mahler's Fifth and Ninth Symphonies and *Das Lied von der Erde*, it is certainly possible that Bernstein attended one or more Mahler programs.

A rich passage in Bernstein's later correspondence with Copland points to the younger figure's strong relationship with Mahler's works in the early 1940s, particularly with *Das Lied von der Erde*—a composition with which Bernstein apparently identified closely during that period. In a letter to Copland on November 12, 1959, Bernstein singled out the symphonic song cycle as a work that continued to resonate, calling it "still one in a million" and referring to having learned about "new music" from Copland twenty years in the past:

> Thence to Mahler (I bought lots of albums of Mahler, & I've been listening & crying as I listen—Das Lied is still one in a million). . . . Mahler makes me think of you, hard, and of our music, which I don't think I really understand the direction of any more (or the purpose); & I long to talk to you & have you explain it to me, & reassure me that new music is just as exciting as it was when you showed me all about it 20 years ago.[34]

I will return to this excerpt later in discussing the 1960 Mahler festival, but one conclusion to draw here is that twenty years earlier—around 1940, when Copland evidently discussed Mahler with him—the two had established *Das Lied von der Erde* as a mutual favorite. That particular composition may have featured in their discussions and score-reading sessions, just as it had for Copland in Boulanger's studio. This interpretation helps contextualize a striking passage from a letter Bernstein wrote in 1943, this one to Serge Koussevitzky's assistant Olga Naumova, who later became Koussevitzky's wife. He told Naumova that he "had a dream last night of an all-Bernstein concert with the B.S.O, conducting my symphony [the "Jeremiah"], playing a concerto, and conducting 'Das Lied von der Erde,' of all things. What a great joy! (The books would call it 'repressed neurotic ambition'!)"[35] This fervid desire to conduct *Das Lied* (he finally did so with the Israel Philharmonic Orchestra in 1950) suggests a reference point not only in the conductors who had already performed it by 1943, such as Koussevitzky and Walter, but also in Copland. Moreover, it signals relationships with Bernstein's broader network of mentors who were composers, including Marc Blitzstein, who wrote positively about Mahler's *Das Lied von der Erde* in the periodical *Modern Music* in 1936 and 1943.[36] At the 1960 Mahler festival, although Bruno Walter conducted the entire work, it was Bernstein who conducted the third song, "Von der Jugend" (sung by tenor William Lewis) as well as the closing section of "Der Abschied" (contralto Helen Raab) as part of the Young People's Concert on Mahler.

Bernstein's explanation of the conclusion of *Das Lied* in the Young People's Concert seems to draw on Copland's interpretation of the same passage. Echoing Copland's commentary on Mahler seen in chapter 3, Bernstein told his audience that Mahler was both "the end of the whole romantic nineteenth century tradition of composers" and "the beginning of modern music." The end of "Der Abschied," he said, "reminds you of the old German music and at the same time gives you very strong hints of the new music that is to come." (As we saw in chapter 3, Copland, in discussing the same piece, quoted Wilfrid Mellers's observation that Mahler's music reflected "the end of a world" as well as "the birth-pangs of a new.") Referring to its "magic stillness," Bernstein called the close of *Das Lied* "one of the most beautiful endings any piece of music has ever had." He also expanded on Copland's statement that at the end of *Das Lied* Mahler "knew, deep down inside himself, that he was saying a final farewell to the 19th century. All his music reinvokes the past glories of that golden age, but with an added note of regret for a wonderful epoch that was gone without hope of recall." As Bernstein said of the same passage,

> it is like Mahler's own personal farewell to the old romantic kind of German music, as if he knows it's all over, and now must begin a new kind of music, which he begins then and there, and it comes out sounding very original. But at the same time, he doesn't want to say goodbye to the old music. He loves all that Wagner and Schubert so much. So he says goodbye sadly, unwillingly, so that at the end of the piece when the singer says the German word *ewig*, meaning forever, she sings it over and over again as if not wishing to let go of this beauty . . . so that finally the music dies out on this word without

> seeming to end at all. It's almost like magic, this marvelous ending. You really have the feeling that it goes on and on forever, even after it's stopped.[37]

In chapter 5 I examined passages in Copland's music that take after this moment in Mahler, with its descending motive and wash of pitches that defy clear resolution. In the "Jeremiah," which Bernstein fantasized conducting alongside *Das Lied* back in 1943, we can observe the same sort of "magic stillness." Example 7.1 shows the end of the symphony's final movement, "Lamentation." Here, descending seconds—this time preceded by leaps—drive the melodic material. Starting at the third measure from the end of the composition, the bell-like combination of piano and clarinet punctuates the texture of sustained strings, echoing both *Das Lied* and similar moments in Copland's music, and the final ambiguous sonority fades into the distance. If Bernstein, following Copland, saw the end of "Der Abschied" in part as a kind of lament, this explains in part the similar gesture at the end of the "Lamentation."

In light of the evidence linking Copland and Bernstein to Mahler's music, Copland comes into view as a clear reference point for Bernstein's intense relationship with another specific work by Mahler: the Second Symphony. It was the first Mahler piece that Bernstein programmed as a conductor; he presented it with the New York City Symphony at the City Center on September 22, 1947, and, as Christopher Jarrett Page has discussed in detail, it became Bernstein's specialty.[38] After leading the Second Symphony in New York, Bernstein programmed it as a guest conductor with the Boston Symphony Orchestra at Symphony Hall in the spring of 1948, at Tanglewood that summer, and once more in the spring of 1949.[39] Until the 1960 Mahler festival with the New York Philharmonic, the Second Symphony was the only numbered Mahler symphony he conducted in its entirety.[40] As noted above, in a 1955 program that included this composition and Copland's *Canticle of Freedom,* Bernstein is said to have shortchanged Copland's work in rehearsal to dwell on the Mahler work, after which the discontented Copland skipped the performance. Bernstein continued to perform the Second Symphony during the following decade and beyond; in addition to concluding his own chapter of the 1960 Mahler festival with a performance of it, he conducted it for a national television audience in the United States after the assassination of John F. Kennedy in 1963.[41]

Bernstein's experience as an assistant conductor to Artur Rodzinski in 1943, when Rodzinski conducted Mahler's Second Symphony with the New York Philharmonic on December 2–3, was certainly one

Example 7.1. Bernstein, Symphony no. 1, “Jeremiah,” mvt. 3, “Lamentation,” 20+1 to 20+8.

of his early exposures to that composition. But Copland emerges as a significant figure in the context of Bernstein's relationship with this work. Copland had had a long history with the composition before he met Bernstein; as we have seen, it was a performance of the Second Symphony that drove Copland to publish his *New York Times* letter back in 1925. He also featured the Second Symphony in his New School lecture series from January and February of 1939—around the same time that Copland and Bernstein played movements from Mahler's Seventh Symphony at the piano. Although surviving material on their lessons is scarce, these details suggest that the Second Symphony was among several of Mahler's works that could have had a place in those sessions.

Serge Koussevitzky's relationship with Copland and Bernstein underscores the strong connection Bernstein developed with Mahler's Second Symphony. Indeed, Copland's recommendation of Mahler to Koussevitzky adds context to Bernstein's fascination with that work. In the 1940–41 season, Koussevitzky intended to program the work, which had not been heard in Symphony Hall since 1918, when Karl Muck conducted it there.[42] For unknown reasons, the Second Symphony ultimately did not appear on any BSO program that season. But the summer before, in 1940, Copland started teaching at Koussevitzky's Berkshire Music Center at Tanglewood—and Bernstein began as Koussevitzky's conducting student. As Bernstein recalled, "Aaron and I were close anyway, and that's what that first summer at Tanglewood seems to be about—meeting Koussevitzky, becoming insanely close like his son. He adored Aaron, Aaron adored him, and that summer for me was about them."[43] These details dovetail with a remark by the *New York Post* music columnist Harriett Johnson, who reported in 1959 that she recalled Bernstein telling her that he "fell in love with the 'Resurrection' Symphony . . . while studying it with Koussevitzky at Tanglewood."[44] Given that Copland discussed Mahler's music with both Bernstein and Koussevitzky and encouraged the latter to program it, there was indeed ample opportunity for the three of them to survey the Second Symphony during the summer of 1940.

When Bernstein did perform Mahler's Second, Copland was supportive—despite evidence that, out of context, might reasonably be interpreted to mean Copland was uneasy about Mahler's prominence in Bernstein's repertoire, which typically highlighted American works. Two days after the 1947 New York City Symphony performance in which Bernstein first conducted Mahler, Copland wrote to him from Rio de Janeiro and asked, "How did G. M. sound in the City Center?" In the same letter, though, he gently chided Bernstein, writing, "Couldn't find a single Amer. work mentioned in any of your preliminary announcements. It's a mistake."[45] Eleven years later, on

November 13, 1958, Bernstein conducted the Orchestre national de France in Mahler's Second Symphony at the Théâtre des Champs-Élysées, as part of the Semaines musicales de Paris festival; the September before the festival, Copland wrote to Bernstein from London that he had heard from the festival organizer, Jack Bornoff, about Bernstein's plans to conduct Mahler's Second Symphony and was "tempted to come over to get a glimpse of you." Here again, though, Copland conveyed unease at the scarcity of American music programs in the festival, and he asked Bernstein to add American music to his Mahler program in Paris in 1958.[46]

Copland's remark to Bernstein in this letter—"Maybe you could squeeze in ten minutes worth [of American music] in front of the Mahler [Second]—what do you think?"—has been understood to mean, as Howard Pollack has suggested, that Copland "may well have disapproved of the way in which Bernstein's involvement with Mahler had begun to displace his earlier devotion to American music."[47] But it seems that in asking Bernstein to perform American works, Copland was prompting him to raise their profile by conducting them alongside the music of Mahler, rather than implying a conflict in Bernstein's enthusiasm for both Mahler and American music. Indeed, in the same letter, Copland praised Bernstein's plans to feature American works with the New York Philharmonic in the coming season, writing of those plans that he "got a real bang out of the changed picture they present," adding, "What you're doing looks terrif [*sic*] on paper and ought to make musical history in America."[48] As for the 1947 letter in which Copland called Bernstein's apparent neglect of American music for that season "a mistake," Copland surely knew that Bernstein was eager to perform American works, as Bernstein had already offered performances of works by Randall Thompson, David Diamond, and Marc Blitzstein during his time with the New York City Symphony; it seems unlikely that in this case it was Bernstein's Mahler in particular that worried Copland. In his own programming as a conductor, Copland drew associations between Mahler and American works, as evidenced by his pairing of Mahler's *Kindertotenlieder* with his own *Short Symphony* at the Ojai festival on May 25, 1958 (just months before the Paris letter). Copland also lavished praise on Mahler during the same period with his lecture on *Das Lied* for the CBC in 1957. And as we have seen, at least one of Bernstein's early experiences in hearing Mahler was in a program with recent American works, including Copland's *Billy the Kid*. Thus, even if Copland did take notice of Bernstein's increasingly strong relationship with Mahler, he may have simply been coaxing his protégé to place that relationship in the service of American music.

By the time of the New York Philharmonic in its Mahler festival in 1960, much had changed in Bernstein's and Copland's musical outlooks since they had examined music together in the late 1930s and early 1940s. Bernstein's focus was now dominated by the change in stature of tonal composition. Bernstein later suggested that Copland's employment of twelve-tone methods in the late 1950s disturbed his hopes for the future of tonality and, for that matter, all of art music—especially since Bernstein identified deeply with Copland's compositions. According to Bernstein, Copland's 1957 twelve-tone *Piano Fantasy* was a difficult pill to swallow. Looking back in the 1980s, Bernstein called Copland's music "so natural for me to play or conduct—as though I could have composed it myself, so to speak," that is, until the *Piano Fantasy*, which Bernstein considered "the first piece that I felt I couldn't have composed."[49] In a 1970 article, Bernstein viewed Copland's turn to serialism as the older composer's undoing (without specifically naming the *Piano Fantasy*):

> When he started writing twelve-tone, I figured that it was inevitable—everybody has to fool with serialism. God knows I spent my whole sabbatical in 1964 in a desperate attempt at it; I've actually thrown away more twelve-tone pieces and bits of pieces than I have written otherwise. But still I asked him, "Of all people, why you—you who are so instinctive, so spontaneous? Why are you bothering with tone rows and with the rules of retrograde and inversion, and all that?" And he answered me, "Because I need more chords. I've run out of chords." And that lasted for four more pieces and then he didn't write any more. How sad for him. How awful for us.[50]

Bernstein's retrospective censure of Copland is somewhat surprising. Not only did Copland seem to consider the *Piano Fantasy* to be a tonal work, but at that point in his career he viewed twelve-tone writing as a "method" rather than a "style," and one that could be part of "a very freely interpreted tonalism." This assessment came from a *New York Times* article on the *Piano Fantasy* in which Copland also wrote that "a good case could be made for the view that the over-all tonal orientation is that of E major."[51] In a review in *Times*, Howard Taubman agreed with Copland's assessment, writing, "Mr. Copland uses twelve-tone devices, but he does not follow them slavishly. Often the piece has a tonal feeling."[52] And Bernstein had already commented positively on Copland's use of twelve-tone writing. In 1951, he had written to Copland about his *Piano Quartet* (1950) that he felt "rather close to the tonal way in which you are handling tone-rows (I've done it too, here and there)."[53] Moreover, Bernstein was already partial to Copland's earlier *Piano Variations*; his history with that work was profound, as he played it from memory when the two first met on Copland's birthday in 1937. The *Piano Variations* indeed shares several characteristics with the *Piano Fantasy*, as Marilyn Kae Hutchison observed in a comparative study of Copland's piano works; these include the "declamatory style" of its opening, the overall "lean texture and sonority," and the appearance of serial techniques (albeit more prominently in the *Piano Fantasy*).[54] (Reflecting on the *Piano Variations* in 1968, the same year as Hutchison's study, Copland considered the composition to have represented the beginning of his "interest in serial writing."[55] Of course, as Emily Abrams Ansari has suggested, such connections could reflect a desire on Copland's part to view his more recent twelve-tone works, like *Inscape* and *Connotations*, as part of a unified artistic output dating back to his earlier years.)[56]

Given Bernstein's substantial encounter with twelve-tone writing in his own music, it is possible that in looking back, he overstated his aversion to the *Piano Fantasy*; it did, after all, appear later the same year that Bernstein told a national audience in his lecture on modern music for the Omnibus series that perhaps a "synthesis" between tonal and atonal writing "points the direction for the future of modern music, and toward a new kind of beauty"—and the *Piano Fantasy* would seem to have offered such a synthesis.[57] Also, to place into context his claim in 1970 of having "thrown away more twelve-tone bits of pieces than I have written otherwise," his output up to 1957 included tone rows in such works as the Symphony no. 2, "Age of Anxiety," and *Candide*.[58] On the other hand, perhaps as far back as 1957 Bernstein was skeptical enough of elaborate twelve-tone explorations that an arguably tonal work like the *Piano Fantasy*—even if it resembled the *Piano Variations*—was beyond the pale for him.

Whether justified or exaggerated, Bernstein's anxieties about the direction of new music after the *Piano Fantasy* emerge clearly in his letter to Copland on November 12, 1959 (quoted above), about two months before the beginning of the Mahler festival early the next year. It is possible that, in addition to the *Piano Fantasy*, events like the 1958 publication of Milton Babbitt's essay "Who Cares if You Listen?," which rejected the idea that new art music needed popular appeal, contributed to Bernstein's distress about the state of modern composition. As we have already seen, it was about twenty years before, in the late 1930s and early 1940s, that Copland was pointing Bernstein toward Mahler's music, presumably as a precedent for the new music of that era. Copland's *El Salón México* (1936) and *Appalachian Spring* (1944), both from those decades, had featured in Bernstein's televised lecture on modern music from 1957 as examples of music that he claimed had revitalized tonality; notably, he highlighted no works from after the mid-1940s.[59]

In that sense, Bernstein's letter to Copland in 1959 implies that, in his own version of recent music history, he nostalgically linked Copland's compositions, especially from the 1930s and 1940s, to Mahler—leaving more recent works like the *Piano Fantasy* out of the picture.

Bernstein's apparent longing for Copland to clarify and redeem new music—which Bernstein called "our music"—transformed into his direct but unacknowledged appropriation of Copland's words and ideas to explain Mahler to his audiences at the Mahler Festival. The festival's most prominent public representation of Mahler was, of course, the televised Young People's Concert "Who Is Gustav Mahler?" Bernstein thus immediately put himself front-and-center in the world of American Mahler advocacy despite conducting only a small subset of Mahler's works in the festival (and delivering some preview lectures). In fact, Bruno Walter and especially Dimitri Mitropoulos, already recognized as Mahler conductors in New York with numerous performances in the 1940 and 1950s (including Mitropoulos's American premiere of Mahler's Sixth in 1947), covered most of the music. At the festival, Mitropoulos led the First, Fifth, and Ninth symphonies as well as the Adagio of the Tenth, while Bruno Walter conducted *Das Lied*; Bernstein performed the Second and Fourth symphonies and several lieder.

Turning to the preview lecture on Mahler's Fourth Symphony that he delivered on January 28, 1960, Bernstein's introduction to Mahler reads as having been modeled directly on a passage from Copland's *Our New Music* from 1941.[60] Indeed, the excerpts are so similar as to suggest the possibility that Copland's writings served as Bernstein's direct source. First, here is the excerpt from Copland's book:

> Mahler's faults as a composer have been dwelt upon *ad nauseam.* Admittedly, he is long-winded, trite, bombastic; he lacks taste, and sometimes he plagiarizes unblushingly, filching his material from Schubert, Mozart, Bruckner, or any other of a half dozen of his favorites. It is music that is full of human frailties, no doubt. But when all is said, there remains something extraordinarily touching about the man's work, something that makes one willing to put up with the weaknesses. Perhaps this is because his music is so very Mahlerlike in every detail. All his nine symphonies are suffused with personality—he had his own way of saying and of doing everything.[61]

Here is Bernstein's apparently paraphrased version:

> We also hear the old arguments against his music being readvanced: the symphonies are too long, too loud, too banal in their material, too overdeveloped, too underdeveloped, they're not really sympho-

> nies at all; they're cheap, bombastic, emotionally extravagant, heart-on-sleeve. Sure: we know all that. But with all its faults, the music is great—the utterance of a genius, an authentic original. No amount of carping about how derivative the music is of Mozart, Schubert, Wagner, and the lot can possibly erase the shining fact that it comes out always sounding like Mahler, with that extraordinary individual personality constantly uppermost. Nobody else could have written it—nobody, ever. It is a treasure-trove of originality; and we are proud that this two month Festival is helping people find it out.[62]

Bernstein's argument follows precisely the same trajectory as Copland's, from admitting the validity of typical criticisms of Mahler's music to the claim that, despite those apparent failings, Mahler's music was original ("Mahlerlike" for Copland, and "always sounding like Mahler," for Bernstein) and expressed the composer's unique "personality."

Further examples show Bernstein to have incorporated Copland's views on Mahler into an outlook on music history that downplayed the importance of twelve-tone music after World War II—a history in which "our music," or the music of Bernstein, Copland, and other Americans, could be perceived as modern despite also being tonal. Copland had written almost twenty years before the Mahler festival in *Our New Music* that of the five composers he considered late romantics—Richard Strauss, Alexander Scriabin, Gabriel Fauré, Jean Sibelius, and Mahler—the latter "had most to give to the music of the future" despite being "more frankly the romantic than any of the others."[63] Copland then elaborated on what, precisely, separated Mahler from the nineteenth century:

> It was because his music was so contrapuntally conceived, without the typical nineteenth-century habit of underpinning the melodies with blocked-out harmonies such as we find continuously in Rimski-Korsakov or Franck—it was because Mahler worked primarily with a maze of separate strands independent of all such chordal underpinning that his instrumentation possesses that sharply etched and clarified sonority that may be heard again and again in the music of later composers. . . . The use of the orchestra as a many-voiced body in this particular way was typical of the age of Bach and Handel. Thus, as far as orchestral practice is concerned, Mahler bridges the gap between the composers of the early eighteenth century and the neoclassicists of our own time.[64]

In 1960, Bernstein distilled Copland's argument for a less technically proficient audience, writing that although Mahler was easily linked to romanticism, his significant contribution to music history—through counterpoint—was to twentieth-century neoclassicism:

> But let me say that perhaps the chief area of influence has been, strangely enough, an anti-romantic one. Imagine, Mahler; who is always pictured as the super-romantic of them all, the most Wagnerian, Schubertian, Beethovenian, that same Mahler was the one who planted the seeds of the new clarity, the new objectivity, of 20th-century music. He did it in many ways; but mainly through his linear writing, a style of such economy, transparency, and reliance on horizontal writing, or counterpoint, that he fed directly into the new music of our time, that we call neo-classic.[65]

Here, Bernstein expanded on Copland's argument for Mahler's relevance to twentieth-century composition. In 1941, Copland had defined neoclassicism as a highly influential trend, inaugurated by Igor Stravinsky with his *Octet* of 1923, toward "adopting the ideals, forms, and textures of the preromantic era."[66] By the early 1960s, however, Copland also viewed neoclassicism as having run its course; in notes for a 1961 lecture on twentieth-century composition, in a section on post–World War II music, he referred to the "end of neo-classicism as such" and said that twelve-tone writing "dominates musical thinking of today."[67]

By calling neoclassicism "the new music of our time" in 1960, with a definite article that implicitly excluded other possible directions, Bernstein was adapting Copland's defense of Mahler to support his own claim that tonality remained as much a factor in new composition in 1960 as it had been twenty years before. This is because of the links Bernstein had already drawn between neoclassicism and modern tonal composition. In his 1957 Omnibus lecture on modern music, Bernstein traced neoclassicism back to Stravinsky's *Octet* and connected it to what he called "modern tonal music," by which he meant music in which "old-fashioned tonality" was made "fresh and new."[68] He used examples from a range of works from the mid-1940s and earlier, by composers including Copland, Roy Harris, Sergei Prokofiev, Paul Hindemith, and Stravinsky, to demonstrate this supposed reanimation of tonality through diatonicism, modal writing, unusual rhythms, and pointed dissonance.[69] As Bernstein's argument ran, atonal music had emerged out of a moribund romanticism, and neoclassicism was a central part of the reaction to the extremes of that romanticism—a reaction that, according to Bernstein, helped preserve tonality as a crucial element of modern composition.[70]

Solidifying his proposed link between Mahler and the pre–twelve-tone music of Copland and others, Bernstein in 1960 identified "a typical Mahler sound" as "the sound of modern music, fresh, lean, and full of clean air."[71] For Bernstein, new music had to be tonal to emanate this "clean air"; atonal music (and by extension for Bernstein, twelve-tone music), as he had told his Omnibus audience of Arnold Schoenberg's *Pierrot lunaire*, had the opposite effect: "Somewhere in the middle of this piece you have a great desire to run and open a window, breathe in a lungful of healthy, clean air."[72] For a composition to gain admittance to Bernstein's realm of "modern music" in the years before the Mahler festival, then, a commitment to tonality was an implicit requirement—one that Copland's recent twelve-tone experiment, the *Piano Fantasy*, apparently did not meet but that his earlier music did. Thus, by invoking Mahler's "clean air" and arguing for its relationship to tonal music, Bernstein established a lineage that stretched from Mahler to Copland—at least to the pre-*Piano Fantasy* Copland.

A commitment to tonality in Bernstein's preferred music did not preclude special effects that might temporarily disrupt the solid sense of a tonal center, and Mahler again was a precedent for such effects among twentieth-century tonal modernists, at least according to Bernstein. He spoke in the January 28, 1960, lecture at the Mahler festival about "modernisms" in the scherzo of Mahler's Fourth Symphony. These included his employment of modes (which Bernstein connected to Debussy and Ravel) and what Bernstein called "wrong notes," or "peculiar notes that lend this little country dance a wry, sour quality, such as has been so evident in modern music, especially of the bitter or satiric kind."[73] With "wrong notes," likely a way of referring to nondiatonic pitches that stand out in the musical fabric, Bernstein may have had in mind the music of Shostakovich. In the 1957 Omnibus lecture, he had already provided an example of this phenomenon in the Polka from Shostakovich's *Golden Age* ballet (1929–30), deploying the term "funny wrong notes"—conspicuous nondiatonic pitches—to bring to life his idea that it was "only natural that a reaction a reaction against German romanticism should involve a certain amount of poking fun and satire."[74]

A further instance of borrowing from Copland's texts illustrates just how firmly Bernstein hoped to establish a Mahler–Copland tonal-modernist lineage. In 1941, Copland had written that Mahler's achievements in orchestration "are to be found again in the orchestral works of Schoenberg, of Honegger, or even of very recent composers like Shostakovitch or the young Englishman Benjamin Britten."[75] In the 1960 preview lecture on Mahler, Bernstein repeated Copland's list of Mahler's successors but added Copland's own name: "Mahler's influence on modern music is not limited to the composers we have named [Schoenberg, Berg, and Webern]; his influence has been enormous on such varied and non-Viennese types as Britten, Copland, Honegger, Shostakovich—oh, very much Shostakovich."[76] In light of Bernstein's broader appropriation of Copland's ideas about Mahler, his addition of Copland to the list of Mahler's musical descendants was perhaps a subtle acknowledgment of Copland's role in shaping his ideas about a composer whom he was in the process of introducing to millions.

Bernstein's claim for Mahler as an ancestor of a large list of twentieth-century composers, including both the Second Viennese School and others, reflects his growing investment at that time in the idea of a dichotomy between tonal and atonal music.[77] Mahler had long been seen primarily as a forerunner of the Second Viennese School, and Bernstein recognized that he was in a position to temper rather than deny that relationship. In 1947, Dika Newlin—a Schoenberg pupil—published *Bruckner, Mahler, Schoenberg,* where she submitted that the three composers in the title formed a direct lineage in music history. In program notes for the Mahler Festival's January 14, 1960, concert, Newlin called Mahler the source of the twelve-tone trend by then operative in Stravinsky's music; and she defined Mahler's historical and contemporary relevance by pointing to his use of ten different pitch classes in the opening viola solo of the Tenth Symphony.[78] Similarly, New York Philharmonic program annotator Howard Shanet, in his piece "Conversation Piece: Why a Mahler Festival?" (published in the program booklet for Bernstein's concert of Mahler's Fourth Symphony), wrote that Mahler's symphonies "contain a surprising number of modern elements, imbedded in the old-fashioned romantic ones—and precisely those modern elements that have been adopted by the composers of the 'New Viennese' school." Shanet proposed specific links between Mahler and the Second Viennese School, connecting elements like Mahler's "kaleidoscopic orchestration" to Schoenberg's and Webern's *Klangfarbenmelodie.*[79] Bernstein's statement in his preview lecture that Mahler's importance was "not limited to" the Second Viennese School was a response to Shanet's notes. Bernstein referred directly to Shanet's commentary and acknowledged that the link Shanet drew between Mahler and those figures was "true, as far as it goes," but he also stated that adding names like Britten, Copland, and Honegger was a way to "round out the picture."

Bernstein's commentary on Mahler during the 1960 festival, therefore, concerned his own relationship with his American mentor as much as it did the legacy of Mahler. His incorporation of elements of Copland's text into his own lectures certainly reveals the extent to which Copland was a central source of his ideas about, and a profound part of his engagement with, Mahler's music. But it also illuminates Bernstein's comment in his letter to Copland in late 1959, where he revealed that listening to Mahler brought Copland to mind in a way that foregrounded his own anxieties about the directions in which contemporary composition was heading. By looking back to his earlier encounter with Mahler under Copland's supervision, and to Copland's own music from that period, Bernstein's borrowing of textual material from Copland to bolster his case for Mahler emerges as an important node in a complex aesthetic argument about twentieth-century music and its future.

Bernstein's reputation for leading emotionally uninhibited performances of Mahler makes his apparent distancing of Mahler from romanticism in 1960 seem surprising; the passionate excess in his Mahler interpretations is a quality that would appear to contradict his claim for Mahler as an ancestor of neoclassicism. In a 1963 review, Benjamin Boretz observed that in Bernstein's performances and recordings, "the fascinating inner polyphony of the music is completely suppressed into a mere accompaniment to the eventless, reiterated 'top' line, each of whose repetitions is treated with an inflated expressivity that . . . painfully exaggerates Mahler's hard-lost failures into a set of posturing caricatures."[80] Bernstein himself might well have agreed with aspects of Boretz's assessment. Speaking about the Ninth Symphony in 1971, Bernstein said, "I have tried in the past in performances of this and other Mahler symphonies to underplay early climaxes, to save, also for my own sanity, for the sake of the orchestra's, so they don't give their all and have nothing left. It's impossible with Mahler. You have to give everything you have emotionally to bar 39, and eight bars later even more."[81] Bernstein's notoriety as a sentimentalist in his Mahler performances has lasted into the twenty-first century. Leon Botstein wrote that "Bernstein's Mahler advocacy tended toward the maudlin" and situated it within a broader "embrace of Mahler as a model in the use of premodernist musical means and time."[82] (Of course, such sweeping assessments of Bernstein's Mahler do offer a misleadingly one-sided picture, suggesting that it lacked any nuance and moderation. For instance, Michael Steinberg, reviewing a performance of Mahler's Seventh Symphony, wrote that Bernstein "conducted with magnificent sense of pace and design, with great verve, and also with restraint."[83] Another reviewer called Bernstein's 1960 recording of the Fourth Symphony with the New York Philharmonic "effortlessly paced and superbly phrased," and added that the "balance is carefully maintained with none of the over-accentuation which can easily destroy the lyrical spirit of the score.")[84]

For Bernstein in the years following the Mahler festival, tonality came to represent a return to a premodernist past. In the Omnibus lecture on modern music from 1957, Bernstein had considered tonality to be central to modern musical composition, with serialism clearly placed at the sidelines. In that lecture, even though he did present "a picture of modern music divided into two camps, tonal and atonal," he did, as seen above, wonder if a "synthesis" between tonal and atonal writing "points the direction for the future of modern music, and toward a new kind of beauty."[85] With his use of twelve-tone writing "here and there," as he wrote Copland in 1951, Bernstein was likely referring to pieces he had already written at that point and that contained tone rows, such as the "Galop" from *Fancy Free* (1944) and "The Dirge" from "Age of Anxiety." At the start of the "Galop," all twelve pitches sound in the context of what emerges clearly as a B-flat-major harmony.[86] The row heard at the start of "The Dirge" is reminiscent of Alban Berg's Violin Concerto in its stacking of thirds, offering hints—if elusive ones—of tonal focus.[87]

Just before the Mahler festival, as evidenced in his 1959 letter to Copland expressing concern about modern music, Bernstein was beginning to grow more insecure about the future of tonality. And this anxiety continued to develop after the festival. Turning to the year 1965, after a soul-searching sabbatical from his conducting duties at the New York Philharmonic, Bernstein asked readers of the *New York Times,* "Is tonality dead forever? Is the international community of composers really, deeply ready to accept that death?"[88] The next year, he wrote that "tonal music lies in abeyance, dormant."[89] But he expressed hope that "we will come back to [tonality] in a new relationship, renewed by the catharsis of our agony," and that the loss of tonality would be only temporary.[90] He likened the "musical crisis" to a "crisis of faith."[91]

To alleviate his own concerns about the future of tonality, Bernstein homed in on Mahler, expanding on his idea that Mahler was a forerunner of twentieth-century tonality. His 1967 article on Mahler in *High Fidelity,* "Mahler: His Time Has Come," makes far more of Mahler's broader relevance than did his earlier commentary on the music. In one of his most powerful passages about Mahler's significance, he claimed that the music somehow foreshadowed twentieth-century events in its combination of "innate violence" with "the aching nostalgia of youthful dreams." Among other difficult circumstances, "it is only after . . . the simultaneous advance of democracy with our increasing inability to stop making war," Bernstein wrote, making in part a pointed reference to the devastating conflict in Vietnam that continued at the time of his writing, "that we can finally listen to Mahler's music and understand that it foretold all."[92]

It was in the same article that Bernstein credited Mahler with having delivered tonality's musical eulogy, with tonality perhaps serving as a musical analogue for the sense of goodness that Bernstein feared had vanished, or was at risk of vanishing, in the twentieth century;

here the sense is palpable that Mahler's tonal idiom evoked for Bernstein the futile wish to return to a time more innocent than Bernstein's own: "Mahler was granted the honor of having the last word, uttering the final sigh, letting fall the last living tear, saying the final good-by. To what? To life as he knew it and wanted to remember it, to unspoiled nature, to faith in redemption; but also to *music* as he knew it and remembered it, to the unspoiled nature of tonal beauty, to faith in its future—good-by to all that."[93] For Bernstein, it was Mahler's Ninth Symphony in particular that represented this supposedly hesitant farewell to tonal music—and here again, the legacy of Copland's views on Mahler's romanticism turns up. As we have seen, Copland had written in *Our New Music* that at the closing of both *Das Lied* and the Ninth Symphony, Mahler "knew, deep down inside himself, that he was saying a final farewell to the 19th century. All his music reinvokes the past glories of that golden age, but with an added note of regret for a wonderful epoch that was gone without hope of recall."[94] Bernstein already borrowed this idea in his 1960 Young People's Concert for his introduction to "Der Abschied" from *Das Lied von der Erde.* But now replacing "19th century" with "tonality," Bernstein claimed in his Norton Lectures at Harvard University in 1973 that in writing the Ninth Symphony, Mahler was "agonizing over his reluctant and protracted farewell to tonality."[95] He called the final movement "a prayer, Mahler's last chorale, his closing hymn, so to speak; and it prays for the restoration of life, of tonality, of faith."[96]

Perhaps the emotional intensity many have observed in his performances of Mahler was, in part, his strategy for enacting what he called Mahler's reluctant and protracted send-off to tonality—and for praying for its restoration through catharsis. As we have seen, his interpretation of Mahler as a precedent for twentieth-century tonal composition had its roots in Copland's linkage of Mahler with neoclassicism. With Copland's turn to twelve-tone music, and Bernstein's growing fear about the future of tonal writing in contemporary music, Bernstein's embrace of tonality in Mahler became desperate. But it remained rooted in Copland's discussion of Mahler's music—this time, the romantic interpretation of Mahler's music as a nostalgic farewell. Bernstein's romantic approach to Mahler may thus be seen as part of a Copland-inspired response to the twelve-tone music of Copland and others, which Bernstein feared had helped expel tonality from modern music.

Bernstein's attraction to Mahler and his shifting sense of tonality's future add a new perspective to the contrasting use of twelve-tone techniques in two of his own works, one from before the crisis of tonality was in full swing, and one from the height of the crisis: *West Side Story* (1957) and Symphony no. 3, "Kaddish" (1963). Bernstein's best-known tone row, if not one audiences would have immediately recognized as a row, appeared in *West Side Story*'s "Cool" as the subject of its central fugue.[97] With its frequent semitones and sequences, the fugue subject fits into the chromatic context both of "Cool" and of the musical as a whole, and it melds with the song's primary melodic material.[98] Here, Bernstein fused twelve-tone writing, tonality, jazz, and classical contrapuntal techniques into a coherent, expressive whole. In doing so, he reconciled twelve-tone composition with tonality and neoclassicism in a synthesis reminiscent of the one that he proposed, in the Omnibus lecture from the same year, might propel modern music forward. A similar case from around the same time is "Quiet" from *Candide* (1956), where the tone row that opens the piece is more reminiscent in its flood of semitones of "The People That Walked in Darkness" from Handel's *Messiah* than of a typical twelve-tone passage.[99]

As Emily Abrams Ansari has written in a compelling discussion of Bernstein's twelve-tone writing and its political implications, his use of a tone row in *West Side Story* "carries none of the heavy existential associations that it bears in 'Kaddish', nor does it feel like it is engaged in a battle with the surrounding tonal material."[100] Indeed, by contrast to his earlier employment of twelve-tone materials, Bernstein's use of tone rows in "Kaddish" reflects the same ideas of tonal sanctity that drove his attitude toward Mahler's Ninth Symphony. In a general sense, Bernstein's debt to Mahler in "Kaddish" is plainly evident. Its combination of orchestra, multiple choirs, and soloists recalls large-scale works like Mahler's Eighth and Second symphonies. Specifically, its juxtaposition of Hebrew, Aramaic, and English recalls the switch in Mahler's Eighth Symphony from a Latin-texted first part to the German second part. And the sweeping soprano melody in the second Kaddish in particular has been likened to Mahler.[101] Turning to the work's use of twelve-tone writing, Mahler may even be seen as an inspiration for this element, insofar as Bernstein ultimately used twelve-tone writing to fortify his case for the survival of tonal music. As David M. Schiller has discussed, the scherzo's serial writing seems to poke fun at Bernstein's twelve-tone-leaning colleagues, associated as it is with the narrator's text about a world lacking in creative vision.[102] As Bernstein later said of the work's trajectory, in Peter Rosen's 1978 documentary *Reflections*, "one of the main points of the piece is that the agony expressed by the twelve tone music has to give way—this is part of the form of the piece—to tonality and diatonicism even, so that what triumphs in the end, the affirmation of faith, is tonal."[103] The seeds of this idea were certainly present in Bernstein's thinking back in 1957, when in the Omnibus lecture on modern music he referred to diatonic scales as a way of escaping the "twelve-tone nightmare."

If *West Side Story*'s "Cool" testifies to a marrying of twelve-tone writing with a diverse musical fabric, "Kaddish," then, points to an uneasy juxtaposition that has a reference point in Bernstein's conception of Mahler. Indeed, in both "Cool" and "Kaddish," what Bernstein would come to identify as Mahler's signature contrasts—"roughhewn *and* epicene, subtle *and* blatant, refined, raw, objective, maudlin, brash, shy, grandiose, self-annihilating, confident, insecure, adjective, opposite, adjective, opposite"—may be seen as parallels for Bernstein's own layering of seemingly disparate musical practices.[104] Following Ansari's interpretation of Bernstein's "Kaddish"—that his "approach to tonality and serialism demonstrates that a functional stylistic détente is impossible in this context"—one might apply Bernstein's conflicting Mahler categories to his own music: "adjective, opposite" perhaps, then, included "twelve-tone, diatonic."[105] Going further, Bernstein's self-identification with Mahler, along with his recognition that Mahler was readily viewed as a twelve-tone ancestor, raises the possibility that Bernstein considered what he perceived as Mahler's rejection of atonality to have been a precedent for his twelve-tone explorations; this interpretation expands on David M. Schiller's point that "in insisting that the effects of Mahler's dualisms can be heard in his music, specifically in Mahler's handling of tonality, Bernstein explains his own predicament as a composer: Bernstein too is torn between Romanticism and Modernism."[106] In the Young People's Concert in 1960, Bernstein revealed that strong sense of self-identification with Mahler:

> Some people say that Mahler's own music sounds too much like all the composers he used to conduct . . . and that he just remembered their music and imitated it when he wrote his own. They say that anyway a conductor's head is too full of everyone else's music so how can he write original stuff of his own. Naturally I don't agree with these people at all. I think Mahler's music is terrific and very original, too. . . . Still, I admit it's a problem to be both a conductor and a composer. There never seems to be enough time and energy to be both things. I ought to know because I have the same problem myself. And that's one of the reasons I'm so sympathetic to Mahler. I understand his problem. It's like being two different men locked up in the same body. One man is a conductor and the other is a composer. And they're both one fellow called Mahler, or Bernstein.[107]

While he portrayed Mahler as having tested the waters of atonality—he even asked in his *High Fidelity* article if the Tenth Symphony contained "signs that he was about to go over the hill, and encamp with Schoenberg"—it was Bernstein himself who was constantly examining what it might mean to "encamp with Schoenberg" through his own works.[108]

Perhaps Bernstein attributed to Mahler a sense of pained farewell to tonality that he himself toyed with in works like the "Kaddish." In other words, in this composition Bernstein placed himself—just as he viewed Mahler—at the edge of tonality, refusing to cross over fully into an atonal universe.

Despite making clear his deep discomfort with twelve-tone composition, Bernstein—like a moth to the flame—continually grasped toward twelve-tone techniques in his music. Indeed, tone rows feature in Bernstein's music throughout his career, including in *Mass* (1971) and *A Quiet Place* (1983).[109] In writing twelve-tone music, Bernstein perhaps reenacted what he saw as Mahler's farewell to tonality in the same way that Copland repeatedly rehearsed Mahler's farewell to romanticism in his works. More important, the victory of tonality over atonality in "Kaddish" helped Bernstein maintain a narrative of twentieth-century music in which the shift away from tonality after Mahler was *not* inevitable. With Copland as its leading American torchbearer, and thus as an important successor of Mahler, tonality had remained alive, well, and unthreatened for Bernstein. If beginning in the 1950s Bernstein's sense of security about tonality seems to have unraveled, spurred perhaps in part by his impressions of Copland's *Piano Fantasy*, then his forceful defense of tonality against atonality might be read as his reassertion of a Mahler–Copland–Bernstein axis in twentieth-century music.

Since Bernstein once pointed to Copland's *Piano Quartet* (unlike the *Piano Fantasy*) as a laudable model for the mingling of twelve-tone and tonal sensibilities, this chamber work serves as a useful lens through which to appreciate Bernstein's complex and changing attitude toward twelve-tone writing in his own music. In the larger context of Cold War politics and the questioning of binaries, Jennifer DeLapp-Birkett has argued cogently that the *Piano Quartet* is "a microcosm of the decades-long struggle between tonality and atonality," adding that it "seems to explore the common ground and the distinctions between these characters and their attendant ideologies as Copland saw them in 1950."[110] DeLapp-Birkett cites Copland's review in 1949, a year before composing the *Piano Quartet*, of the composer Rene Leibowitz's book *Schoenberg and His School*—a book that argues vigorously for the importance of twelve-tone writing. In his review, Copland asked, prefiguring Bernstein's post-sabbatical musing, "Has the tonal system really been exhausted and should it be abandoned or are there still hidden resources to be tapped?"[111] The *Piano Quartet* might thus be read as Copland's initial compositional response to his own question about tonality and its future, one in which he answered that twelve-tone writing might offer a new vehicle for tonal music to thrive (and one that Bernstein, as we have seen, agreed with, at least temporarily). Bernstein's limited use of tone rows in *Candide* and *West Side Story*, by carefully blending twelve-tone writing and tonality, suggests a similar mentality. In "Kaddish," on the other hand, Bernstein—despite following Copland's lead in placing twelve-tone and tonal elements in the same work—heightens a sense of a disconnect between these aesthetic worlds, a disconnect that was present to some extent in the *Piano Quartet*; as DeLapp-Birkett has argued about that work's third movement, "it is as if Copland portrays tonality and atonality as separate characters, pitted against each other in a struggle." But while Bernstein played winners and losers in "Kaddish," in Copland we observe "a process aimed at reconciling the differences between serialism and tonality."[112]

If "Kaddish" was Bernstein's hard-earned affirmation of faith in tonality (with its concomitant defeat of twelve-tone writing, at least for the time being) and Mahler's Ninth one of its spiritual antecedents, then *Chichester Psalms* (1965) celebrated that affirmation. Bernstein wrote this work during his sabbatical and associated it with his ruminations on the supposed death of tonality. He waxed poetic in the *New York Times* on how this work helped him navigate his tonal crisis and reject (temporarily) twelve-tone modernism, writing that he "brooded and mused" on "the death in our time of tonality" and on "serial strictures, the dearth of romance." He considered the result of his soul-searching, the *Chichester Psalms*, to be "a simple and modest affair/ Tonal and tuneful and somewhat square." Bernstein was proud to call it his own despite acknowledging that it might not be acceptable to more adventurous musicians ("Certain to sicken a stout John Cager"). He concluded that it was his "youngest child, old-fashioned and sweet/ And he stands on his own two tonal feet."[113] Here, Bernstein performed through straightforward verse what his dedication to tonality demonstrated through music—pride in certain aspects of tradition, and faith that techniques perceived as old-fashioned could continue to seem fresh. At the same time, he had already established himself as a credible musician who knew the current trends of modernism—including the "strictures of serialism"—and had chosen to reject them in favor of "romance" and "old-fashioned" composition. For Bernstein, the decision to conduct Mahler and to compose tonal music went hand in hand with a return to romantic expression in the face of twelve-tone experimentation. He later said of the final movement of Mahler's Ninth Symphony, which he first conducted with the New York Philharmonic on November 25, 1965, "This is tonality unashamed."[114] Given his *Times* poem, he might as well have been speaking of his own *Chichester Psalms*. That Bernstein and others could compose tonal music after Mahler's supposed farewell to tonality was no contradiction; it was a reflection of Bernstein's positioning of Mahler at the end of the Austro-German tradition of tonal music rather than a statement that tonality itself was extinct in the middle of the twentieth century.

The opening of *Chichester Psalms* might be profitably understood in this context as a recomposed version of the beginning of Mahler's Eighth Symphony for a newly revitalized mid-twentieth-century conception of tonality. Jack Gottlieb has observed that Bernstein's opening "pays homage to the similarly affirmative opening" of that Mahler work.[115] That Bernstein might have turned to aspects of Mahler's Eighth, a work that also sets sacred texts, as a model for his setting of psalms is not surprising; he conducted the first part of that symphony with the New York Philharmonic in September of 1962 at the opening of Lincoln Center. As seen in example 7.2a (from Mahler's Eighth Symphony, which reproduces ex. 4.1) and example 7.2b (from Bernstein's *Chichester Psalms*), the two passages share noticeable details of melodic contour and orchestration. A striking instrumental eruption sets the stage, and the soprano lines descend a fourth before an upward leap and a following descent. The brass respond with a similar gesture, supported by timpani, before the return of the voices. Differences abound too; Bernstein has strings double voices and employs an array of percussion instruments, forgoing the organ, while Mahler's orchestration at this moment in the work is more transparent and includes imitation between the trumpets and trombones.

More important, Bernstein's opening is anything but straightforwardly tonal, despite his promise in the *New York Times* poem. Mahler presents an unambiguous E-flat-major opening with a predictable turn to the dominant at the first choir's return. In Bernstein's harmonically complex opening phrase, on the other hand, the B-flat-major key signature marks a highly dissonant musical fabric. B♭ in soprano, alto, and bass clash with the A in the tenor, lending the first syllable of "Urah" (Awake) with the fitting quality of a wake-up call, a dissonant version of the imperative "Veni" (Come) in Mahler's symphony. Parallel sevenths between tenor and bass add to the passage's piquancy, while the A♭ in soprano and alto suggests either the B-flat Mixolydian mode or a competing E-flat-major flavor. The pervasive dissonance in this opening gesture clarifies Bernstein's claim that the *Chichester Psalms* stood "on its own two tonal feet," as it draws on Bernstein's argument for tonality in modern music in his Omnibus lecture from 1957—his insistence, as seen above, that pointed dissonance could enliven tonality. There, for example, he combined the "Star-Spangled Banner" and "America" ("My Country 'Tis of Thee") at the piano in the same key, playing one melody in each hand and generating pungent dissonances

Example 7.2a. Mahler, Eighth Symphony, part 1, mm. 1–8.

Example 7.2b. Bernstein, *Chichester Psalms*, mvt. 1, mm. 1–5.

between the melodies. "If you want to be modern," he added (admitting that "this procedure is ridiculously oversimplified"), "it's simple: just don't fix it. Leave all the dissonant clashes in."[116] The clashing lines that commence *Chichester Psalms* suggest a similar transformation of fairly traditional melodic building blocks into "modern music," with the contours and textures of Mahler's Eighth serving as a direct jumping-off point for Bernstein's tonality-rejuvenating sabbatical project.

Even if Bernstein felt a certain distance from Copland's music by the 1960s, it was thanks to Copland's argument connecting Mahler to modernism that Bernstein had a framework for linking Mahler to the survival of tonality in the first place. At the same time, Copland's claim that Mahler's music was a farewell to the nineteenth century prepared Bernstein to make a similar claim for Mahler as a farewell to tonality. For the better part of the 1950s, Bernstein seemed confident about tonality and its relationship to modern composition—even twelve-tone music. But as he came to fear that atonality, through serialism, really was superseding tonal music in new composition, he refashioned Copland's conception of Mahler, turning Mahler into the last great exponent of tonality. Now, Mahler, as an uncompromisingly tonal predecessor, became for Bernstein a refreshing *escape* from aspects of modernist composition that pointed toward serialism and atonality. Performing Mahler was thus a torturous act of hanging on to a sacred tonal heritage.

Leon Botstein wrote of Bernstein's advocacy of Mahler that "in the 1960s it coincided with his increasing resentment at the rise of radical modernism."[117] A complete understanding of how Bernstein came to champion Mahler as a forerunner of modern tonal writing as opposed to twelve-tone writing is inseparable from an awareness of his relationship with Copland, who worked with Bernstein primarily as a composition teacher, and who established Mahler as a proto-modernist but also as a romanticist. In sum, beginning in 1925, Copland shaped an argument connecting Mahler to a cluster of contemporary composers. His own multifaceted interest in Mahler coincided with his mentoring of Bernstein as a composer in the late 1930s and early 1940s. As Bernstein began performing Mahler's Second Symphony in the late 1940s, Copland supported Bernstein's decision to perform those works and urged him to associate them with American compositions. At the New York Philharmonic Mahler festival in 1960, Bernstein's longstanding affinity with Copland's music—particularly in the context of his own anxiety about twelve-tone composition—was a central facet of his argument for Mahler's importance. His case for the preservation of tonality, in turn, may have informed what has frequently been viewed as Bernstein's overtly emotional performance practice of Mahler as well as his treatment of tonality and tone rows in his own music.

As this chapter centers on aspects of Bernstein's activities as a composer and Mahler conductor that can be linked directly to Copland, Bernstein's activities after the 1970s are beyond its scope. His engagement with Mahler's music certainly continued through numerous performances and recordings with several orchestras. One particular area of interest that deserves further study is his own sense of shared Jewish identity with Mahler. Indeed, this relationship could certainly figure into "Jeremiah," "Kaddish," and *Chichester Psalms* (the latter of which sets text in Hebrew), given these works' connections to Mahler.[118] To be sure, the fact that Copland and several other important predecessors in Bernstein's life as a Mahlerian—including Walter, Koussevitzky, Rodzinski, and Reiner—were Jewish is a crucial detail. It was later in his career, in the 1984 television "essay" *The Little Drummer Boy,* that this aspect of his identification with Mahler developed fully, but Mahler's Jewishness was certainly on Bernstein's radar screen much earlier. At the Young People's Concert in 1960, for instance, he told his audience that they would find in Mahler both "German sounding" music and "Slavic and Jewish sounds," setting up these categories as opposites. Before that, as conductor of the Israel Philharmonic Orchestra, Bernstein highlighted Mahler's music regularly.[119] And, at Bernstein's first Mahler performance—the Second Symphony at the City Center in 1947—the program was "dedicated to the Resurrection of Palestine."[120] Copland did not encourage Bernstein to explore his Jewish identity through his music, but it is certainly plausible that Bernstein drew on his Jewish musical ancestry in Copland and Mahler in constructing his professional persona.[121]

That Copland should have been so present in Bernstein's Mahler advocacy is at once both glaringly obvious and oddly nonintuitive. As a member of multiple communities, including conductors and composers, Bernstein surely had numerous sources for his interest in, knowledge about, and conceptions of Mahler.[122] It should come as no surprise that Copland, as one of his closest mentors, directly informed this aspect of Bernstein's musical life. Yet a historiographical tendency to treat conducting and composing as endeavors detached from each other helps explain why the conductor-based lineage has dominated the discussion of Bernstein's involvement with Mahler's music. The loose ancestry of conducting mentors is a part of the story, but it is only one of the many appropriate contexts in which to understand the pathways by which ideas about Mahler's significance circulated. Here in particular, the profound link between Bernstein's case for Mahler and his enduring anxieties about tonal composition emerges only through an approach that integrates, rather than divides, the standard categories of conductor and composer.

Of course, much about Bernstein's complex relationship with Mahler, including issues of Jewish identity, remains to be studied beyond the Copland-centered discussion in this chapter. Applying a new lens to Bernstein's relationship with Mahler's music paves the way for fruitful inquiries into Mahler's reception and other aspects of twentieth-century music, especially by interpreting archival materials that shed light on personal relationships that are too easily overlooked. The specific results of any conversations between Bernstein and Copland, Mitropoulos, Walter, and others about *Das Lied* or any other Mahler work are impossible to pin down; further research may well add other figures who were important for Bernstein, such as Renée Longy-Miquelle, Walter Piston, and Marc Blitzstein, to this list.[123] But the evidence presented here affords a glimpse into the significant role such discussions played in shaping the legacy of Mahler in particular. These conversations defy the typically fixed classifications—as conductors, composers, or otherwise—of the musicians who participated in them. And in doing so, they add a new dimension to our understanding of how figures engaged with music and transformed its reception.

CONCLUSION

This study has considered Copland's Mahler advocacy in several different contexts, including as a student, a teacher, a critic, a composer, an advisor, and a mentor. But Copland also brought Mahler to audiences in the most direct way possible: as a conductor. In the 1950s, quite late in his own career as an established composer, Copland began to conduct major orchestras on a regular basis.[1] Although he is not typically viewed as a composer-conductor today, conducting was an integral part of his musical persona, and one that was closely tied to his composing. Looking back in the mid-1980s, Copland spoke of the intersection between those two activities. "You spend most of your life watching conductors conduct your music," he said. "Finally you get the feeling that, gee, I'd just like to get up there just once and conduct my music the way I dreamt it. . . . When I finally got the courage to do it, I found that it was a great source of pleasure."[2]

For Copland as conductor, Mahler's music served as a bridge between the grand transatlantic romantic tradition and the modernist impulses of the twentieth century. Indeed, Mahler's songs and symphonies appeared in Copland's programs in significant ways that suggested particular linkages among Mahler, American music, and romanticism. One of Copland's apparent favorites was the Adagietto from Mahler's Fifth Symphony. Perhaps following his own advice to "pick and choose among the separate movements" of Mahler's symphonies, Copland conducted the Adagietto worldwide with several orchestras—the Orquestra Sinfônica Brasileira in Rio de Janeiro on July 28, 1962; the Chicago Symphony Orchestra in Ravinia on July 6, 1963; and the New York Philharmonic's Promenade concerts on June 1, 5, and 6, 1973.[3] In these programs he frequently conducted American works alongside Mahler. The Brazil program included Bernstein's *Candide* overture, Charles Ives's *Unanswered Question*, Brahms's *Variations on a Theme by Haydn*, and Copland's own *Tender Land Suite* and *Lincoln Portrait* (the latter with Paolo Santos narrating). In the Chicago program, he conducted Berlioz's *Roman Carnival Overture*, the Brahms *Variations*, Ives's *Unanswered Question*, and his own *Red Pony* suite and *Lincoln Portrait* (this time with Governor Otto Kerner narrating). In the New York program, Copland conducted his *El Salón México* and portions of *Rodeo*, as well as Bernstein's *Candide* Overture, Sergei Prokofiev's *Lieutenant Kijé* suite, and Carl Maria von Weber's Concertino in E-flat major, op. 26, alongside the Mahler. These programs connected nineteenth-century French and Austro-German composers, including Mahler, to twentieth-century international modernism. In his review of the latter performance, Allen Hughes called Prokofiev and Copland "two master orchestrators of the 20th century." Strikingly, Hughes contrasted the strings-only scoring of the Mahler movement with the "color" of the other works.[4]

Copland's relationship with Mahler as a conductor actually developed before the 1960s, at the Ojai Music Festival in Southern California. In 1958, as we have seen, Copland led the Ojai Festival Symphony Orchestra in Mahler's *Kindertotenlieder* and the first West Coast performance of his own *Short Symphony*. On May 23, 1976, Copland conducted members of the Los Angeles Philharmonic in Mahler's Fourth Symphony (with Polly Jo Baker singing the fourth movement); the *Symphonic Ode* was also on that program. Martin Bernheimer's review of the concert in the *Los Angeles Times* shows a surprising contrast between the two composers' reception—a contrast that suggests the potential of the music of both Copland and Mahler to cross typical boundaries. Bernheimer wrote of the Fourth Symphony that it was "Mahler devoid of heroics or dash, Mahler on an unaccustomed intimate scale, Mahler of infinite tenderness and just a touch of melancholy." Meanwhile, Copland's *Symphonic Ode* was labeled "big and bombastic."[5] The latter comment employed the same kind of terminology that had irritated Copland when critics used it to describe Mahler more than fifty years earlier. Copland, it seems, had successfully transformed Mahler from a longwinded composer of late-romantic monstrosities to a restrained master of small-scale expression. And in the process, Copland's own music took on Mahler's previous reputation for symphonic opulence.

Bernheimer's remark on the *Symphonic Ode* links the piece firmly to the romantic tradition and contrasts sharply with John Adams's comment, quoted in the introduction of this book, that "Copland's orchestral works are like pieces of Shaker furniture, simple to the point of being humble, but sturdy and effective and free of excess emotional baggage. They are typical of the American grain, not unlike the prose of Ernest Hemingway or the poetry of Robert Frost."[6] Depending on one's priorities and biases, one might indeed hear the *Symphonic Ode* as either "free of excess emotional baggage" or "big and bombastic," or a bit of both. Copland's music—like Mahler's—is both bombastic and delicate, grandiose and modest, romantic and modern. He, along with others in his network who followed his lead, found in Mahler, either directly or indirectly, a crucial precedent for the ambiguities that infuse twentieth-century American composition.

NOTES

Introduction

1. Copland, *New York Times*, April 5, 1925.
2. See Murchison, *American Stravinsky*.
3. Crist and Shirley, *Selected Correspondence*, 247.
4. Berger, *Aaron Copland*, 39.
5. Adams, *Hallelujah Junction*, 182.
6. Tilson Thomas et al., *Keeping Score*.
7. Bernstein, "What Is American Music?"
8. Fauser, "Aaron Copland."
9. Oja, *Making Music Modern*, 237–51.
10. Murchison, *American Stravinsky*.
11. Riley and Smith, *Nation and Classical Music*, 84–85.
12. Hubbs, *Queer Composition*, 108–9 and 140–41.
13. Gilman, *Edward MacDowell*, 85.
14. Magee, *Charles Ives Reconsidered*, 38–66.
15. Shadle, *Orchestrating the Nation*, 265–66.
16. Levy, *Frontier Figures*.
17. See Murchison, *American Stravinsky*, 73; Hubbs, *Queer Composition*, 144–45; and Tischler, *An American Music*, 182.
18. Copland, "Music and the Human Spirit," 29.
19. Downes, *New York Times*, October 19, 1941.
20. See Messing, *Neoclassicism in Music*.
21. Horowitz, *Classical Music in America*, 266.
22. Gilliam, "Viennese Opera Composer," 225.
23. Gienow-Hecht, *Sound Diplomacy*, 206–7. Also see Tischler, *An American Music*, 68–91.
24. Copland, "Stravinsky's Dynamism," 165.
25. Copland, 164–65.
26. Oja, *Making Music Modern*, 4.
27. Albright, *Untwisting*, 29.
28. See Johnson, *Mahler's Voices*, 102; and Franklin, *Reclaiming Late-Romantic Music*, 19 and 23.
29. Berger, *Aaron Copland*, 39–40.
30. Thomson. "Greatest Music Teacher," 42.
31. See Keller, "Bernstein and Mahler."

Chapter One

1. See La Grange, *Gustav Mahler*, 587–89, and Horowitz, *Classical Music in America*, 193.

2. Krehbiel, *New York Tribune*, December 18, 1909.

3. *New York Tribune*, November 7, 1904.

4. Krehbiel, *New York Tribune*, December 13, 1909.

5. Horowitz, *Moral Fire*, 114–18.

6. Krehbiel, *New York Tribune*, May 21, 1911.

7. Krehbiel, *New York Tribune*, December 13, 1909.

8. Aldrich, *New York Times*, November 6, 1904.

9. Wister, *Philadelphia Orchestra*, 107–8.

10. Pollack, *Aaron Copland*, 32–33.

11. Aaron Copland, "Forms of Modern Music," Copland Collection, Music Division, Library of Congress, Washington, DC, 211/35. In this book, materials in the Leonard Bernstein, Aaron Copland, and Serge Koussevitzky collections at the Library of Congress are identified by the box number, a slash, and the number of the folder in which the item resides. For items available in the library's online collections of these figures, a digital ID (searchable at http://www.loc.gov) is provided instead of the collection name and box and folder numbers.

12. Wister, *Philadelphia Orchestra*, 108.

13. Society of Friends of Music, *Gustav Mahler*, 16–17.

14. Society of Friends of Music, 7, 22, and 14.

15. Krehbiel, *Bohemians*, 22. The event was reported in Henry Krehbiel's book as an informal "smoker," but the club's meeting minutes for January 4, 1909, in mentioning Mahler's acceptance of the Club's invitation, called the potential event a "dinner," which would have been a larger and more formal affair (The Bohemians Minutes, May 4, 1907–May 7, 1923, p. 30 of binder, Bohemians Club Collection, JPB 11-15, Box 9, New York Public Library, New York; also see Krehbiel, *Bohemians*, 12–13, on these categories). There was clearly room for flexibility in the planning stages of these events; the minutes for February 6, 1911, describe approval of a smoker for Victor Herbert to be held March 11, 1911; that event turned out to be a dinner (p. 53 of the minutes). In Mahler's case, it probably was a smoker, with "dinner" referenced casually. A smoker could involve dinner; the minutes of December 5, 1908, report on a smoker at Lüchow's, but on the same event, we read "Following the dinner" (p. 29 of the minutes).

16. Copland and Perlis, *Copland: 1900 through 1942*, 27.

17. Dickinson, "Composer in Interview," 11.

18. Copland and Perlis, *Copland: 1900 through 1942*, 27–28.

19. Mathers, "Solid Basic Training," 48.

20. Jacobi, "Rubin Goldmark," 50. See also Pollack, *Aaron Copland*, 35; and Mathers, "Solid Basic Training," 8.

21. Jacobi, "In Defense of Modernism," 221.
22. Copland, "Composer from Brooklyn," 522.
23. Copland, "Rubin Goldmark," 16.
24. Krehbiel, *Bohemians*, 10.
25. *New York Times*, November 25, 1917.
26. Paul, "Converging Paths," 175.
27. Henderson, *New York Herald*, March 5, 1922.
28. Copland, "Composer from Brooklyn," 522.
29. See Coster, "Mengelberg's Mahler."
30. Roman, *Gustav Mahler's American Years*, 280.
31. Gilman, "Music of the Month," 122.
32. Aldrich, *New York Times*, March 9, 1923.
33. Aldrich, *New York Times*, January 28, 1924. On the American reception of Mahler's songs, see Reilly, "Mahler in America," 426.
34. Doering, *Great Orchestrator*, 101.

Chapter Two

1. Dickinson, "Composer in Interview," 11.
2. Copland, letter to his parents, November 3, 1921, Music Division, Library of Congress, Washington, DC, digital ID copland corr0028.
3. See Herta Blaukopf, "Amsterdam"; and Nikkels, "Mahler and Holland," 326–37.
4. Pasler, *Writing through Music*, 313; La Grange, "Mahler and France," 148–49; and La Grange, *Gustav Mahler*, 724–25.
5. La Grange, *Gustav Mahler*, 735–57.
6. See La Grange, "Mahler and France," 148–50.
7. La Grange, "Mahler and France," 149–50. On Dukas's praise for Mahler, see La Grange, *Gustav Mahler*, 413.
8. See Fauser, *Politics of Musical Identity*, 65–66; Ellis, *Interpreting the Musical Past*, 142; Schmid, "À bas Wagner," 77–91; Hart, "Symphony and National Identity," 131–48; and Pasler, *Composing the Citizen*, 288–89.
9. See Brooks, *Musical Work*, 91–97.
10. "L'architecture, l'esthétique de Mahler, par sa dimension, son expansion, sont contraires à l'esprit français, fait de mesure, d'harmonie" (Boulanger, "Le jubilé," 83). I am grateful to Jeanice Brooks for providing me with a copy of this article. Unless otherwise noted, all translations here are my own, with helpful corrections and suggestions from Magali Bergolla, Louis Epstein, and anonymous readers. This passage is quoted in Vignal, *Mahler*, 6. It also appears in Giuliani, "Les enregistrements," 198, n. 49, and with more context from the review itself in Stricker, "La critique," 133–34.

11. See Oja, *Making Music Modern*, 238; and Pollack, *Aaron Copland*, 36. This detail turns up in the Mahler literature in Mitchell, "Mahler Renaissance," 560.

12. Francis, *Teaching Stravinsky*, 5.

13. Edwards, *Flawed Words and Stubborn Sounds*, 49.

14. The tendency in Mahler reception to focus on concerts and published reactions has been noted in Paul, "Converging Paths," v. For examples see Reilly, "Mahler in America" (one of Paul's examples) and Coster, "Mengelberg's Mahler Performances." For examples beyond Mahler's music, see Bailey, "For the Serious Listeners," and Bashford, "Late Beethoven."

15. La Grange, "Mahler and France," 151. Confronting this narrow perspective, the story of Mahler's reception through various printed editions of Mahler's works is explored in Zychowicz, "Mahler Reception."

16. Everist, *Mozart's Ghosts*, 3.

17. Brooks, "Nadia Boulanger," 415–20.

18. Paul, "Converging Paths," 134–40.

19. Links between the Mahler festival and the Paris Peace Conference have been suggested before, including at the time of the festival itself. See Paul, "Converging Paths," 134; and Samaroff Stokowski, *An American Musician's Story*, 162–63.

20. "L'italien parlait en français et les deux viennois en allemand. Une étroite solidarité spirituelle réunissait ces ennemis de la veille. Et à la sortie de cette même manifestation on pouvait voir le français Florent Schmitt se promener bras-dessus bras-dessous avec l'autrichien Arnold Schönberg" (Casella, "Chroniques et notes). Paul cited a similar account, by Olga Samaroff Stokowski, of a meeting between Schmitt and the German conductor Hermann Abendroth. See Paul, "Converging Paths," 134; and Samaroff Stokowski, *An American Musician's Story*, 166.

21. Paul, "Converging Paths," 140; and Op de Coul, "Modern Chamber Music," 1:83.

22. Paul, "Converging Paths," 134.

23. This material is quoted from the manifesto as reproduced in Op de Coul, "Modern Chamber Music," I.84.

24. Op de Coul, I.77.

25. *Vijf Concerten van Internationale Moderne Kamermuziek Tijdens Het Mahler-Feest (6–21 Mei 1920)*, Georganiseerd Door Alexander Schmuller (Amsterdam, 1920), found in the Médiathèque Nadia Boulanger du Conservatoire national supérieur musique et danse in Lyon, France, UFNB L 18 CON. The inside title page includes Boulanger's initials, the word Amsterdam, and the year 1920, all in her hand.

26. Letter from Willem Mengelberg, January 6, 1920, Fonds Boulanger, Bibliothèque nationale de France, Paris, NLA 85, 108.

27. This list is found in the planning documents for the Mahler festival, preserved in the Royal Concertgebouw Orchestra's collection at the

Amsterdam City Archives (Archief van het Concertgebouw N.V., Stukken betreffende uitnodiging van gasten, 2.20.8.1.1.4.3006, Stadsarchief Amsterdam, Netherlands).

28. Potter, *Nadia and Lili Boulanger*, 1–17.

29. Rosenstiel, *Nadia Boulanger*, 56.

30. Rosenstiel, 98.

31. "Il est impossible d'imaginer une plus émouvante interprétation du *Chant de la Terre*" (Boulanger, "Le jubilé," 182).

32. Rosenstiel, *Nadia Boulanger*, 130.

33. Boulanger, "Lectures," 121n1.

34. Casella, *L'evoluzione*, 51, example 72.

35. Halbreich, *Honegger*, 40. I am grateful to Robert Piencikowski for drawing my attention to this matter.

36. As quoted and translated in Orenstein, *A Ravel Reader*, 420. On Ravel's relationship with Mahler's music, also see Fulcher, "Composer as Intellectual," 216.

37. Combe, "Les Symphonies de Mahler."

38. Kelly, *Music and Ultra-Modernism*, 73.

39. "Mahler a-t-il 'du genie'? Oui, certainement—mais ce génie est-il de caractère universel?" (Boulanger, "Le jubilé," 183).

40. "Il est certain qu'en ce qui concerne Mahler et les artistes français, il y a une part d'inconnaissance, et une part d'incompatabilité" (Boulanger, "Le jubilé," 183).

41. See Kelly, *Music and Ultra-Modernism*, 124; and Fulcher, *Composer as Intellectual*, 20–22.

42. "L'architecture, l'esthétique de Mahler, par sa dimension, son expansion, sont contraires à l'esprit français, fait de mesure, d'harmonie. En d'autres termes, ici le style doit dominer le sentiment tandis que là tout doit s'effacer devant lui: D'où une manière de néo-romantisme que les races latines semblent fuir, de même qu'elles essaient de renoncer à la prédominance du 'moi'" (Boulanger, "Le jubilé," 183).

43. Recent discussions of neoclassicism reveal its resonance well beyond stylistic considerations after World War I. See Levitz, *Modernist Mysteries*, 17–27; Kelly, *Music and Ultra-Modernism*, 224–25; and Fulcher, *Composer as Intellectual*, 170. For background on the division of Teutonic and Latin in French discourse, see Ellis, *Interpreting the Musical Past*, 212–15.

44. Boulanger, "Le jubilé," 182.

45. Mahler-Feestboek (Amsterdam, 1920), Médiathèque Nadia Boulanger. Her count of 156 instrumentalists is on p. 7. The inside title page of the book contains her initials and the year 1920 in her hand.

46. "Toute tentative dans ce domaine aide donc au rapprochement intellectuel qui doit, non pas neutraliser les races, mais leur permettre de déterminer les raisons de leurs différentes individualités" (Boulanger, Le jubilé," 182).

47. Vaughan Williams, *Beethoven's Choral Symphony*, 100. On internationalism after World War I, see Fauser, *Sounds of War*, 136; and Fulcher, *Composer as Intellectual*, 126.

48. "D'aucuns, agissant vis-à-vis de Mahler comme vis-à-vis de Liszt et de Brahms, ont pris le parti de condamner son oeuvre sans en rien connaître, ou presque, d'autres, avec la meilleure foi du monde, se sont heurtés à une sorte d'impossibilité d'adaptation qui doit avoir une cause" (Boulanger, "Le jubilé," 183).

49. "Notre indépendance est une des nos fiertés—elle nous permet d'oublier nos griefs commes nos sympathies dans le désir sincère de comprendre bien" (Boulanger, "Le jubilé, 183).

50. "Ce n'est pas méconnaître Mahler que reconnaître ce qui nous sépare parfois de lui" (Boulanger, "Le jubilé, 183).

51. "Les conditions d'existence exigent que chaque peuple s'efforce de comprendre la mentalité des autres peuples" (Boulanger, "Le jubilé," 182).

52. "Force le respect, car avec une sincérité indéniable elle s'est exprimée fortement, elle attire les coeurs, car elle a concentré en elle les plus grands sentiments humains. L'inquietude de l'homme devant sa propre misère, devant l'inconnu qu'il entrevoit de toutes parts, sa douleur devant la mort et son amour pour l'enfant sont les premiers qu'on reconnaisse. Ensuite, sa résignation sereine et croyante, sa force hautaine et solitaire, que traversent de sauvages sursauts de révolte, de passion, apparaissent, et enfin, sa foi, cette foi donnant de la paix à tous les deuils, du rayonnement à tous les bonheurs. Que tout ceci ne soit pas parfois terni par une tournure mélodique contestable, par des longueurs et des lourdeurs, est impossible à soutenir, mais faut-il s'acharner à critiquer quand on peut aimer? . . . Or, il y a mille raisons d'aimer Mahler qui, en tout cas, est un des grands parmi les compositeurs modernes—efforçons-nous de ressentir l'émotion profonde de son oeuvre" (Boulanger, "Le jubilé, 183).

53. Combe, "Les Symphonies," 55.

54. Fauser, "Aaron Copland," 536.

55. Francis, "Everything Had to Change."

56. Boulanger, "Lectures," 124.

57. Boulanger, 121.

58. Fauser, "Aaron Copland," 537.

59. Copland and Perlis, *Copland: 1900 through 1942*, 65.

60. Francis, "A Dialogue Begins," 35–41. On Boulanger's analyses, see also Brooks, *Musical Work*, 45–59.

61. Boulanger, "Concerts Koussevitzky," as quoted in Messing, *Neoclassicism in Music*, 133.

62. Boulanger, "Lectures," 145.

63. Brooks, *Musical Work*, 131. Also see Musk, "Regionalism."

64. Ellis, *Interpreting the Musical Past*, 102–5.

65. Oja, *Making Music Modern*, 237–51.

66. Thomson, "Greatest Music Teacher," 42.

67. Copland and Perlis, *Copland: 1900 through 1942*, 63–64.

68. Copland and Perlis, 65.

69. Copland, article in *Fontainebleau Alumni Bulletin*, May 1930, as quoted in Leonard, *Conservatoire Américain*, 22. Also see Fauser, "Aaron Copland," 536.

70. Fauser, "Aaron Copland," 535

71. Copland, letter to Boulanger, September 22, 1922, Music Division, Library of Congress, Washington, DC, digital ID copland corr0056. See also Pollack, *Aaron Copland*, 63.

72. Copland, letter to Boulanger, September 22, 1922. Also see Fauser, "Aaron Copland," 535; and Pollack, *Aaron Copland*, 66.

73. Copland, *New York Times*, April 5, 1925. Mengelberg conducted the Second Symphony on March 28 and April 5, 1925. The soloists were Marie Sundelius and Mme Charles Cahier. Copland's letter, though never before analyzed in detail, is reprinted in Kostelanetz, *Copland*, 149–50, and it is discussed, among other places, in Reilly, "Mahler in America," 432n39; Pollack, *Aaron Copland*, 63; Oja, *Making Music Modern*, 240; and Paul, "Converging Paths," 177–78.

74. Copland, letter to Nadia Boulanger, April 3, 1925, Music Division, Library of Congress, Washington, DC, digital ID copland corr0064. This letter is reprinted in Crist and Shirley, *Selected Correspondence*, 46–48.

75. Copland actually referred to the "scherzo" of the Ninth Symphony, but the uncompromising counterpoint of the third movement (Rondo-Burleske) makes it likely he was referring to that movement as the particularly modern one, even though the second movement is more typically called the scherzo. This possibility is proposed in Pollack, *Aaron Copland*, 577n15.

76. Nadia Boulanger, letter to Aaron Copland, 1925, Copland Collection, Music Division, Library of Congress, Washington, DC, 248/9.

77. Copland, letter to Nadia Boulanger, January 5, 1927, Fonds Boulanger, Bibliothèque nationale de France, Paris, NLA 294, 24.

78. Copland, letter to Nadia Boulanger, August 22, 1927, Fonds Boulanger, Bibliothèque nationale de France, Paris, NLA 63, 126–27. Four days before writing this letter, Copland drew the same contrast between Mahler and Strauss in a letter to the American composer Roger Sessions and his wife Barbara. The latter appears in Kostelanetz, *Copland*, 315–16; and Crist and Shirley, *Selected Correspondence*, 56–57. Copland and Sessions are thought to have met at Boulanger's studio in 1926; they soon formed an artistic partnership of their own with the Copland–Sessions Concerts, which began in New York in 1928 and highlighted contemporary American music. See Pollack, *Aaron Copland*, 165, 600n18. On the Copland–Sessions Concerts, see Oja, *Making Music Modern*, 195–97.

79. Thomson, *Musical Scene*, 94. Also see Reilly, "Mahler in America," 431–32.

80. See Pollack, *Aaron Copland*, 520.

81. Mitchell, *Songs and Symphonies*, 69.

82. See DeVoto, "Debussy Sound," 190.

83. Perlis and Van Cleve, *Composers' Voices*, 255–56.

84. Rosenstiel, *Nadia Boulanger*, 336.

85. Gottlieb, e-mail messages to the author, June 25 and 29, 2009.

86. Schonberg, *New York Times*, July 4, 1989.

87. Kosman, *San Francisco Chronicle*, June 7, 1998.

88. La Grange, e-mail message to the author, April 15, 2010.

89. Pedagogy, History of Music, 1935, Talma Notebooks, Louise Talma Collection, Music Division, Library of Congress, Washington, DC. I am grateful to Kimberly Francis for drawing my attention to these materials.

90. On the broader shift from internationalism to nationalism during World War II, see Fauser, *Sounds of War*, 7; and Francis, *Teaching Stravinsky*, 120.

91. See Francis, *Teaching Stravinsky*, 69–70.

92. See Brooks, *Musical Work*, 142.

93. On Boulanger's time in the United States, see Rosenstiel, *Nadia Boulanger*, 307–30. On her travels to England, see Spycket, *Boulanger*, 140–42.

Chapter Three

1. Copland, *New York Times*, April 5, 1925.

2. See Coster, "Mengelberg's Mahler."

3. Gilman, *New York Herald Tribune*, March 30, 1925.

4. Sanborn, *Telegram Mail*, April 6, 1925, as quoted in Coster, "Mengelberg's Mahler," 285.

5. Langley, "Justice for Gustav Mahler," 164.

6. In addition to the Mahler festival in Amsterdam in 1920, there was a similar festival in Vienna the same year, and another in Wiesbaden, Germany, in 1921.

7. Oja, *Making Music Modern*, 241.

8. Langley, "Justice for Gustav Mahler," 161–62.

9. Langley, 162.

10. Paul, "Converging Paths," 177–78.

11. Oja, *Making Music Modern*, 232–35. Also see Messing, "Polemic as History."

12. Oja, 234.

13. Aldrich, *New York Times*, February 11, 1906.

14. Aldrich, *New York Times*, March 9, 1923.

15. Copland, "Modern Orchestration," 43.

16. Copland and Perlis, *Copland: 1900 through 1942*, 91.

17. On the American popularity of *Pacific 231*, see Oja, *Making Music Modern*, 65 and 418n12.

18. Downes, *New York Times*, November 3, 1924.

19. Oja, *Making Music Modern*, 54.

20. Perlis and Van Cleve, *Composers' Voices*, 302–3.

21. Boulanger, "Lectures," 147–48.

22. Copland, letter to Boulanger, August 26, 1924, Music Division, Library of Congress, Washington, DC, digital ID copland corr0062.

23. Pollack, *Aaron Copland*, 125.

24. Oja, *Making Music Modern*, 305.

25. Copland, "Composer from Brooklyn," 548.

26. Damrosch, *My Musical Life*, 354–55. Also see Reilly, "Mahler in America," 423.

27. Ivry, *Poulenc*, 38.

28. Milhaud and Rostand, *Interviews*, 52.

29. As quoted in Halbreich, *Honegger*, 310.

30. Pollack, *Aaron Copland*, 67.

31. Oja, *Making Music Modern*, 65.

32. See Johnson, *Mahler's Voices*, 28.

33. Copland, *Our New Music*, 35.

34. Tomatz, "Rubin Goldmark, Postromantic," 61.

35. See Rutkoff and Scott, *New School*, 63 and 80–82.

36. Oja, *Making Music Modern*, 198.

37. Bick, "New School," 130.

38. See Oja, *Making Music Modern*, 304–5, and Bick, "New School," 144.

39. Cone, "Conversation with Aaron Copland," 65.

40. *New York Times*, January 16, 1927. See *The New School for Social Research, Announcement, Spring Term 1927*, General Course Catalogs, New School Archives, Digital Collections (http://digitalarchives.library.newschool.edu/index.php/Detail/objects/NS050101_ns1927sp), p. 21.

41. *The New School for Social Research, Inc.: 1933 Spring*, General Course Catalogs, New School Archives, Digital Collections (http://digitalarchives.library.newschool.edu/index.php/Detail/objects/NS050101_ns1933sp), p. 28.

42. Copland, Lecture 10 in "Aesthetics of Modern Music," Copland Collection, Music Division, Library of Congress, Washington, DC, 210/8, 46–50. See Bick, "New School," 144n59. In Copland and Perlis, *Copland: 1900 through 1942*, 139, it is actually labeled "The Appreciation of Modern Music," and it was reported there that enrollment for the course was 68.

43. In the quotations from Copland's notes, I have retained the the truncated language of his handwritten notes. For the sake of readability, I have silently removed Copland's inconsistent capitalizations of several

words. In some cases, frayed edges on lecture pages mean that small amounts of text have been lost.

44. *The New School for Social Research Announcement, 1927 Fall*, General Course Catalogs, New School Archives, Digital Collections (http://digitalarchives.library.newschool.edu/index.php/Detail/objects/NS050101_ns1927fa), p. 29.

45. Copland, Lecture 4 in "Masterworks of Modern Music," Copland Collection, Music Division, Library of Congress, Washington, DC, 212/23, 16–19.

46. *Musical America*, April 2, 1921.

47. Copland, "Music between the Wars," 57.

48. Copland, *Our New Music*, 34.

49. Copland and Perlis, *Copland: 1900 through 1942*, 183.

50. Copland, Lecture 3 in "Forms of Modern Music," Copland Collection, Music Division, Library of Congress, Washington, DC, 211/35, 17–22.

51. *The New School for Social Research, Announcement, 1929–1930, Fall*, General Course Catalogs, New School Archives, Digital Collections (http://digitalarchives.library.newschool.edu/index.php/Detail/objects/NS050101_ns1929fa), p. 25.

52. Copland, *What to Listen for in Music*, 196.

53. *The New School for Social Research, 1935–1936*, General Course Catalogs, New School Archives, Digital Collections (http://digitalarchives.library.newschool.edu/index.php/Detail/objects/NS050101_ns1935ye), p. 55. Notes for the Mahler session itself appear as Lecture 2 in "Music of Today," Copland Collection, Music Division, Library of Congress, Washington, DC, 213/17, 7–11 (p. 9 mistakenly resides in 212/23, with "Masterworks of Modern Music").

54. Fauser, *Sounds of War*, 136.

55. Pollack, *Aaron Copland*, 67–68.

56. Copland "Music between the Wars," 58–59.

57. Oja, *Making Music Modern*, 244. Also see Tischler, *An American Music*, 107.

58. Crist, "Aaron Copland and the Popular Front."

59. Copland, "Modern Orchestration Surveyed," 43.

60. Crist, *Music for the Common Man*, 74.

61. Copland, Lecture 7 in "Symphonic Masterpieces," Copland Collection, Music Division, Library of Congress, Washington, DC, 214/40, 23–25.

62. *Curriculum, The New School for Social Research, Spring 1939*, General Course catalogs, New School Archives, Digital Collections (http://digitalarchives.library.newschool.edu/index.php/Detail/objects/NS050101_ns1939sp), p. 15.

63. Copland, "Composer from Brooklyn," 550; and Crist, "Aaron Copland and the Popular Front," 410.

64. Fauser, *Sounds of War*, 255–57.

65. See Fauser, 264–67; and Crist, "Third Symphony," 377–78.

66. *Curriculum: The New School for Social Research, Spring 1939*, p. 15.

67. Rutkoff and Scott, *New School*, 26.

68. Copland, letter to Nadia Boulanger, October 16, 1927, Music Division, Library of Congress, Washington, DC, digital ID copland corr0094.

69. Cone, "Conversation with Aaron Copland," 65.

70. Copland, *Our New Music*, 32–33.

71. Copland, 62.

72. Copland, 32.

73. Copland, 30.

74. See Fauser, "Aaron Copland," 543.

75. Pollack, *Aaron Copland*, 222.

76. Downes, *New York Times*, October 19, 1941.

77. "Mahler (XX Cent[ury])," Music Division, Library of Congress, Washington, DC, digital IDs copland writ0077 and writ0078. I am grateful to Robin Elliott, Allan Morris, and Sara Scott Turner for their assistance in locating information on this lecture. The two groups of lectures notes indicated here appear to have been for the same lecture.

78. "Mahler (XX Cent[ury])," Music Division, Library of Congress, Washington, DC, digital ID copland writ0078.

79. Copland, *Our New Music*, 63.

80. Copland, *New York Times*, October 20, 1957.

81. Goldberg, *Los Angeles Times*, May 26, 1958.

Chapter Four

1. Locke, "Two Interviews," 211–12.

2. Pollack, *Aaron Copland*, 142–45.

3. Copland and Perlis, *Copland: 1900 through 1942*, 162.

4. Goldstein, *Price of Whiteness*, 119–22.

5. Levy, *Frontier Figures*, 300–302. Also see Murchison, *American Stravinsky*, 131–47, and Botstein, *Copland Reconfigured*, 454–71.

6. Mason, "American Music."

7. Copland, *Our New Music*, 83.

8. Copland, "What Is Jewish Music?"

9. Pollack, *Aaron Copland*, 524.

10. Pollack, 523–24.

11. Copland, letter to Bernstein, Music Division, Library of Congress, Washington, DC, digital ID lbcorr 01080. See Pollack, *Aaron Copland*, 522–23.

12. Goldstein, *Price of Whiteness*, 166–67.

13. Goldstein, 190.

14. Copland, "Memorial," 147.

15. Copland and Perlis, *Copland: 1900 through 1942*, 32.

16. Copland, "Memorial," 148.
17. Rosenfeld, *Musical Portraits*, 285–86.
18. Rosenfeld, 287.
19. Rosenfeld, 289.
20. Rosenfeld, 293–94.
21. Rosenfeld, 206–8.
22. Rosenfeld, 209.
23. Rosenfeld, 214.
24. Rosenfeld, *Musical Chronicle*, 244–45.
25. See Oja, *Making Music Modern*, 307–8.
26. Rosenfeld, *Musical Portraits*, 287.
27. Copland, "Jewish Composers in the Western World," Copland Collection, Music Division, Library of Congress, Washington, DC, 212/17.
28. Copland, *Our New Music*, 32.
29. Rosenfeld, *Musical Portraits*, 217–20.
30. Copland, *Our New Music*, 31.
31. Rosenfeld, *Musical Portraits*, 215.
32. Rosenfeld, 220.
33. Rosenfeld, "Tragedy," 266.
34. Rosenfeld, *Musical Portraits*, 220.
35. Copland, *Our New Music*, 31–32
36. Rosenfeld, *Musical Portraits*, 211 and 213.
37. Rosenfeld, *Musical Chronicle*, 239 and 241.
38. Rosenfeld, *Musical Portraits*, 214.
39. Rosenfeld, *Musical Chronicle*, 240.
40. Rosenfeld, *Musical Portraits*, 209.
41. Rosenfeld, *Musical Chronicle*, 241.
42. Rosenfeld, *Musical Portraits*, 213.
43. Rosenfeld, *Musical Chronicle*, 239.
44. Rosenfeld, *Musical Portraits*, 221.
45. Rosenfeld, 266.
46. Oja, *Making Music Modern*, 125–126.
47. Copland and Perlis, *Copland: 1900 through 1942*, 165.
48. Copland and Perlis, 183.
49. Cone, "Conversation with Aaron Copland," 64.
50. Pollack, *Aaron Copland*, 524.
51. Pollack, 524.

Chapter Five

1. Copland and Perlis, *Copland: Since 1943*, 159.
2. "Mahler (XX Cent[ury])," Music Division, Library of Congress, Washington, DC, digital ID copland writ0078.

3. Mellers, "Mahler," 349.

4. Copland, Lecture 2 in "Music of Today," Copland Collection, Music Division, Library of Congress, Washington, DC, 213/17, 7–11

5. Copland, *Our New Music*, 30.

6. Tilson Thomas, "Mahler in America."

7. Feder, *Mahler*, 151.

8. Johnson, "Status of Subject," 111.

9. La Grange, *Gustav Mahler*, 1411.

10. Copland and Diether, "Record Collecting," 66–67.

11. Johnson, "Status of Subject," 112–13.

12. Johnson, 112.

13. See Pesson, "Mahler and Debussy," 167.

14. Copland and Perlis, *Copland: 1900 through 1942*, 119–20.

15. Copland and Perlis, 120.

16. "Mahler (XX Cent[ury])," Music Division, Library of Congress, Washington DC, digital ID copland writ0078.

17. Copland and Perlis, 120.

18. See Banfield, "Broadway Sound," 154, where a link is suggested between *Das Lied* and such descending passages in *Music for the Theatre* and elsewhere in Copland's oeuvre.

19. Copland and Perlis, *Copland: 1900 through 1942*, 120.

20. Copland and Perlis, 124–25.

21. Starr, "Solitary Contemplation," 297.

22. Starr, 300 and 315.

23. Starr, 314.

24. Crist, *Music for the Common Man*, 171–72.

25. I am grateful to David Conte for pointing out to me a relationship between the treatment of diatonicism at the end of *Das Lied* and the beginning of *Appalachian Spring*.

26. Grofé, "Grand Canyon Suite," 16.

27. Toliver, "Eco-ing in the Canyon," 347.

28. As quoted in Toliver, 360.

29. Riley and Smith, *Nation and Classical Music*, 133.

30. Riley and Smith, 132.

31. Riley and Smith, 135.

32. Riley and Smith, 136.

33. Starr, "Solitary Contemplation," 300.

34. See Lebrecht, *Why Mahler?*, 253.

35. Holloway, "Howard's Way," 54.

36. Pollack, *Aaron Copland*, 484.

37. Copland and Diether, "Record Collecting."

38. Pisani, "Creating Native American Identities," 256.

39. Lerner, "Wide Open Spaces," 482– 83.

40. Crist, *Music for the Common Man*, 124.

41. Lerner, "Wide Open Spaces," 503 and 514n88.

42. Schiff, *New York Times,* November 4, 2001.

43. Copland, *What to Listen for in Music,* 196.

44. Copland and Perlis, *Copland: Since 1943,* 68. In his article on Mahler's American reception, Edward R. Reilly wrote of Copland that "many of his own works betray little, if any, trace of Mahler's influence," but that "certain compositions, such as the Third Symphony, do suggest his admiration for Mahler's textures and scoring" (Reilly, "Mahler in America," 436).

45. Pollack, *Aaron Copland,* 415.

46. Copland and Perlis, *Copland: 1900 through 1942,* 165.

47. Copland and Perlis, 183.

48. Pollack, *Aaron Copland,* 149. On the same page, Pollack also suggested of the *Ode* that "in contrast to Mahler, the piece is terrifically sober and austere."

49. "Mahler (XX Cent[ury])," Music Division, Library of Congress, Washington, DC, digital ID copland writ0077.

50. Copland, letter to Natalie Koussevitzky, October 29, 1931, Music Division, Library of Congress, Washington, DC, digital ID copland corr0159.

51. Aaron Copland, letter to Nadia Boulanger, January 5, 1927, Fonds Boulanger, Bibliothèque nationale de France, Paris, NLA 294, 24.

52. Copland, letter to Nadia Boulanger, April 3, 1925, Music Division, Library of Congress, Washington, DC, digital ID copland corr0064. This letter is reprinted in Crist and Shirley, *Selected Correspondence,* 46–48.

Chapter Six

1. La Grange, *Gustav Mahler,* 141 and 364–65.

2. La Grange, 153 and 677.

3. See Lang, "Mahler's American Debut," 240–62.

4. Baltimore newspapers reported that the BSO performed the Adagietto as a separate piece at its concert at the Lyric Opera House. See *Baltimore Sun,* February 15, 1906, in Boston Symphony Orchestra Archives scrapbooks, vol. 23, 163.

5. See Kaplan, "Adagietto," 380n6.

6. Except where stated otherwise, information in this section on dates of the BSO's Mahler performances was culled from a report generated in November 2007 from the computerized repertory database at the Boston Symphony Orchestra Archives. I wish to thank Bridget Carr at the BSO Archives for providing me with this report.

7. These performances took place December 7–8, 1928; December 26–27, 1930; November 6–7, 1936; and February 12–13, 1937. The 1937 performance took place at Carnegie Hall in New York.

8. Koussevitzky conducted the Ninth Symphony on October 16–17, 1931; November 9, 1931; November 19, 1931 (at Carnegie Hall); January 9, 1932 (at Carnegie Hall); December 8–9, 1933; Marcy 27–28, 1936; February 28–March 1, 1941; and March 13, 1941 (at Carnegie Hall). He also performed the symphony's fourth movement as a stand-alone on April 2, 1936 (at Carnegie Hall) and December 8–9, 1939.

9. The dates of his performances of the Fifth Symphony were October 22–23, 1937; March 4–5, 1938; March 10, 1938 (at Carnegie Hall); and March 1–2, 1940.

10. Mitropoulos conducted Mahler's First Symphony January 31–February 1, 1936, and Walter conducted it January 15–16, 1942. Among Burgin's performances of Mahler's works were *Das Lied* on December 3–4, 1943; the third and fourth movements of the Fourth Symphony in late January and early February of 1942; and the Fifth Symphony November 19–21, 1948.

11. Performances at Symphony Hall took place February 6–7, 1948, and March 25–26, 1949. The Tanglewood performance was August 1, 1948.

12. Koussevitzky conducted the Seventh Symphony October 15–16, 1948. The *Das Lied* performance took place at Tanglewood on August 6, 1949.

13. See Reilly, "Mahler in America," 428–29.

14. Reilly, 429.

15. Crawford, *America's Musical Life*, 582.

16. Exceptions include a brief mention in Reilly, "Mahler in America," 429–30, and a more detailed summary in Page, "Resurrection," 99–124.

17. Flerlage, "America and Gustav Mahler," 426.

18. See Moses Smith, *Koussevitzky*, 36–37.

19. Lourié, *Serge Koussevitzky*, 50.

20. Moses Smith, *Koussevitzky*, 64–67.

21. Copland, "Serge Koussevitzky," 255.

22. Copland and Perlis, *Copland: 1900 through 1942*, 92.

23. See Leichtentritt, *Serge Koussevitzky*, 151–57, and Moses Smith, *Koussevitzky*, 338.

24. *Boston Globe*, September 16, 1923.

25. *Boston Globe*, September 13, 1924.

26. See the list of premieres on the Boston Symphony Orchestra's website, at http://www.bso.org/brands/bso/about-us/historyarchives/archival-collection/american-premieres-at-the-bso/american-premieres-the-1920s.aspx. Also see, Moses Smith, *Koussevitzky*, 147–48.

27. *Boston Globe*, September 21, 1924.

28. *Boston Herald*, September 13, 1924, found in "Programs, Clippings and Pictures, May 1924 to August 1939," a compilation of materials relating to Koussevitzky. The compilation resides in the Music Department at the Boston Public Library.

29. *Boston Globe*, September 28, 1924.

30. Roberts, *Boston Globe*, January 17, 1925.

31. Somervell, *Boston Globe*, October 9, 1927.

32. *Boston Globe*, April 29, 1928.

33. *Boston Globe*, October 27, 1929.

34. Roberts, *Boston Globe*, April 5, 1930.

35. Roberts, *Boston Globe*, January 17, 1925.

36. Moses Smith, *Koussevitzky*, 164–67.

37. Downes, *New York Times*, November 25, 1928. See Moses Smith, *Koussevitzky*, 170. One of the assistants was Nicolas Slonimsky, who appeared sitting at the piano in a picture in the *Boston Globe* under the headline, "'My Secretary Knows More than I Do'—The Boss" (Corinne Danforth, *Boston Globe*, January 16, 1927). This *Globe* piece did not suggest that Slonimsky was actually filling Koussevitzky's musical duties, but it apparently angered Koussevitzky, anyway. See Moses Smith, *Koussevitzky*, 171–72.

38. Downes, *New York Times*, November 25, 1928.

39. Fecher, *Diary of H. L. Mencken*, 24–25. Courtesy of Sebastian Stockman.

40. See Moses Smith, *Koussevitzky*, 164.

41. George Henry Lovett Smith, *Boston Evening Transcript*, June 22, 1935, as it appeared in Boston Symphony Orchestra Season Announcement 1935–36, BSO Printed Matter, Boston Symphony Orchestra Archives, Boston, MA.

42. Moses Smith, *Koussevitzky*, 184. See Boston Symphony Orchestra, Programme, Forty-Fourth Season, 1924–1925, 1981. The count includes instances in which works were repeated, but it does not distinguish between works Koussevitzky conducted and those that were programmed that season but not conducted by Koussevitzky.

43. Boston Symphony Orchestra, Programme, Forty-Third Season, 1923–1924, 1792. As with the count for Koussevitzky, this one includes instances in which works were repeated, but it does not distinguish between works Monteux conducted and those that were programmed that season but that Monteux did not conduct.

44. *Boston Globe*, October 1, 1930.

45. *Boston Post*, October 1, 1931. This article is found in the Boston Symphony Orchestra Archives scrapbooks, vol. 54, 10.

46. *New York Times*, September 27, 1931.

47. *New York Herald Tribune*, September 30, 1931. This article is found in the Boston Symphony Orchestra Archives scrapbooks, vol. 54, 6.

48. Grey, *New York Times*, July 27, 1930.

49. Downes, *New York Times*, April 11, 1926.

50. See Banks, "Mahler and Viennese Modernism."

51. *Boston Evening Transcript*, January 13, 1932. This article is found in the Boston Symphony Orchestra archives scrapbooks, vol. 54, 95. Here, the caption (under pictures of both sides of the medal) reads "Medal of Honor Bestowed upon Dr. Koussevitzky Last Saturday in New York by the Bruckner-Mahler Society of America to Mark His Production in Boston

and New York, This Season, of Mahler's Ninth Symphony. In Appreciation as Well of His Zeal for Both Composers."

52. This conclusion is implied in Kurt Blaukopf, *Mahler*, 243, and Reilly, "Mahler in America," 429–30. Also see Engel, "New Symphonic Horizons," 3.

53. Taubman, *New York Times*, July 20, 1931.

54. Engel, *Gustav Mahler*, 118. On Engel's role in founding the group, see the memorial note after the table of contents in *Chord and Discord* 2, no. 7 (1954).

55. Koussevitzky, "Dr. Serge Koussevitzky on Mahler," 15.

56. Document in Koussevitzky Archive, Music Division, Library of Congress, Washington, DC, 13/20. This document by Copland was quoted in Pollack, *Aaron Copland*, 63, and it was discussed as Koussevitzky's own in Page, "Resurrection," 14–15. The passage in Copland's handwriting is nearly identical to the one printed in *Chord and Discord*; the only significant difference is that in the handwritten version, after "every artist," the words "who deserves the name" appear, but are faded.

57. Copland, letter to Boulanger, July 25, 1923, Music Division, Library of Congress, Washington, DC, digital ID copland corr0058, as quoted and translated in Crist and Shirley, *Selected Correspondence*, 40.

58. Koussevitzky, letter to Copland, November 29, 1928, Copland Collection, Music Division, Library of Congress, Washington, DC, 257/27.

59. Letter to Serge Koussevitzky, n.d., Music Division, Library of Congress, Washington, DC, digital ID copland corr0517. Although it is undated, the letter was clearly a reply to Koussevitzky's.

60. Letter to Serge Koussevitzky, December 4, 1928, Music Division, Library of Congress, Washington, DC, digital ID copland corr0118.

61. The letter was appeared in Boston Symphony Orchestra, Programme, Fifty-First Season, 1931–1932, 100–102.

62. Letter to Aaron Copland, February 14, 1928, Copland Collection, Music Division, Library of Congress, Washington, DC, 257/27.

63. Letter to Aaron Copland, February 15, 1928, Copland Collection, Music Division, Library of Congress, Washington, DC, 257/27. On Copland's encounter with *Oedipus Rex* in 1927, see Pollack, *Aaron Copland*, 139.

64. Koussevitzky, letter to Aaron Copland, November 29, 1928, Copland Collection, Music Division, Library of Congress, Washington, DC, 257/27

65. See Moses Smith, *Koussevitzky*, 209.

66. Copland's notes for his New School lecture on Mussorgsky's work from that fall are found in "Masterworks of Modern Music," Copland Collection, Music Division, Library of Congress, Washington, DC, 212/23.

67. Pollack, *Aaron Copland*, 34

68. Brant, transcript of interview with Vincent Plush, 45.

69. Pollack, *Aaron Copland*, 123.

70. Crist and Shirley, *Selected Correspondence*, 67.

71. Pollack, *Aaron Copland*, 204.

72. Moses Smith, *Boston American*, December 8, 1928. This article is found in the Boston Symphony Orchestra Archives scrapbooks, vol. 51, 37.

73. Roberts, *Boston Globe*, December 8, 1928.

74. Sloper, *Christian Science Monitor*, December 8, 1928. This article is found in the Boston Symphony Orchestra Archives scrapbooks, vol. 51, 37.

75. Moses Smith, *Boston American*, December 8, 1928.

76. Meyer, *Boston Evening Transcript*, December 27, 1930. This article is found in the Boston Symphony Orchestra archives scrapbooks, vol. 53, 87.

77. Moses Smith, *Boston American*, October 17, 1931. This article is found in the Boston Symphony Orchestra Archives scrapbooks, vol. 54, 22.

78. Roberts, *Boston Globe*, October 17, 1931.

79. Warren Storey Smith, *Boston Post*, October 17, 1931. This article is found in the Boston Symphony Orchestra Archives scrapbooks vol. 54, 22. Smith was referring to former BSO conductor Karl Muck's concerts of the Fifth Symphony.

80. Hale, *Boston Herald*, October 17, 1931. This article is found in the Boston Symphony Orchestra Archives scrapbooks, vol. 54, 21.

81. *Boston Evening Transcript*, October 17, 1931. This article is found in the Boston Symphony Orchestra Archives scrapbooks, vol. 54, 22. The author of the review is identified only by the initials J. D.

82. Moses Smith, *Boston American*, October 17, 1931.

83. Sloper, *Christian Science Monitor*, October 17, 1931. This article is found in the Boston Symphony Orchestra Archives scrapbooks, vol. 54, 21.

84. Durgin, *Boston Globe*, November 7, 1936.

85. This was reported in the December 1936 volume of *Chord and Discord*.

86. See Reilly, "Mahler in America," 429–30.

87. Ewen, *Dictators*, 97.

88. Durgin, *Boston Globe*, November 27, 1948.

89. Ewen, *Dictators*, 97.

90. Krehbiel, *New York Tribune*, May 10, 1914, and Hackett, *Chicago Evening Post*, April 16, 1921. The latter article is found in the clippings files of the Chicago Symphony Orchestra's Rosenthal Archives.

91. Straus, *New York Times*, April 13, 1942.

92. A list of timings affixed to the penultimate leaf of Leonard Bernstein's score of the Second Symphony held at the New York Philharmonic Archives, available online in the Leon Levy Digital Collection, indicates that this performance was abridged (http://archives.nyphil.org, ID:1819).

93. Koussevitzky, "Poetry and Music," 3.

94. Copland, *What to Listen for in Music*, 196.

95. Rosenfeld, "After Mahler's 'Ninth,'" 245.

96. The movement timing is listed as 14:32 under the date October 15, 1948, but under October 16, 1948, the last movement is labeled "with cut" next to a time of 9:07.

97. Floros, *Mahler*, 290.

98. See Pickett, "Mahler on Record," 349.

99. Floros, *Mahler*, 287.

100. Hale, *Boston Herald*, October 17, 1931.

101. Copland, *New York Times*, September 21, 1952.

102. On Koussevitzky's preferences, see Horowitz, *Classical Music in America*, 302.

Chapter Seven

1. See Hart, *Orpheus*, 400; Horowitz, *Classical Music in America*, 479; Reilly, "Mahler in America," 434; Keller, "Bernstein and Mahler," 191; and Page, "Resurrection."

2. Keller, "Bernstein and Mahler," 177.

3. Page, "Resurrection," 114.

4. Seldes, *Leonard Bernstein*, 146. On Walter, also see Ryding and Pechefsky, *Bruno Walter*, 318 and 400; and Page, "Resurrection," 194–95.

5. Peyser, *Bernstein*, 298; and Hubbs, "Bernstein, Homophobia, Historiography," 30.

6. See Laird and Lin, *Leonard Bernstein*, 4; Pollack, *Aaron Copland*, 194–197; and Julia Smith, *Aaron Copland*, 289.

7. See Copland and Perlis, *Copland: Since 1943*, 232; Page and Page, *Selected Letters*, 198; Burton, *Leonard Bernstein*, 255; Pollack, *Aaron Copland*, 198; Secrest, *Leonard Bernstein*, 307; and Page, "Resurrection," 152–54.

8. See interview with Phillip Ramey in Copland and Perlis, *Copland: Since 1943*, 353; and Pollack, *Aaron Copland*, 198.

9. Seldes, *Leonard Bernstein*, 145. The passage Seldes quoted comes from Aaron Copland, *Our New Music* (New York, 1941), 31.

10. Pollack, Review of Barry Seldes, 762.

11. Schiff, *New York Times*, November 4, 2001.

12. See Meckna, "Copland, Sessions, and Modern Music," 198–204; and Meckna, "Rise of the Composer-Critic."

13. Meckna, "Copland, Sessions, and Modern Music," 204.

14. See, for example, the biographical summary in Laird and Lin, *Leonard Bernstein*, where the account of life and works is divided into sections on Bernstein as conductor, composer, educator and commentator, and pianist; and Gradenwitz, *Infinite Variety*, where a separate section on Bernstein as a performer precedes a discussion of his compositions. A notable exception is Joseph Horowitz, who suggested that Bernstein's programming choices at the New York Philharmonic related to his concerns as a composer (Horowitz, "As Music Director," 142–51).

15. Hubbs, "Bernstein," 24.

16. On Copland as Bernstein's compositional influence, see, for example, Pollack, *Aaron Copland,* 194; and Schiller, *Bloch, Schoenberg, and Bernstein,* 163–65.

17. See Bernstein, "Who Is Gustav Mahler," and the discussions in Page, "Resurrection," 238; Keller, "Bernstein and Mahler," 174–75; Paul, "Converging Paths," 373–74; and Myers, *Leonard Bernstein,* 53.

18. Brant, interview with Vincent Plush, 45 and 64–66. Also see Pollack, *Aaron Copland,* 186–88.

19. Brant, letter to Copland, September 22, 1930, Copland Collection, Music Division, Library of Congress, Washington, DC, 249/1.

20. Adler, e-mail messages to author, November 14 and 15, 2010.

21. Adler, *Study of Orchestration,* 512–13.

22. Bernstein, letter to Copland, November 19, 1938, Copland Collection, Music Division, Library of Congress, Washington, DC, 247/1, as quoted in Burton, *Leonard Bernstein,* 50. On Bernstein's thesis and its relationship with his concert programming, see Horowitz, "As Music Director," 142.

23. Interview with Bernstein in Copland and Perlis, *Copland: 1900 through 1942,* 339. Also see Pollack, *Aaron Copland,* 194.

24. Copland, letter to Bernstein, Music Division, Library of Congress, Washington, DC, digital ID musbernstein 100065052.

25. Parmenter, *New York Times,* November 10, 1940.

26. See Pollack, *Aaron Copland,* 195.

27. According to Fülöp, *Mahler Discography,* 172–73, the earliest LP release of Mahler's Seventh Symphony was by Hans Rosbaud and the Berlin Radio Symphony Orchestra, recorded in 1952.

28. Bernstein, "Aaron Copland," 54.

29. Copland, letter to Bernstein, September 1939, Music Division, Library of Congress, Washington, DC, digital ID lbcorr 01080.

30. Bernstein, letter to Copland, Copland Collection, Music Division, Library of Congress, Washington, DC, 247/1. The standard German form of the third word would actually be "Ungeduldiges."

31. See Perlis, "Dear Aaron, Dear Lenny," and Pollack, *Aaron Copland,* 195. Bernstein also used the greetings "Aaron, liebchen" and "Aaronchen, liebchen" around this time. See Simone, *Leonard Bernstein Letters,* 85 and 89.

32. Durgin, *Boston Globe,* January 31, 1942.

33. Peyser, *Bernstein,* 57.

34. Bernstein, letter to Copland, November 12, 1959, Copland Collection, Music Division, Library of Congress, Washington, DC, 247/2. See Simone, *Leonard Bernstein Letters,* 422–23; and Pollack, *Aaron Copland,* 196.

35. Bernstein, letter to Olga Naumova [1943], Koussevitzky Archive, Music Division, Library of Congress, Washington, DC, 6/5. See Page, "Resurrection," 113.

36. Blitzstein, "New York Medley," 39, and Blitzstein, "London," 118. I am grateful to Howard Pollack for drawing my attention to materials relating to Blitzstein's encounters with Mahler's music. Blitzstein wrote to Nadia Boulanger in 1927 that he had been studying Mahler's Sixth Symphony and *Das Lied von der Erde* with Arnold Schoenberg; see Pollack, *Blitzstein,* 31.

37. Bernstein, "Who Is Gustav Mahler?"

38. Page, "Resurrection," 56–57 and 146.

39. Page, 99–112.

40. Page, 146. Bernstein included the opening of the First Symphony's third movement in the Young People's Concert "Humor in Music" in 1959.

41. Page, 212–13 and 244–54.

42. *Boston Globe,* 22 September 1940.

43. Interview with Bernstein in Copland and Perlis, *Copland: 1900 through 1942,* 340.

44. Johnson, *New York Post,* April 14, 1959. See Page, "Resurrection," 50.

45. Copland, letter to Bernstein, September 24, 1947, Music Division, Library of Congress, Washington, DC, digital ID lbcorr 01125. See Crist and Shirley, *Selected Correspondence,* 184.

46. Copland, letter to Bernstein, September 23, 1958, Music Division, Library of Congress, Washington, DC, digital ID lbcorr 01133.

47. Pollack, *Aaron Copland,* 198.

48. See Horowitz, "As Music Director," 140–42.

49. Interview with Bernstein in Copland and Perlis, *Copland: 1900 through 1942,* 334.

50. Bernstein, "Aaron Copland," 55. See Copland and Perlis, *Copland: Since 1943,* 367–68; and Perlis, "Dear Aaron, Dear Lenny," 174–75.

51. Copland, *New York Times,* October 20, 1957.

52. Taubman, *New York Times,* October 26, 1957.

53. Bernstein, letter to Copland, November 14, 1951, Copland Collection, Music Division, Library of Congress, Washington, DC, 247/1. See Pollack, *Aaron Copland,* 197; Copland and Perlis, *Copland: Since 1943,* 154; and Simone, *Leonard Bernstein Letters,* 292–93.

54. Hutchison, "Stylistic and Pianistic Evaluation," 11–12.

55. Copland and Cone, "Conversation with Aaron Copland."

56. Ansari, *Sound of a Superpower,* 139

57. Bernstein, *Joy of Music,* 222. See Ansari, *Sound of a Superpower,* 175.

58. See Helen Smith, *There's a Place for Us,* 248.

59. See Bernstein, *Joy of Music,* 180–224.

60. Also see the preview version of these passages in Copland, "Five Post-Romantics." Bernstein himself sometimes contributed to *Modern Music.*

61. Copland, *Our New Music,* 31–32.

62. Bernstein, "New York Philharmonic Preview," typescript with emendations in pencil and blue pencil, January 28, 1960, Music Division, Library

of Congress, Washington, DC, digital ID lbtep 0302. See Page, "Resurrection," 193–99.

63. Copland, *Our New Music,* 30.

64. Copland, 32–33.

65. Bernstein, "New York Philharmonic Preview." Also see Seldes, *Leonard Bernstein,* 104–5.

66. Copland, *Our New Music,* 102.

67. Copland, "Compositional Techniques in the 20th Cent[ury]," Copland Collection, Music Division, Library of Congress, Washington, DC, 210/39.

68. Bernstein, *Joy of Music,* 209–10.

69. Bernstein, 210–16.

70. Bernstein, 202–10.

71. Bernstein, "New York Philharmonic Preview."

72. Bernstein, *Joy of Music,* 203.

73. Bernstein, "New York Philharmonic Preview."

74. Bernstein, *Joy of Music,* 208.

75. Copland, *Our New Music,* 33–34.

76. Bernstein, "New York Philharmonic Preview."

77. See Ansari, *Sound of a Superpower,* 175–77.

78. Newlin, "Mahler and Beyond."

79. Shanet, "Conversation Piece."

80. Boretz, "Records," 536.

81. The passage is from the film *Four Ways to Say Farewell,* as quoted in Keller, "Bernstein and Mahler," 176, where Bernstein's performance practice is discussed further.

82. Botstein, "Whose Gustav Mahler?," 17.

83. Steinberg, *Boston Globe,* December 19, 1965.

84. Kelly, *Boston Globe,* August 7, 1960.

85. Bernstein, *Joy of Music,* 222. See Ansari, *Sound of a Superpower,* 175.

86. Helen Smith, *There's a Place for Us,* 247n7. Also see Gottlieb, *Working with Bernstein,* 146.

87. See Bushard, *Waterfront,* 185n35.

88. Bernstein, "What I Thought," *New York Times,* October 24, 1965. For an overview of changes in Bernstein's musical outlook, see Horowitz, *Classical Music in America,* 480–82.

89. Bernstein, *Infinite Variety,* 10.

90. Bernstein, 13.

91. Bernstein, 13. Also see Schiller, *Bloch, Schoenberg, and Bernstein,* 146.

92. Bernstein, "Mahler: His Time Has Come," 52. See Seldes, *Leonard Bernstein,* 104–6.

93. Bernstein, 54.

94. Copland, *Our New Music,* 30.

95. Bernstein, *Unanswered Question,* 265. Barry Seldes also noted this similarity between Copland's passage from *Our New Music* and Bernstein's

discussion of Mahler in the Norton Lectures. See Seldes, *Leonard Bernstein,* 133 and 241n8.

96. Bernstein, *Unanswered Question,* 319.

97. See Helen Smith, *There's a Place for Us, 165–67; and Swayne, Orpheus in Manhattan, 317.*

98. See Helen Smith, 166.

99. Helen Smith, 126 and 249–50.

100. Ansari, *Sound of a Superpower,* 185.

101. See, for instance, LaFave, *Experiencing Leonard Bernstein,* 144.

102. Schiller, *Bloch, Schoenberg, and Bernstein,* 158.

103. See Ansari, *Sound of a Superpower,* 179.

104. Bernstein, "Mahler: His Time Has Come," 53.

105. Ansari, *Sound of a Superpower,* 177. Schiller interprets "Kaddish" differently, arguing that it aimed for a reconciliation of twelve-tone writing and tonality. See Schiller, *Bloch, Schoenberg, and Bernstein,* 159–162.

106. Schiller, *Bloch, Schoenberg, and Bernstein,* 149–50.

107. Bernstein, "Who Is Gustav Mahler?"

108. See Paul, "Converging Paths," 174, where the author notes that "the promulgated image of the composer was a thinly self-disguised portrait of the promoter." On Bernstein's use of military metaphors, see Ansari, *Sound of a Superpower,* 175.

109. See Helen Smith, *There's a Place for Us,* 247–54.

110. DeLapp[-Birkett], "Copland in the Fifties," 221. Also see DeLapp-Birkett, "Copland and the Politics of Twelve-Tone Composition."

111. Copland, *New York Times,* November 27, 1949.

112. DeLapp[-Birkett], "Copland in the Fifties, 209.

113. Bernstein, "And What I Did," *New York Times,* October 24, 1965. See Ansari, *Sound of a Superpower,* 180–81.

114. Bernstein, *Unanswered Question,* 319.

115. Gottlieb, *Working with Bernstein,* 332.

116. Bernstein, *Joy of Music,* 214.

117. Botstein, "Whose Gustav Mahler?," 17.

118. Gottlieb, "Symbols of Faith," 292–93. See Schiller, *Bloch, Schoenberg, and Bernstein,* 133–34.

119. See Page, "Resurrection," 49–50, for a discussion of Bernstein's ideas (or lack of ideas) about Mahler's Jewishness before his first performances of the music, and pp. 80–98 on Bernstein's performances of Mahler with the Israel Philharmonic.

120. *The Program-Magazine of the New York City Center* 5, no. 3 (week of September 21, 1947): 4. Also see Page, "Resurrection," 56.

121. On Bernstein, Copland, and Jewish identity, see Schiller, *Bloch, Schoenberg, and Bernstein,* 163–65.

122. David C. Paul identified the columnist Kurt List as one possible source for Bernstein's ideas about Mahler's significance. See Paul, "Converging Paths," 373.

123. Walter Piston's widely circulating treatise on orchestration contains examples of Mahler's music; see Piston, *Orchestration.* On Longy-Miquelle, see Schiff, *New York Times,* November 4, 2001.

Conclusion

1. See Pollack, *Aaron Copland,* 532–41.
2. Miller, *Aaron Copland.*
3. Copland's catalog of his programs may be found in the Copland Collection, Music Division, Library of Congress, Washington, DC, 243/11–12; the Brazil and Chicago concerts are listed there.
4. Hughes, *New York Times,* June 3, 1973.
5. Bernheimer, *Los Angeles Times,* May 30, 1976.
6. Adams, *Hallelujah Junction,* 182.

BIBLIOGRAPHY

Adams, John. *Hallelujah Junction: Composing an American Life.* New York: Farrar, Straus, and Giroux, 2008.

Adler, Samuel. *The Study of Orchestration.* New York: Norton, 1982.

Albright, Daniel. *Untwisting the Serpent.* Chicago: University of Chicago Press, 2000.

Aldrich, Richard. "Gustav Mahler—His Personality and His Symphony." *New York Times,* November 6, 1904.

———. "Music." *New York Times,* March 9, 1923.

———. "Music." *New York Times,* January 28, 1924.

———. "A New Symphony by Gustav Mahler." *New York Times,* February 11, 1906.

Ansari, Emily Abrams. *The Sound of a Superpower: Musical Americanism and the Cold War.* New York: Oxford University Press, 2018.

Bailey, Walter B. "'For the serious listeners who swear neither at nor by Schoenberg': Music Criticism, the Great War, and the Dawning of a New Attitude toward Schoenberg and Ultra-Modern Music in New York City." *Journal of Musicology* 32 (2015): 279–322.

Baltimore Sun. "Was Musical Triumph: Boston Symphony Orchestra Pleases Large Audience." February 15, 1906.

Banfield, Stephen. "Copland and the Broadway Sound." In *Copland Connotations: Studies and Interviews,* edited by Peter Dickinson, 153–64. Woodbridge, Suffolk, UK: Boydell & Brewer, 2002.

Banks, Paul. "Mahler and Viennese Modernism." In *On Mahler and Britten: Essays in Honour of Donald Mitchell on His Seventieth Birthday,*" edited by Philip Reed. Woodbridge, Suffolk, UK: Boydell & Brewer, 1995.

Bashford, Christina. "The Late Beethoven Quartets and the London Press, 1836–ca. 1850." *Musical Quarterly* 84 (2000): 84–122.

Berger, Arthur. *Aaron Copland.* New York: Oxford University Press, 1953.

———. *Reflections of an American Composer.* Berkeley, CA.: University of California Press, 2002.

Bernheimer, Martin. "Ojai '76: Musical Sprawl in Need of a Ruthless Mastermind." *Los Angeles Times.* May 30, 1976.

Bernstein, Leonard. "Aaron Copland: An Intimate Sketch." *High Fidelity* 20 (November 1970): 53–55.

———. "Bernstein: What I Thought . . ." *New York Times*, October 24, 1965.

———. ". . . And What I Did." *New York Times*, October 24, 1965.

———. *The Infinite Variety of Music*. New York: Amadeus, 2007.

———. "Introduction to Modern Music," *Omnibus: The Historic TV Broadcasts on 4 DVDs*. Port Washington, NY: E1 Entertainment, 2010. Video.

———. *The Joy of Music*. New York: Simon & Schuster, 1959.

———. "Mahler: His Time Has Come." *High Fidelity/Musical America* 17 (1967): 51–54.

———. *The Unanswered Question: Six Talks at Harvard*. Cambridge, MA: Harvard University Press, 1976.

———. "What Is American Music?" *Leonard Bernstein's Young People's Concerts with the New York Philharmonic*. West Long Branch, NJ: Kultur International Films, 2004. Video.

———. "Who Is Gustav Mahler?" *Leonard Bernstein's Young People's Concerts with the New York Philharmonic*. West Long Branch, NJ: Kultur International Films, 2004. Video.

Bick, Sally. "In the Tradition of Dissent: Music at the New School for Social Research, 1926–1933." *Journal of the American Musicological Society* 66, no. 1 (2013): 129–90.

Blaukopf, Herta. "Amsterdam 1920: Sechs Zeitzeugen feiern Mahler." *Muziek & wetenschap* 5, no. 3 (1995/1996): 347–61.

Blaukopf, Kurt. *Mahler*. Translated by Inge Goodwin. New York: Limelight Editions, 1985.

Blitzstein, Marc. "London: Fourth Winter of the Blackout," *Modern Music* 20 (1943), 117–120.

_____. "New York Medley, Winter, 1935." *Modern Music* 13 (1936): 34–40.

Boretz, Benjamin. "Records." *The Nation*, June 22, 1963, 535–36.

Boston Evening Transcript. "My Time Will Yet Come," January 13, 1932.

———. "New Mahler Symphony Given," October 17, 1931.

Boston Globe. "Boston to Be Center for Modern Music," September 13, 1924.

———. "Brings New Music, Tribute to Symphony," October 1, 1930.

———. "The 47th Symphony Season," April 29, 1928.

———. "Koussevitzky Appointed Conductor," September 16, 1923.

———. "Koussevitzky's First Programs to Prove Versatility," September 28, 1924.

———. "Koussevitzky Gives More Details of Symphony Plans," September 22, 1940.

———. "New Symphony Conductor Says His Programs Will Be Different," September 21, 1924

———. "Tolerating Modernist Music," October 27, 1929.

Boston Herald. "Won't Shock Music Lovers," September 13, 1924.

Boston Post. "Few Novelties for Symphony," October 1, 1931.

Botstein, Leon. "Copland Reconfigured." In *Aaron Copland and His World,* edited by Carol J. Oja and Judith Tick, 439–83. Princeton, NJ: Princeton University Press, 2005.

———. "Whose Gustav Mahler? Reception, Interpretation, and History." In *Mahler and His World,* edited by Karen Painter, 1–53. Princeton, NJ: Princeton University Press, 2002.

Boulanger, Nadia. "Concerts Koussevitzky." *Le monde musical,* November 1923. Quoted and translated in Scott Messing, *Neoclassicism in Music: From the Genesis of the Concept through the Schoenberg/Stravinsky Polemic.* Ann Arbor: UMI Research Press, 1988.

———. "Le jubilé de W. Mengelberg." *Le monde musical* (June 1920): 182–83.

———. "Lectures on Modern Music." *Rice Institute Pamphlet 13, no. 2 (1926): 113–95.*

Brant, Henry. Transcript of interview with Vincent Plush, Santa Barbara, CA. May 11, 1983. Oral History American Music, Yale University.

Brooks, Jeanice. *The Musical Work of Nadia Boulanger: Performing Past and Future Between the World Wars.* New York: Cambridge University Press, 2013.

———. "Nadia Boulanger and the Salon of the Princesse de Polignac." *Journal of the American Musicological Society* 46 (1993): 415–68.

Burton, Humphrey. *Leonard Bernstein.* New York: Doubleday, 1994.

Bushard, Anthony. *Leonard Bernstein's* On the Waterfront*: A Film Score Guide.* Lanham, MD: Rowman & Littlefield, 2013.

Casella, Alfredo. "Chroniques et notes—Le 'Mahlerfest' d'Amsterdam." *Revue musicale* 1, no. 1 (November 1, 1920).

———. *L'evoluzione della musica: A traverso la storia della cadenza perfetta.* London: J. & W. Chester, 1924.

Combe, Édouard. "Les symphonies de Mahler." *La revue musicale* 3 (July 1922): 42–56.

Cone, Edward T. "Conversation with Aaron Copland." *Perspectives of New Music* 6, no. 2 (1968): 57–72.

Copland, Aaron. "Composer from Brooklyn: An Autobiographical Sketch." *Magazine of Art* 32 (September 1939): 522–23 and 548–50.

———. "Defends the Music of Mahler," letter to the editor. *New York Times,* April 5, 1925.

———. "Fantasy for Piano." *New York Times,* October 20, 1957.

———. 'Five Post-Romantics,' *Modern Music* 18 (May 1941), 218–24.

———. "An Indictment of the Fourth B." *New York Times,* September 21, 1952.

———. "Memorial to Paul Rosenfeld." *Notes* 4, no. 2 (1947): 147–151.

———. "Modern Orchestration Surveyed," *Modern Music* 8 (1930): 41–44.

———. "Music and the Human Spirit." In *Aaron Copland: A Reader: Selected Writings: 1923–1972*, edited by Richard Kostelanetz, 26–32. New York: Routledge, 2004.

———. "Music between the Wars." In *Aaron Copland: A Reader: Selected Writings, 1923–1972*, edited by Richard Kostelanetz, 38–69. New York: Routledge, 2004.

———. *Our New Music.* New York: Whittlesey House, 1941.

———. "Rubin Goldmark: A Tribute," *The Juilliard Review* 3, no. 3 (1956): 15–16.

———. "Serge Koussevitzky and the American Composer," *Musical Quarterly* 30 (1944): 255–69.

———. "Stravinsky's Dynamism." In *Aaron Copland: A Reader: Selected Writings, 1923–1972*, edited by Richard Kostelanetz, 162–65. New York: Routledge, 2004.

———. "What Is Jewish Music?" *New York Herald Tribune*, October 2, 1949.

———. *What to Listen for in Music.* Rev. ed. New York: McGraw Hill, 1988.

———. "The World of A-Tonality." *New York Times*, November 27, 1949.

Copland, Aaron, and Jack Diether. "Guide to Record Collecting: Aaron Copland Suggests a Mahler Discography." *Hi-Fi Music at Home*, March–April 1957.

Copland, Aaron, and Vivian Perlis, *Copland: 1900 through 1942.* New York: St. Martin's, 1999.

———. *Copland: Since 1943.* New York: St. Martin's, 1999.

Coster, Aarnout. "Mengelberg's Mahler performances in America 1921–1930." In *Das Gustav-Mahler-Fest Hamburg 1989*, edited by Matthias Theodor Vogt, 279–90. Kassel: Bärenreiter, 1991.

Crawford, Richard. *America's Musical Life: A History.* New York: Norton, 2001.

Crist, Elizabeth B. "Aaron Copland and the Popular Front." *Journal of the American Musicological Society* 56 (2003): 409–65.

———. "Aaron Copland's Third Symphony from Sketch to Score." *Journal of Musicology* 18, no. 3 (2001): 377–405

———. *Music for the Common Man: Aaron Copland During the Depression and War.* New York: Oxford University Press, 2005.

Crist, Elizabeth B., and Wayne Shirley, eds. *The Selected Correspondence of Aaron Copland.* New Haven, CT: Yale University Press, 2006.

Damrosch, Walter. *My Musical Life.* New York: Charles Scribner's Sons, 1923.

Danforth, Corinne. "'My Secretary Knows More than I Do'—The Boss." *Boston Globe*, January 16, 1927.

DeLapp[-Birkett], Jennifer L. "Copland in the Fifties: Music and Ideology in the McCarthy Era." PhD diss., University of Michigan, 1997.

DeLapp-Birkett, Jennifer. "Copland and the Politics of Twelve-Tone Composition in the Early Cold War United States." *Journal of Musicological Research* 27 (2008): 31–62.

DeVoto, Mark. "The Debussy Sound: Colour, Texture, Gesture." In *The Cambridge Companion to Debussy*, edited by Simon Tretzise, 179–96. Cambridge, UK: Cambridge University Press, 2003.

Dickinson, Peter. "Composer in Interview: Aaron Copland." *Tempo* 57, no. 224 (2003): 11–15.

Doering, James M. *The Great Orchestrator: Arthur Judson and American Arts Management*. Urbana: University of Illinois Press, 2013.

Downes, Olin. "A Composer States His Position." *New York Times*, October 19, 1941.

———. "A Conductor's Musicianship." *New York Times*, November 25, 1928.

———. "Music: Locomotive Symphony Repeated." *New York Times*. November 3, 1924.

———. "Programs of an Orchestra Season, Qualities of Works of Modern Men." *New York Times*, April 11, 1926.

C. W. D. [Cyrus W. Durgin], "Symphony Hall." *Boston Globe*, November 7, 1936.

———. "Symphony Hall." *Boston Globe*, January 31, 1942.

Durgin, Cyrus. "Mayes Cello Soloist at Symphony; Liszt's 'Faust' Score Revised," *Boston Globe*, November 27, 1948.

Edwards, Allen. *Flawed Words and Stubborn Sounds: A Conversation with Elliott Carter*. New York: Norton, 1971.

Ellis, Katharine. *Interpreting the Musical Past: Early Music in Nineteenth-Century France*. New York: Oxford University Press, 2008.

Engel, Gabriel. *Gustav Mahler, Song-Symphonist*. New York: Bruckner Society of America, 1932.

———. "New Symphonic Horizons." *Chord and Discord* 1, no. 1 (1932): 1–4.

Everist, Mark. *Mozart's Ghosts: Haunting the Halls of Musical Culture*. New York: Oxford University Press, 2012.

Ewen, David. *Dictators of the Baton*. Chicago: Alliance Book Corporation, 1943.

Fauser, Annegret. "Aaron Copland, Nadia Boulanger, and the Making of an 'American' Composer." *Musical Quarterly* 89 (2006): 524–54.

———. *The Politics of Musical Identity: Selected Essays*. London: Routledge, 2015.

———. *Sounds of War: Music in the United States During World War II.* New York: Oxford University Press, 2013.

Fecher, Charles A., ed. *The Diary of H. L. Mencken.* New York: A. A. Knopf, 1989.

Feder, Stuart. *Gustav Mahler: A Life in Crisis.* New Haven, CT: Yale University Press, 2004.

Flerlage, Raeburn. "America and Gustav Mahler." *American Music Lover* 7, no. 12 (1941): 426–29.

Floros, Constantin. *Gustav Mahler: The Symphonies.* Translated by Vernon and Jutta Wicker. Portland, OR: Amadeus Press, 1993.

Francis, Kimberly. "A Dialogue Begins: Nadia Boulanger, Igor Stravinsky, and the *Symphonie de psaumes.*" *Women & Music: A Journal of Gender and Culture* 14 (2010): 22–44.

———. "'Everything Had to Change': Nadia Boulanger's Translation of Modernism in the Rice Lecture Series, 1925." *Journal of the Society for American Music* 7 (2013): 363–81.

———. *Teaching Stravinsky: Nadia Boulanger and the Consecration of a Modernist Icon.* New York: Oxford University Press, 2015.

Franklin, Peter. *Reclaiming Late-Romantic Music: Singing Devils and Distant Sounds.* Berkeley: University of California Press, 2014.

Fulcher, Jane F. "The Composer as Intellectual: Ideological Inscriptions in French Interwar Neoclassicism." *Journal of Musicology* 17 (1999): 197–230.

———. *The Composer as Intellectual: Music and Ideology in France, 1914–1940.* New York: Oxford University Press, 2005.

Fülöp, Péter. *Mahler Discography.* Toronto: Mikrokosmos, 2010.

Gienow-Hecht, Jessica. *Sound Diplomacy: Music and Emotions in Transatlantic Relations, 1850–1920.* Chicago: University of Chicago Press, 2009.

Gilliam, Bryan. "A Viennese Opera Composer in Hollywood: Korngold's Double Exile in America." In *Driven into Paradise: The Musical Migration from Nazi Germany to the United States,* edited by Reinhold Brinkmann and Christoph Wolff, 223–42. Berkeley: University of California Press, 1999.

Gilman, Lawrence. *Edward MacDowell: A Study.* New York: John Lane, 1908.

———. "Music," *New York Herald Tribune.* March 30, 1925.

———. "Music of the Month: Concerning Mahler." *North American Review* 214 (1921): 122–28.

Giuliani, Elizabeth. "Les enregistrements de Nadia Boulanger: Une conception et une pratique originales de l'interprétation musicale." In *Nadia Boulanger et Lili Boulanger: Témoignages et études,* edited by Alexandra Laederich, 191–202. Lyon: Symétrie, 2007.

Goldberg, Albert. "Copland and Bumbry Star in Ojai Finale. *Los Angeles Times*, May 26, 1958.

Goldstein, Eric L. *The Price of Whiteness: Jews, Race, and American Identity*. Princeton, NJ: Princeton University Press, 2006.

Gottlieb, Jack. "Symbols of Faith in the Music of Leonard Bernstein." *Musical Quarterly* 66 (1980): 287–95.

———. *Working with Bernstein*. New York: Amadeus Press, 2010.

Gradenwitz, Peter. *Leonard Bernstein: The Infinite Variety of a Musician*. New York: Oswald Wolff, 1987.

Grey, Robert G. "Bruckner and Mahler," letter to the editor. *New York Times*, July 27, 1930.

Grofé, Ferde. "Story of the Grand Canyon Suite." *Arizona Highways* 71, no. 4 (1995): 14–16.

Hackett, Karleton. "Orchestra Plays Mahler's Music in Brilliant Style." *Chicago Evening Post*, April 16, 1921.

Halbreich, Harry. *Arthur Honegger*. Translated by Roger Nichols. Portland, OR: Amadeus Press, 1999.

Hale, Philip. "Music." *Boston Herald*, October 17, 1931.

Hart, Brian. "The Symphony and National Identity in Early Twentieth-Century France." In *French Music, Culture, and National Identity, 1870–1939*, edited by Barbara Kelly, 131–48. Rochester, NY: University of Rochester Press, 2008.

Hart, Philip. *Orpheus in the New World: The Symphony Orchestra as an American Cultural Institution*. New York: Norton, 1973.

Henderson, W. J. "Mahlerians Trying to Cudgel Public into Adoring His Music." *New York Herald*, March 5, 1922.

Holloway, Robin. "Howard's Way," *Musical Times* 141 (2000): 51–58.

Horowitz, Joseph. "As Music Director: A Quest for Meaning and Identity." In *Leonard Bernstein: How a Modern Renaissance Man Transformed Music and the World during His New York Philharmonic Years*, edited by Barbara B. Haws and Burton Bernstein, 135–51. New York: Collins, 2008.

———. *Classical Music in America: A History*. New York: Norton, 2007.

———. *Moral Fire: Musical Portraits from America's Fin de Siècle*. Berkeley: University of California Press, 2012.

Hubbs, Nadine. "Bernstein, Homophobia, Historiography." *Women & Music*, 13 (2009): 24–42.

———. *The Queer Composition of America's Sound: Gay Modernists, American Music, and National Identity*. Berkeley: University of California Press, 2004.

Hughes, Allen. "Music in Review." *New York Times*, June 3, 1973.

Huneker, James. *Overtones: A Book of Temperaments.* New York: Charles Scribner's Sons, 1912.

Hutchison, Merilyn Kae. "A Stylistic and Pianistic Evaluation of Copland's *Piano Fantasy.*" Master's thesis, North Texas State University, 1968.

Ivry, Paul. *Francis Poulenc.* London: Phaidon, 1996.

Jacobi, Frederick. "In Defense of Modernism," *Modern Music* 17 (May–June 1940): 221–25.

———. "Rubin Goldmark: A Tribute." *Modern Music* 13 (March–April 1936): 49–50.

Johnson, Harriett. "Philharmonic Fetes Mahler in '59–'60." *New York Post,* April 14, 1959.

Johnson, Julian. "The Status of Subject in Mahler's Ninth Symphony." *19th-Century Music* 8, no. 2 (1994): 108–120.

———. *Mahler's Voices: Expression and Irony in the Songs and Symphonies.* New York: Oxford University Press, 2009.

Kaplan, Gilbert. "Adagietto: 'From Mahler With Love.'" In *Perspectives on Gustav Mahler,* edited by Jeremy Barham, 379–400. Aldershot, UK: Ashgate, 2005.

Keller, James M. "Bernstein and Mahler: Channeling a Prophet." In *Leonard Bernstein: How a Modern Renaissance Man Transformed Music and the World During His New York Philharmonic Years,* edited by Barbara B. Haws and Burton Bernstein, 173–91. New York: Collins, 2008.

Kelly, Barbara. *Music and Ultra-Modernism in France: A Fragile Consensus, 1913–1939.* Rochester, NY: Boydell & Brewer, 2013.

Kelly, Kevin. "Bernstein Conducts Mahler 4th." *Boston Globe,* August 7, 1960.

Kosman, Joshua. "Mahler to the Max." *San Francisco Chronicle,* June 7, 1998.

Kostelanetz, Richard, ed. *Aaron Copland: A Reader: Selected Writings: 1923–1972.* New York: Routledge, 2004.

Koussevitzky, Serge. "Dr. Serge Koussevitzky on Mahler." *Chord and Discord,* 1, no. 1 (February 1932): 15.

———. "Poetry and Music; Musical Interpretation; and Some Remarks About American Orchestras." *Proceedings of the American Academy of Arts and Sciences* 73, no. 1 (1938): 1–4.

H. E. K. [Henry E. Krehbiel], "Death of Mr. Mahler." *New York Tribune.* May 21, 1911.

———. "Music: Absolute and Programmatic." *New York Tribune,* December 18, 1909.

———. "Music: The Philharmonic Society." *New York Tribune,* December 13, 1909.

Krehbiel, H. E. "Mahler's Symphony Heard First Time." *New York Tribune*, May 10, 1914.

Krehbiel, Henry E. *"The Bohemians" (New York Musicians' Club): A Historical Narrative and Record.* New York: n.p., 1921.

La Grange, Henry-Louis de. *Gustav Mahler, vol. 4: A New Life Cut Short (1907–1911).* New York: Oxford University Press, 2008.

———. "Mahler and France." In *The Mahler Companion*, edited by Donald Mitchell and Andrew Nicholson, 138–52. New York: Oxford University Press, 1999.

LaFave, Kenneth. *Experiencing Leonard Bernstein: A Listener's Companion.* Lanham, MD: Rowman & Littlefield, 2015.

Laird, Paul R. and Hsun Lin. *Leonard Bernstein: A Research and Information Guide.* Second edition. New York: Routledge, 2015.

Lang, Zoë, ed. "Mahler's American Debut: The Reception of the Fourth and Fifth Symphonies." In Mahler and His World, edited by Karen Painter, 227–63. Princeton, NJ: Princeton University Press, 2002.

Langley, Allen Lincoln. "Justice for Gustav Mahler." *Musical Quarterly* 12, no. 2 (1926): 153–65.

Lebrecht, Norman. *Why Mahler? How One Man and Ten Symphonies Changed Our World.* New York: Pantheon, 2010.

Leichtentritt, Hugo. *Serge Koussevitzky, the Boston Symphony Orchestra, and the New American Music.* Cambridge, MA: Harvard University Press, 1946.

Leonard, Kendra Preston. *The Conservatoire Américain: A History.* Lanham, MD: Scarecrow Press, 2007.

Lerner, Neil. "Copland's Music of Wide Open Spaces: Surveying the Pastoral Trope in Hollywood." *Musical Quarterly* 85 (2001): 477–515.

Levitz, Tamara. *Modernist Mysteries: Perséphone.* New York: Oxford University Press, 2012.

Levy, Beth. *Frontier Figures: American Music and the Mythology of the American West.* Berkeley: University of California Press, 2012.

Locke, Ralph P. "Aaron Copland: Two Interviews (1970, 1972) & Three Letters." *Journal of the American Liszt Society* 54–56 (2003–5): 201–17.

Lourié, Arthur. *Serge Koussevitzky and His Epoch.* New York: A. A. Knopf, 1931.

Magee, Gayle Sherwood. *Charles Ives Reconsidered.* Urbana: University of Illinois Press, 2008.

Mason, Daniel Gregory. "Is American Music Growing Up?" *Arts & Decoration, November 1920.*

Mathers, Daniel E. "Solid Basic Training: Aaron Copland's Studies with Rubin Goldmark." *American Music* 33, no. 1 (2015): 1–67.

Meckna, Michael. "Copland, Sessions, and Modern Music: The Rise of the Composer-Critic in America." *American Music* 3 (1985): 198–204.

———. "The Rise of the Composer-Critic: Aaron Copland, Roger Sessions, Virgil Thomson, and Elliott Carter in the Periodical 'Modern Music,' 1924–1946." PhD diss., University of California, Santa Barbara, 1984.

Mellers, Wilfrid. "Mahler as Key Figure." *Scrutiny* 9 (March 1941): 343–51.

Messing, Scott. *Neoclassicism in Music: From the Genesis of the Concept through the Schoenberg/Stravinsky Polemic.* Ann Arbor: UMI Research Press, 1988.

———. "Polemic as History: The Case of Neoclassicism." *Journal of Musicology 9 (1991): 481–97.*

A. H. M. [Meyer, Alfred H.] "Again Mahler and His 'Song of the Earth.'" *Boston Evening Transcript,* December 27, 1930.

Milhaud, Darius, and Claude Rostand. *Interviews with Claude Rostand.* Translated by Jane Hohfeld Galante. Oakland, CA: Center for the Book at Mills College, 2002.

Miller, Allan, dir. *Aaron Copland: A Self-Portrait.* Princeton, NJ: Films for the Humanities, 1986. Video.

Mitchell, Donald. "The Mahler Renaissance in England: Its Origins and Chronology." In *The Mahler Companion,* edited by Donald Mitchell and Andrew Nicholson, 547–64. New York: Oxford University Press, 1999.

———. *Songs and Symphonies of Life and Death.* Berkeley: University of California Press, 1985.

Murchison, Gayle. *The American Stravinsky: The Style and Aesthetics of Copland's New American Music, the Early Works, 1921–1938.* Ann Arbor: University of Michigan Press, 2012.

Musical America. "New Philharmonic Will Have 120 Men and 4 Conductors," April 2, 1921.

Musk, Andrea. "Regionalism, Latinité and the French Musical Tradition: Déodat de Sévérac's *Héliogabale.*" In *Nineteenth-Century Music Studies,* edited by Jim Samson and Bennett Zon, 226–49. Aldershot, UK: Ashgate, 2002.

Myers, Paul. *Leonard Bernstein.* London: Phaidon, 1998.

New York Herald Tribune. "Dr. Koussevitzky Arrives to Open Eighth Season." September 30, 1931.

New York Times. "Many Choral Programs." November 25, 1917.

———. "Music Notes Near at Hand." January 16, 1927.

———. "Plans of Four Orchestras." September 27, 1931.

New York Tribune. "Music. The New-York Symphony Orchestra." November 7, 1904.

Newlin, Dika. *Bruckner, Mahler, Schoenberg.* New York: Norton, 1947.

———. "Conversation Piece: Mahler and Beyond." Notes on the Programs, 2–4. New York: New York Philharmonic, January 14, 15, and 17, 1960.

Nikkels, Eveline. "Mahler and Holland." In The Mahler Companion, edited by Donald Mitchell and Andrew Nicholson, 326–37. New York: Oxford University Press, 1999.

Oja, Carol J. *Making Music Modern: New York in the 1920s.* New York: Oxford University Press, 2000.

Op de Coul, Paul. "Modern Chamber Music at the 1920 Mahler Festival: A Prelude to the International Society for Contemporary Music." In *Gustav Mahler: The World Listens,* edited by Donald Mitchell, I.77–84. Haarlem: TEMA Uitgevers, 1995.

Orenstein, Arbie, ed. *A Ravel Reader: Correspondence, Articles, Interviews.* Mineola, NY: Dover, 2003.

Page, Christopher Jarrett. "Leonard Bernstein and the Resurrection of Gustav Mahler." PhD diss., University of California, Los Angeles, 2000.

Page, Tim and Vanessa Weeks Page. *Selected Letters of Virgil Thomson.* New York: Summit, 1988.

Parmenter, Ross. "NBC Orchestra Heard." *New York Times,* November 10, 1940.

Pasler, Jann. Composing the Citizen: Music as Public Utility in Third Republic France. Berkeley: University of California Press, 2009.

———. Writing through Music: Essays on Music, Culture, and Politics. New York: Oxford University Press, 2008.

Paul, David C. "Converging Paths to the Canon: Charles Ives, Gustav Mahler, and American Culture." PhD diss., University of California at Berkeley, 2006.

Perlis, Vivian. "Dear Aaron, Dear Lenny: A Friendship in Letters." In *Aaron Copland and His World,* edited by Carol J. Oja and Judith Tick, 151–78. Princeton, NJ: Princeton University Press, 2005.

Perlis, Vivian, and Libby Van Cleve. *Composers' Voices from Ives to Ellington: An Oral History of American Music.* New Haven, CT: Yale University Press, 2005.

Pesson, Gérard. "Mahler and Debussy: Transcendence and Emotion." Translated by Peter Righton. In *The Mahler Companion,* edited by Donald Mitchell and Andrew Nicholson, 153–70. New York: Oxford University Press, 1999.

Peyser, Joan. *Bernstein: A Biography.* New York: Beech Tree, 1987.

Pickett, David. "Mahler on Record: The Spirit or the Letter?" In *Perspectives on Gustav Mahler,* edited by Jeremy Barham, 345–77. Burlington, VT: Ashgate, 2005.

Pisani, Michael V. "I'm an Indian Too: Creating Native American Identities in Nineteenth- and Early Twentieth-Century Music." In *The Exotic in Western Art Music*, edited by Jonathan Bellman, 218–57. Boston: Northeastern University Press, 1998.

Piston, Walter. *Orchestration*. New York: Norton, 1955.

Pollack, Howard. *Aaron Copland: The Life and Work of an Uncommon Man*. Urbana: University of Illinois Press, 2000.

———. *Marc Blitzstein: His Life, His Work, His World*. New York: Oxford University Press, 2012.

———. Review of Barry Seldes, "Leonard Bernstein: The Political Life of an American Musician." *Notes* 66 (2010): 762–64.

Potter, Caroline. *Nadia and Lili Boulanger*. Burlington, VT: Ashgate, 2006.

Reilly, Edward R. "Mahler in America." In *The Mahler Companion*, edited by Donald Mitchell and Andrew Nicholson, 422–37. New York: Oxford University Press, 1999.

Riley, Matthew, and Anthony D. Smith. *Nation and Classical Music: From Handel to Copland*. Woodbridge, Suffolk, UK: Boydell Press, 2016.

P. R. [Penfield Roberts]. "Beethoven Fills Symphony Program." *Boston Globe*. January 17, 1925

———. "German Program at Symphony Concert." *Boston Globe*, March 7, 1925.

———. "Mahler Novelty at Symphony Concert." *Boston Globe*, December 8, 1928.

———. "Schnabel Heard at Symphony Concert," *Boston Globe*, April 5, 1930.

———. "Symphony Hall." *Boston Globe*, October 17, 1931.

Roman, Zoltan. *Gustav Mahler's American Years, 1907–1911: A Documentary History*. Stuyvesant, NY: Pendragon, 1989.

Rosen, Peter, dir. *Leonard Bernstein: Reflections*. EuroArts International, 2010. Video.

Rosenfeld, Paul. "After Mahler's 'Ninth.'" *The New Republic*, January 13, 1932.

———. *Musical Portraits*. New York: Harcourt, Brace, & Howe, 1920.

———. *Musical Chronicle (1917–1923)*. New York: Harcourt, Brace, 1923.

———. "The Tragedy of Gustav Mahler." *The New Republic*. April 8, 1916.

Rosenstiel, Léonie. *Nadia Boulanger: A Life in Music*. New York: Norton, 1982.

Rutkoff, Peter M., and William B. Scott. *New School: A History of the New School for Social Research*. New York: Free Press, 1986.

Ryding, Erik, and Rebecca Pechefsky. *Bruno Walter: A World Elsewhere*. New Haven, CT: Yale University Press, 2001

Samaroff Stokowski, Olga. *An American Musician's Story*. New York: Norton, 1939.

Sanborn, Pitts. Review of Mahler's Second Symphony. *New York Telegram-Mail.* April 6, 1925.

Schiff, David. "The Man Who Mainstreamed Mahler." *New York Times*, November 4, 2001.

Schiller, David M. *Bloch, Schoenberg, and Bernstein: Assimilating Jewish Music.* New York: Oxford University Press, 2003.

Schmid, Marion. "À bas Wagner! The French Press Campaign against Wagner during World War I." In *French Music, Culture, and National Identity, 1870–1939*, edited by Barbara Kelly, 77–91. Rochester, NY: University of Rochester Press, 2008.

Secrest, Merle. *Leonard Bernstein: A Life.* New York: A. A. Knopf, 1994.

Seldes, Barry. *Leonard Bernstein: The Political Life of an American Musician.* Berkeley: University of California Press, 2009.

Schonberg, Harold C. "Making Mahler Loved in France." *New York Times*, July 4, 1989.

Shadle, Douglas W. *Orchestrating the Nation.* New York: Oxford University Press, 2016.

Shanet, Howard. "Conversation Piece: Why a Mahler Festival?" Notes on the Programs, 2–4. New York: New York Philharmonic, January 28–31, 1960.

Simone, Nigel, ed. *The Leonard Bernstein Letters.* New Haven, CT: Yale University Press, 2013.

Sloper, Leslie A. "Music." *Christian Science Monitor*, October 17, 1931.

L. A. S. [Leslie A. Sloper]. "'Song of the Earth' in Boston," *Christian Science Monitor.* December 8, 1928.

Smith, George Henry Lovett. "Classic Versus Moderns: An Ever-Fresh Discussion." *Boston Evening Transcript*, June 22, 1935.

Smith, Helen. *There's a Place for Us: The Musical Theatre Works of Leonard Bernstein. Farnham, Surrey, UK: Ashgate, 2011.*

Smith, Julia. *Aaron Copland, His Work and Contribution to American Music.* New York: Dutton, 1955.

Smith, Moses. *Koussevitzky*. New York: Allen, Towne & Heath, 1947.

———. "Mahler Work Novelty at Symphony." *Boston American*, December 8, 1928.

———. "Mahler's Ninth Symphony Wins Favor under Koussevitzky." *Boston American*, October 17, 1931.

Smith, Warren Storey. "Symphony in Mahler's Great 9th." *Boston Post*, October 17, 1931.

Society of Friends of Music. *Gustav Mahler: The Composer, The Conductor, The Man: Appreciations by Distinguished Contemporary Musicians.* New York: Society of Friends of Music, 1916.

Somervell, Stephen. "Traditions—Who Makes Them!" Scoffs Mr. Koussevitzky." *Boston Globe,* October 9, 1927.

Spycket, Jérôme. *Nadia Boulanger.* Translated by M. M. Shriver. Stuyvesant, NY: Pendragon, 1992.

Starr, Larry. "The Voice of Solitary Contemplation: Copland's *Music for the Theatre* Viewed as a Journey of Self-Discovery." *American Music* 20 (2002): 297–316.

Steinberg, Michael. "Bernstein, Philharmonic Give Last 3 Symphonies." *Boston Globe,* December 19, 1965.

Straus, Noel. "Erno Rapee Leads Mahler's Eighth: Playing of Symphony Marks 500th Program of Radio City Music Hall of the Air." *New York Times,* April 13, 1942.

Stricker, Rémy. "La critique de Nadia Boulanger: À la recherche d'une passion objective." In *Nadia Boulanger et Lili Boulanger: Témoignages et études,* edited by Alexandra Laederich, 131–38. Lyon: Symétrie, 2007.

Swayne, Steve. *Orpheus in Manhattan: William Schuman and the Shaping of America's Musical Life.* New York: Oxford University Press, 2011.

Taubman, Howard. "Copland Fantasy for Piano Heard." *New York Times,* October 26, 1957.

———. "Mahler's Music at Stadium." *New York Times,* July 20, 1931.

Tilson Thomas, Michael. *Keeping Score: Copland and the American Sound.* Directed by David Kennard, Joan Saffa, and Gary Halvorson. San Francisco: SFS Media, 2006. Video.

———. "Mahler in America," *Keeping Score.* San Francisco Symphony, 2011. http://www.keepingscore.org/interactive/gustav-mahler/epilogue.

Thomson, Virgil. "'Greatest Music Teacher'—at 75." *Music Educators Journal* 49, no. 1 (1962): 42–44.

———. *The Musical Scene* (New York: A. A. Knopf, 1945).

Tischler, Barbara. *An American Music: The Search for an American Musical Identity.* New York: Oxford University Press, 1986.

Toliver, Brooks. "Eco-ing in the Canyon: Ferde Grofé's *Grand Canyon Suite* and the Transformation of Wilderness." *Journal of the American Musicological Society* 57, no. 2 (2004): 325–368.

Tomatz, David. "Rubin Goldmark, Postromantic: Trial Balances in American Music." PhD diss., Catholic University of America, 1966.

Vaughan Williams, Ralph. *Some Thoughts on Beethoven's Choral Symphony with Writings on Other Musical Subjects.* London: Oxford University Press, 1953.

Vignal, Marc. *Mahler.* Rev. ed. Paris: Seuil, 1995.

Wister, Frances Anne. *Twenty-Five Years of the Philadelphia Orchestra, 1900–1925.* Philadelphia: Women's Committee for the Philadelphia Orchestra, 1925.

Zychowicz, James L. "Mahler Reception in Forty Historic Editions: Significant Holdings in the Newberry Library, Chicago." *Notes* 74 (2017): 36–59.

INDEX

Page numbers in italics indicate illustrations.

Eastman Studies in Music

Ralph P. Locke, Senior Editor
Eastman School of Music

Additional Titles of Interest

Anneliese Landau's Life in Music: Nazi Germany to Émigré California
Lily E. Hirsch

Elliott Carter's What's Next?*: Communication, Cooperation, and Separation*
Guy Capuzzo

European Music and Musicians in New York City, 1840–1900
Edited by John Graziano

George Rochberg, American Composer: Personal Trauma and Artistic Creativity
Amy Lynn Wlodarski

John Kirkpatrick, American Music, and the Printed Page
Drew Massey

The Karl Muck Scandal:
Classical Music and Xenophobia in World War I America
Melissa D. Burrage

Nadia Boulanger and the Stravinskys: A Selected Correspondence
Edited by Kimberly A. Francis

Martinů's Subliminal States:
A Study of the Composer's Writings and Reception,
with a Translation of His "American Diaries"
Thomas D. Svatos

Samuel Barber Remembered: A Centenary Tribute
Peter Dickinson

Verdi in America: "Oberto" through "Rigoletto"
George W. Martin

A complete list of titles in the Eastman Studies in Music series may be found on the University of Rochester Press website, www.urpress.com